Just when you thought Lee Strobel had covered all the bases in his *Case* books, he writes this one. I couldn't put it down! *The Case for Miracles* is magnificent in its presentation of the facts and over the top in its engaging style. I doubt very much that you will read a more encouraging book anytime soon. God is very much in the miracle business in our day, and Strobel demonstrates that beyond a reasonable doubt.

> CRAIG J. HAZEN, PhD, founder and director of
> the MA program in Christian apologetics at Biola
> University and author of *Five Sacred Crossings*

The Case for Miracles is a wonderful addition to Lee Strobel's *Case* series. With his usual journalistic flair and integrity, Strobel chases down the best sources, stories, and evidence for the miraculous. He makes a powerful case for their reality and yet doesn't shy away from addressing the tough issues, such as unanswered prayers. This book is stimulating to the mind and moving to the heart. It's a must-read for believers and skeptics alike.

> SEAN MCDOWELL, PhD, professor, speaker,
> and author or coauthor of more than fifteen books,
> including *Evidence That Demands a Verdict*

Lee Strobel hits another home run as he welcomes us alongside in his honest investigation. For anyone wondering about miracles, this is the book to start with.

> CRAIG S. KEENER, PhD, F. M. and Ada Thompson professor
> of biblical studies at Asbury Theological Seminary and author
> of *Miracles: The Credibility of the New Testament Accounts*

The Case for Miracles is almost a miracle in itself. I mean that it is an astonishingly powerful case for the reality of miracles—including reports on scientific research with which most people are no doubt unfamiliar. Every person interested in the subject of the supernatural must read this book. It demolishes claims that science disproves miracles.

> ROGER E. OLSON, PhD, Foy Valentine professor of
> Christian theology and ethics at George W. Truett
> Theological Seminary, Baylor University

I flat-out defy anyone to read *The Case for Miracles* and not see that miracles exist. This book constitutes what any fair-minded person must be obliged to call "proof," and I recommend it to anyone wondering whether they can really know if God is real and still working among us today.

ERIC METAXAS, #1 *New York Times* bestselling author of
If You Can Keep It: The Forgotten Promise of American Liberty

If your faith was renewed and strengthened by *The Case for Christ*, you will fall on your knees in worship as you read *The Case for Miracles*. Once again, Lee Strobel lays out a clear, perfectly reasoned argument—this time, showing that God is alive and working in miraculous ways in our world right now.

SHEILA WALSH, singer, speaker, TV host, and bestselling author

Here's a masterpiece on miracles—a powerful and persuasive book that refutes skeptics and builds a convincing case that God is still in the miracle business today.

JOSH D. MCDOWELL, author and speaker

Once again, Lee Strobel uses his brilliant mind, calm logic, clear prose, and compelling storytelling to untangle a complex topic. This time he focuses on the fascinating subject of miracles. Both skeptics and believers—actually, anyone who is intellectually honest—will benefit from this fair-minded investigation of the possibility of miracles, their meaning, and the implications for our lives.

DR. RICK WARREN, The Purpose Driven Life

The Case for Miracles is an entertaining, fast-paced defense of God's miraculous action in the world. Lee Strobel's treatment is commendable for its balance, including not only positive evidence for miracles but a skeptic's case against miracles; examining not only stories of contemporary healing but also miraculous works of creation and historical events connected with life of Jesus; and not shying away from cases in which a desperately needed and long-sought miracle was not forthcoming. A moving and convincing treatment.

WILLIAM LANE CRAIG, research professor of
philosophy at Talbot School of Theology and professor
of philosophy at Houston Baptist University

I had a front-row seat watching Lee Strobel walk into our church as an ardent atheist and eventually become a pastor on our senior staff and now a world-renowned Christian apologist. Only God! This book will catalyze your faith!

BILL HYBELS, founder of Willow Creek Church
and the Global Leadership Summit

I love this book! Lee Strobel takes us on a page-turning journey through the elation of documented modern-day miracles to the anguish felt when God is silent. Lee addresses all the hard questions, and even allows the publisher of *Skeptic* magazine to make his best case *against* miracles. So whether you are a true believer or a seasoned skeptic open to evidence, you'll be enlightened and challenged by this brilliant book.

FRANK TUREK, PhD, coauthor of
I Don't Have Enough Faith to Be an Atheist

Lee Strobel's latest book is thick with striking examples of medically verified physical healings and of God's life-changing, supernatural intervention in the lives of ordinary people. The evidence is simply stunning. As usual, Strobel gives the skeptic lots to think about and the Christian lots to be confident in—with a riveting chapter for those whose miracles stay missing. *The Case for Miracles* will certainly change your prayers. It might just change your life.

GREGORY KOUKL, president of Stand to Reason
and author of *The Story of Reality* and *Tactics*

Lee Strobel takes an unconventional approach in *The Case for Miracles* as he confronts head-on the skeptics' arguments and systematically demolishes all of them. But he doesn't stop there; he presents a powerful case for the actual occurrence of miracles and other divine intervention in our lives. He doesn't dodge any of the nagging questions but provides comforting and satisfactory explanations for why God doesn't supernaturally resolve every problem we face and erase all human suffering this side of eternity. This is not merely a feel-good book for hungry believers; it's a thoughtful treatment covering the full scope of the subject—from the subjective, experiential, and anecdotal to the objective, rational, and theological. This book is first-rate—and another superb contribution to Lee's invaluable body of work.

DAVID LIMBAUGH, *New York Times*
bestselling author of *Jesus On Trial*

With his usual flair and readable style, Lee Strobel deals at length with the issue of miracles through a series of interesting interviews, making it clear that it would indeed be a miracle if one could explain all the myriads of testimonies of miracles through the ages by a theory that doesn't involve God. Highly recommended!

BEN WITHERINGTON III, PhD, Amos professor of New Testament for doctrinal studies at Asbury Theological Seminary

Lee Strobel has done it again. In *The Case for Miracles*, he pulls off a theological and apologetic hat trick with respect to topic, evidence, and style. First, the overall question addressed in the book requires courage, if not sheer audacity. He tackles one of the thorniest issues perennially embedded within the arguments between belief and unbelief—the question of miracles. Second, he looks head-on at the evidence for and against(!) miracles in today's world—and the stories are amazing. Finally, as to style, Lee sets forth his case by developing historical, scientific, and biblical materials in a way that not only is readable for a popular audience, but has substantial theological and philosophical content undergirding it. Lee Strobel has, once again, done his homework. I highly recommend this book!

ROBERT B. SLOAN, president of Houston Baptist University

Lee Strobel's new book, *The Case for Miracles*, is a resource that has been needed in the apologetics field for years. The dismissal of Christianity by many young adults is due to the strong bias against the supernatural so prevalent in the classroom and culture. Strobel is known for meticulous research, gripping one-on-one interviews, and compelling apologetic conclusions—and *The Case for Miracles* powerfully delivers on these points. The book offers fresh research about God and the possibility of his intervention in the world. I am confident that Strobel's work is tangibly helping people see beyond the naturalistic bias that has gripped academia for far too long.

ALEX MCFARLAND, director of apologetics and Christian worldview at North Greenville University

This may be my favorite book among the many favorites Lee Strobel has written. Without the miraculous, Christianity crumbles under the weight of its own claims. Once again, Lee brings the curiosity of an investigator, the skill of a legal editor, the mind of a scientist, and the heart of a pastor to make the case for miracles in a way that will compel skeptics, strengthen doubters, and embolden people of faith.

> GENE APPEL, senior pastor of Eastside Christian Church,
> Anaheim, California

Lee Strobel turns his investigative mind toward the question of modern-day miracles, interviewing both Christians and non-Christians to provide a balanced approach. I'm glad to recommend *The Case for Miracles* because I believe that our God still works in the world, both to demonstrate his power to unbelievers and to strengthen the faith of Jesus followers.

> ED STETZER, PhD, Billy Graham distinguished
> chair at Wheaton College

One of the most troubling verses in the Bible says that Jesus taught in his hometown, but "did not do many miracles there because of their lack of faith." Could this be true of *my* life? Of *yours*? A great way to expand your faith is by reading *The Case for Miracles*. This exciting new book will increase your expectancy for God's miraculous activity—even in your own life.

> MARK MITTELBERG, bestselling author of *Confident Faith* and
> *The Questions Christians Hope No One Will Ask (with Answers)*

Over the years, I've struggled with how to thoughtfully articulate a belief in miracles. Some of my struggle comes from having been generally raised with atheistic naturalism. My tendency is to disbelieve first and then ask questions. After reading *The Case for Miracles*, I now see I lacked cohesion to my view of miracles. My attempts at understanding were disjointed and incidental. Lee Strobel investigates miracles from many vantage points, including atheistic skepticism, eyewitness testimony, historical evidence, scientific testability, visions and dreams, evangelical embarrassment, and unanswered prayers. It's a whirlwind of angles written at an accessible level, with Strobel's usual dry wit peppered in along the way. If you've ever wondered about God's miraculous work in his creation, this book is for you.

> MARY JO SHARP, apologetics professor, author,
> and director of Confident Christianity

Also by Lee Strobel

THE CASE FOR
Miracles

A Journalist Investigates
Evidence for the Supernatural

LEE
STROBEL

ZONDERVAN

The Case for Miracles
Copyright © 2018 by Lee Strobel

Requests for information should be addressed to:
Zondervan, *3900 Sparks Dr. SE, Grand Rapids, Michigan 49546*

ISBN 978-0-310-25924-4 (international trade paper edition)

ISBN 978-0-310-35169-6 (audio)

ISBN 978-0-310-34334-9 (ebook)

Library of Congress Cataloging-in-Publication Data

Names: Strobel, Lee, 1952- author.
Title: The case for miracles : a journalist investigates evidence for the supernatural /
    Lee Strobel.
Description: Grand Rapids, Michigan : Zondervan, [2018] | Includes bibliographical
    references and index.
Identifiers: LCCN 2017048503 | ISBN 9780310259183 (hardcover)
Subjects: LCSH: Miracles. | Supernatural.
Classification: LCC BT97.3 .S77 2018 | DDC 231.7/3—dc23
    LC record available at https://lccn.loc.gov/2017048503

Cover design: Curt Diepenhorst
Cover photo: caracterdesign / Getty Images
Interior design: Kait Lamphere

First printing January 2018 / Printed in the United States of America

For Emma Jean Mittelberg
Miracle Girl

Contents

PART 4: The Most Spectacular Miracles

PART 5: Difficulties with Miracles

My guide must be my reason, and at the thought of miracles my reason is rebellious. Personally, I do not believe that Christ laid claim to doing miracles, or asserted that he had miraculous power . . . There is no supernatural.

Thomas A. Edison[1]

Events that we commonly call miracles are not supernatural, but are part of a spectrum of more-or-less improbable natural events. A miracle, in other words, if it occurs at all, is a tremendous stroke of luck.

Richard Dawkins[2]

A scientific law is not a scientific law if it holds only when some supernatural being decides not to intervene.

Stephen Hawking[3]

Miracles in fact are a retelling in small letters of the very same story which is written across the whole world in letters too large for some of us to see.

C. S. Lewis[4]

If [an unbeliever] is confronted with a miracle as an irrefutable fact he would rather disbelieve his own senses than admit the fact.

Fyodor Dostoyevsky[5]

God is not a prisoner of the laws of nature . . . God, who set the regularities there, can himself feed a new event into the system from outside. Science cannot stop Him from doing that.

John Lennox[6]

If miracles exist at all, they exist not for their own sake but for us, to point us toward something beyond. To someone beyond.

Eric Metaxas[7]

"Unless you people see signs and wonders, you will never believe."

Jesus, in John 4:48

The most incredible thing about miracles is that they happen.

G. K. Chesterton[8]

Investigating the Miraculous

Everyone had high hopes for Benjamin after he finished third in his class at a predominantly black high school and scored the highest SAT ranking of any student in twenty years from a Detroit public school.

He could only afford the ten-dollar admission fee to apply to one college, so he chose Yale University and was granted a full scholarship. He thought he was pretty hot stuff—until the end of his first semester.

Ben was failing chemistry, a prerequisite in fulfilling his dream of becoming a physician. Everything depended on the final exam. But he wasn't ready for it, not by a long shot.

That evening, he prayed. "Lord, medicine is the only thing I ever wanted to do," he said. "Would you please tell me what it is *you* really want me to do?"

He intended to study for the exam all night, but sleep overcame him. All seemed lost—until he had a dream: he was alone in an auditorium when a nebulous figure began writing chemistry problems on the blackboard.

"When I went to take the test the next morning, it was like *The Twilight Zone*," he recalled. "I recognized the first problem as one of the ones I had dreamed about. And the next, and the next, and the next—and I aced the exam and got a good mark in chemistry. And I promised the Lord he would never have to do that for me again."

Ben went on to achieve his goal of becoming a physician. By age thirty-three, he became the youngest director of pediatric neurosurgery in the country, performing pioneering operations at Johns Hopkins Hospital. He separated twins conjoined at the brain, performed the first successful neurosurgery on a fetus, developed new methods of treating brain stem and spinal cord tumors, and was awarded the nation's highest civilian honor, the Presidential Medal of Freedom.

A 2014 poll ranked Benjamin Solomon Carson Sr. as among the ten most admired people in America. He even made a bid to become president of the United States, achieving front-runner status in the Republican primary for a season. All because a dream helped him pass a chemistry course nearly fifty years ago.[1]

What do you think? Was this a coincidence? A tall tale exaggerated to promote a political career? Or a miraculous intervention by God?

✳ ✳ ✳

In Equatorial Africa, far from pharmacies and hospitals, a woman died in childbirth, leaving behind a grieving two-year-old daughter and a premature baby in danger of succumbing to the chill of the night. With no incubator, no electricity, and few supplies, the newborn's life was in jeopardy.

A helper filled a hot water bottle to maintain the warmth desperately needed by the infant, but suddenly the rubber burst—and it was the last hot water bottle in the village.

A visiting missionary physician from Northern Ireland, Dr. Helen Roseveare, asked the orphans to pray for the situation—but a faith-filled ten-year-old named Ruth seemed to go too far.

"Please, God, send us a water bottle," she implored. "It'll be no good tomorrow, God, the baby'll be dead; so please send it this afternoon." As if that request was not sufficiently audacious, she added, "And while You are about it, would You please send a dolly for the little girl so she'll know You really love her?"

Recalled Roseveare, "I was put on the spot. Could I honestly say, 'Amen'? I just did not believe that God could do this. Oh, yes, I know that He can do everything. The Bible says so, but there are limits, aren't there?"

The only hope of getting a water bottle would be from a parcel sent from the homeland, but she had never received one during the almost four years she had lived there. "Anyway," she mused, "if anyone did send a parcel, who would put in a hot water bottle? I live on the equator!"

A couple of hours later, a car dropped off a twenty-two-pound package. The orphans helped open it and sort through the contents: some clothing for them, bandages for the leprosy patients, and a bit of food.

Oh, and this: "As I put my hand in again, I felt the . . . could it really be? I grasped it, and pulled it out. Yes. A brand-new rubber, hot water bottle!" said Roseveare. "I cried. I had not asked God to send it; I had not truly believed that He could."

With that, little Ruth rushed forward. "If God has sent the bottle, He must have sent the dolly too!" she exclaimed.

She dug through the packaging and found it at the bottom of the parcel: a beautifully dressed doll. Asked Ruth, "Can I go over with you, Mummy, and give this dolly to that little girl, so she'll know that Jesus really loves her?"

That parcel had been packed *five months earlier* by Roseveare's former Sunday school class. The leader, feeling prompted by God, included the hot water bottle; a girl contributed the doll.

And this package, the only one ever to arrive, was delivered the same day Ruth prayed for it with the faith of a child.[2]

A mere twist of fate? An embellished yarn? Or perhaps a miracle?

✳ ✳ ✳

Duane Miller's greatest enjoyment came from preaching at his small church and singing songs of worship. It wasn't just his livelihood to lead a Baptist congregation in Brenham, Texas; it was his passion, his calling, and his source of joy and satisfaction.

When he awoke with the flu one Sunday morning, his throat was like sandpaper and his voice would "catch" on words. Each syllable was painful to speak. The flu soon disappeared, but his windpipe remained ablaze and his voice reduced to a raspy whisper. His throat felt constricted, as if someone were choking him.

For all practical purposes, Miller's voice was gone. No longer able to preach, he resigned from his pastorate. He eventually landed a government job researching records—a position he then lost because his inability to speak meant he couldn't testify in court about his findings. Insurance stopped covering his treatments, and he faced thousands of dollars in medical bills.

"For the first time in my life, I felt utterly useless. My income, my future, my health, my sense of well-being, all were suddenly beyond my control. It was a terrifying and humbling experience," he said.

Over three years, he was examined by sixty-three physicians. His case was even scrutinized by a Swiss symposium of the world's leading throat specialists. The diagnosis: the flu virus destroyed the nerves of his vocal cords, rendering them limp. When Miller asked about his prognosis for recovery, a doctor told him, "Zero."

Despite Miller's protestations, his former Sunday school class at First Baptist Church of Houston prevailed on him to speak. A special microphone was used to amplify Miller's soft, hoarse, croaky voice—and the class agreed to endure the grating sound because of their love for him and his teaching.

Ironically, his text was Psalm 103, where the third verse reads, God "heals all your diseases." Miller said later, "With my tongue, I was saying, 'I still believe that God heals,' but in my heart, I was screaming, *'But why not me, Lord?'*"

He went on to the next verse, which says the Lord "redeems your life from the pit." He told the class, "I have had and you have had in times past *pit* experiences."

As soon as he said the word *pit*, the choking sensation disappeared. "Now, for the first time in three years, I could breathe freely," he recalled. "I heard a gasp from the crowd, and that's when I, too, realized my voice had come back. I could hear myself!"

His stunned audience began to clap and cheer, shout and laugh; his wife, Joylene, broke down in tears. "I don't understand this right now," Miller stammered—with a fresh, new voice.

The dramatic moment of Miller's recovery had been captured on audiotape, which went viral. Subsequent doctor examinations showed his throat looks like it never had any problems; in fact, against all odds, even the scar tissue has disappeared.

Said one physician, "Even if I could explain how you got your voice back by coincidence—which I can't—I could never explain what happened to the scar tissue."

Today, Miller is pastor of Pinnacle Church, serving the Cedar Creek Lake area of Texas. Ironically, he also hosts a daily program on a Dallas radio station—yes, using his voice to tell others about the God who he is convinced still performs miracles.

"You see, God didn't just restore my life," he said. "He *amplified* it."[3]

At his website, you can listen to the tape of when his voice came back.[4] Then ask, "Is this a supernatural act of God? Or is it better explained as some sort of spontaneous remission that only coincidentally occurred while he was quoting the Bible on healing?"

✻ ✻ ✻

Jennifer Groesbeck, a twenty-five-year-old single mother studying to become a medical assistant, was driving home on a darkened Utah highway in 2015 when her car suddenly struck a concrete barrier and careened off the road.

The red Dodge sedan landed upside down, partially submerged in the icy waters of a river, not visible from the roadway.

Fourteen hours later, a fisherman spotted the wreck and called police. When four officers arrived, they spotted an arm through the car's window, but the severity of the wreck argued against anyone surviving such a horrific accident.

That's when they heard a woman's voice calling out softly, "Help me, we're in here!" The words were as clear as day. Shouted back an officer, "Hang in there! We're trying what we can!"

Now motivated to push harder, their adrenaline fueled by the hope of a survivor, the officers plunged into the near-freezing waters, which at times reached their necks, and used their collective strength to pull the water-laden vehicle onto its side.

What they discovered shocked them. Groesbeck had been killed on impact. But in the backseat, they found an unconscious eighteen-month-old girl, who had hung by her car seat upside down all through the frigid night, the top of her blond hair just inches from the water.

The rescuers formed a human chain to bring the child to safety, where she was briefly hospitalized and later released in good health.

But that voice—where did it come from? Not from Groesbeck, who was long deceased from the crash. Not from the child, who was unconscious—besides, said a rescuer, it was definitely the voice of a woman.

Officer Tyler Beddoes said he wouldn't have believed what

happened if the other rescuers hadn't heard the voice too. "That's the part that really sends me for a whirl," he told reporters. "I'm not a typically religious guy. It's hard to explain—it was definitely something. Where and why it came from, I'm not sure."

Many people didn't hesitate to call it a miracle. But could there be another explanation? Perhaps rescuers mistook the sound of a breeze through the trees. Or maybe the deceased mother somehow momentarily regained life at just the right instant to give the police the extra adrenaline they needed. Or possibly it was a product of the overactive imagination of the officers, whose senses were heightened in the crisis.

A miracle? Beddoes isn't sure, but given the circumstances, even this skeptical cop conceded, "That's what you think of."[5]

❊ ❊ ❊

There are more than a thousand people in the British auditorium. The lights are bright, and old-time gospel music swells from the organ. The healing evangelist speaks in an unknown tongue; he casts out demons; he touches people on the face and they instantly fall backward. There is an unmistakable sense of euphoria and anticipation in the room.

The evangelist, who seems to be responding to some private word of knowledge, begins calling out diseases that are being healed. Soon people line up to testify that their ailments have miraculously disappeared. Someone says their shortsightedness is cured; another reports that a persistent ringing in his ears has been alleviated; a third says his sprained ankle has suddenly been restored to full strength and he can walk again without pain.

The evening has the feel of a charismatic healing service, but with one major difference: the "healing evangelist" is an atheist.

Derren Brown is a former Christian who is now one of England's most famous illusionists. "It is his unparalleled ability as a 'mentalist' that sets him apart," said Christian commentator Justin Brierley. "Using a mixture of suggestion, 'cold reading,' hypnosis and plain old trickery, Brown has the ability to make people believe in God, miracles and the power of prayer."

Brown professed faith in Jesus as a youngster and attended a Pentecostal church, but he became disillusioned when he felt manipulated into speaking in tongues and when his Christian friends cautioned him against his foray into hypnosis. He said his decision to come out as gay wasn't a factor so much as his mounting disbelief in the resurrection of Jesus.

Performance after performance in his stage show *Miracles*, Brown would produce an exciting and stimulating atmosphere. "I thought that if I could create some type of adrenaline, then someone with a bad back is going to tell me that they can't feel the pain," he explained. "It's a chemical thing."

What's more, he added, "They would also hit the floor when I touched them on the face because they have a certain expectation. When you go to these events as a believer you know what's supposed to happen. So I show clips of people doing that. By the time they come up on stage, there's a similar expectation of what they're supposed to do."

Brown insists he isn't trying to dissuade people from faith. Citing nineteenth-century German philosopher Arthur Schopenhauer, he says Christianity can be useful as a folk myth if it helps people make sense of their lives.

"But it has to be presented as real in order for it to work and have a real effect," Brown said. Then he admitted, "That might sound very patronizing, of course, if you believe it to be real."[6]

Do these "fake miracles" discredit other miracle claims? Or

because this atmosphere doesn't resemble how most healings take place, is Brown's show irrelevant to the question of whether some miracles are actually genuine?

* * *

Recently, I was chatting with a former colleague from my days as an atheist and legal editor at the *Chicago Tribune.*

"You were the last person I ever thought would give up journalism to go tell people about Jesus," he said. "You were one of the most skeptical people I knew. If I told you the deli down the block had a good sandwich, you wouldn't believe me until I produced a dozen restaurant reviews, plus a certified chemical analysis of the ingredients from the Food and Drug Administration."

That's an obvious exaggeration, but, yes, my background in journalism and law did tend to amplify my naturally doubting personality. The newsroom, with its prevailing attitude of scoffing skepticism, was an ideal environment for me. And yet, ironically, it was my skepticism that ultimately drove me to faith in Jesus.

That's because my wife Leslie's newfound belief in Christ provoked me to investigate the historical underpinnings of Christianity. I was confident that my strategic objections would end up undermining the entire religion and rescue her from this "cult."

To my dismay, the data of science (from cosmology and physics to biochemistry and human consciousness) convinced me there was a supernatural Creator, while the evidence from history satisfied me that Jesus of Nazareth was resurrected from the dead, confirming his identity as the unique Son of God.

The inexorable conclusion that Christianity is true prompted me to put my trust in Christ and later leave my newspaper career to spend my life telling others the story of his atoning death on their behalf.

However, my skeptical nature didn't entirely dissipate. Did I believe in miracles? Yes, of course, I was convinced that the resurrection and other miracles occurred as the Gospels reported. But that left open the question of whether God is still in the miracle business today.

I did agree with pastor and author Timothy Keller, who said, "There is nothing illogical about miracles if a Creator God exists. If a God exists who is big enough to create the universe in all its complexity and vastness, why should a mere miracle be such a mental stretch?"[7]

Theologically, I was not in the camp of the *cessationists*— Christians who believe that after the apostles died and the New Testament canon was established, signs and wonders ceased and we shouldn't seek them today.[8]

On top of that, I had seen God's mysterious work in my own life. For example, one day during prayer, I felt prompted to get an anonymous five-hundred-dollar cashier's check and send it to a young woman in our church who was struggling to recover from a life of abuse and financial difficulty.

Leslie prayed about it and felt precisely the same urging. We knew this wasn't something conjured from our own minds because that amount constituted almost all of our bank account at the time. Specifically, we felt compelled to mail the check so it would arrive the following Monday.

On Monday morning, before the mail's delivery, the young woman called in an absolute panic. "Please pray for me," she pleaded. "My car broke down Saturday afternoon, and they said it will cost almost five hundred dollars to fix. I just don't have the money. I don't know what to do!"

"Okay," I said, trying to conceal the buoyancy I felt inside. "Leslie and I will pray for you."

That afternoon, she received the anonymous check—and Leslie and I experienced the joy of being the answer to someone's prayers.

Coincidence? I suppose it could have been if it were the only such head-scratching incident we have experienced in our Christian life. To me, it fit an ongoing pattern of God listening and supernaturally responding.

And yet . . .

Feeling Conflicted over Prayer

As a young staff member at Willow Creek Church near Chicago, I was asked to substitute for a pastor in presiding over a monthly prayer session for people seeking healing from God. About a hundred people gathered in our chapel as we put James 5:14 into practice: "Is anyone among you sick? Let them call the elders of the church to pray over them and anoint them with oil in the name of the Lord."

My role would be to offer a general prayer on behalf of everyone assembled; for those who then wanted individual prayer and anointing, several of our elders were on hand afterward.

I have to confess that I felt conflicted. Much of the prayer came easily—asking for God to provide wisdom to the physicians, to comfort those who were suffering, to relieve pain, to strengthen hope and faith, to guide the hands of surgeons, and so forth. All of that, of course, was important.

But when it came to specifically asking God for healing, how bold should I be? How strongly should I phrase my request? My unstated fear: *What if I stick out my neck and beseech God for healing—and nothing happens?* Was I copping out when I concluded my prayer with, "Your will be done"?

Ultimately, I prayed as authentically as I knew how and with as much faith as I could muster. I did explicitly ask God to supernaturally restore the health of all those gathered. But in the back of my mind, I wondered if he would really come through for them in this world. Selfishly, I fretted that my credibility was at stake.

After all, for every person who experiences a miracle like the one that happened to Duane Miller, whose voice was instantaneously restored after several years as he preached, there are many others whose healing won't come until heaven.

In fact, the day Miller's voice was miraculously cured, a thirty-two-year-old father of two children was sitting in that same congregation. He had been diagnosed with a brain tumor. Despite the church's fervent prayers, he died two weeks later.[9]

I couldn't identify with some of my Pentecostal friends who cite Isaiah 53:5—"with his stripes we are healed"—to claim that if someone has sufficient faith in Jesus, then physical healing will surely flow in this life. Of course, that means the reverse would also be true—if they aren't healed, then it's somehow their fault for lacking faith. That's untenable to me.

Miller is as perplexed as anyone why he was selected for such dramatic supernatural action. "I can't give you 'ten principles to prepare for God's healing,'" he said. "It wasn't my faith, it wasn't my response, it wasn't my obedience, I didn't earn a thing. I just received His unearned favor."[10]

Miracles versus Coincidence

Driving through downtown Houston, its streets choked with cars at rush hour, I inched toward a skyscraper where I was due for a meeting—and against all odds, I spotted a vacant parking space adjacent to the door.

A miracle, I mused—and maybe it was. Or maybe it wasn't. The truth is that we often throw around that term too loosely.

I set my computer to search for the key word *miracle* among the news stories on the internet, and invariably all sorts of articles are snagged. Just today, there were such headlines as "Boat captain rescues 'miracle' cat thrown off bridge," "Miracle on Water Street: A doctor witnesses crash, saves man's life," and "Miracle baby born the size of a tennis ball now home." A football player was said to need a "miracle" to resuscitate his sagging career, and a diver who survived after hitting his head on the platform during a competition is called a "miracle man."

What's the best way to define the miraculous? Philosophers and theologians have offered various descriptions. Augustine was poetic, saying a miracle is "whatever appears that is difficult or unusual above the hope and power of them who wonder." Scottish philosopher David Hume was skeptical: "A miracle is a violation of the laws of nature." Oxford's Richard Swinburne was straightforward, calling a miracle "an event of an extraordinary kind brought about by a god and of religious significance."[11]

Personally, I'm partial to the definition offered by the late Richard L. Purtill, professor emeritus of philosophy at Western Washington University: "A miracle is an event (1) brought about by the power of God that is (2) a temporary (3) exception (4) to the ordinary course of nature (5) for the purpose of showing that God has acted in history."[12]

To illustrate his definition, Purtill recounted how he had been prescribed nitroglycerine tablets for a heart condition. The pharmacist said something that stuck in his mind: if two pills taken in succession don't relieve the pain, take a third but immediately call an ambulance.

Not long afterward, he awoke with chest pain. He took one pill and later another, but neither had an effect. He took a third. His wife offered to drive him to the hospital, but he asked her to call 911. She did, the paramedics arrived promptly, and his life was saved.

After he recovered, he had a flat tire on a car trip and his heart stopped while he was changing the tire. He fell unconscious, his head on the freeway. Two passing motorists stopped; both of them just happened to know CPR. One called the paramedics. Purtill's heart was restarted, and his life was spared once more.

Although he said he's grateful to God for the outcome, Purtill stressed that "there was nothing in the events to suggest any nonnatural causes. The pharmacist's remarks, the training of the people who helped me, the medical technology are all things that seem to need no nonnatural explanation."

Consequently, he doesn't consider his preservation to be miraculous. On the other hand, he does believe as a Christian that "God was, as usual, hiding divine action in plain sight amid the ordinary course of events."[13]

So some of what we casually classify as "miracles" really seem closer to fortunate "coincidences," or God at work through routine processes. How can we tell them apart? For me, when I see something extraordinary that has spiritual overtones and is validated by an independent source or event, that's when the "miracle" bell goes off in my mind.

In other words, a dream about a nebulous figure writing chemistry problems on a blackboard isn't miraculous in itself. But if those equations are the very same problems that present themselves on an independently prepared examination the next day, that *does* seem miraculous—especially when the incident occurs after a prayer pleading for God's help.

Spontaneous remissions do happen sometimes in serious illnesses, but they usually take place over a period of time and often do not endure. If a serious illness is instantly and permanently eradicated at the exact moment a prayer for healing is being offered—well, that tends to push the needle over into the "miracle" category for me.

More Than 94 Million "Miracles"

It's not surprising that my former tribe of atheists deny the possibility of the miraculous, although it is startling how many of them are so vocally hostile to the concept.

"For New Atheists and their fellow travelers . . . skepticism has become an evangelical endeavor," said Noah Berlatsky, a contributing writer for *The Atlantic*. "It's not enough to sit in the corner and quietly disbelieve; they must spread their disbelief at the point of rationalism's sharp sword. Like an enlightened imperial conqueror, the skeptic will liberate you from the weight of tradition and superstition—whether you want to be liberated or not."[14]

The late atheist Christopher Hitchens used his considerable wit and rhetorical flair to try to humiliate anyone who dared to publicly affirm that miracles have taken place. In debating Christians, he would ask, "Do you *really* believe that Jesus was born of a virgin? Do you *really* believe that he rose from the dead?"

If the Christian answered yes, Hitchens would declare with a dramatic flourish, "Ladies and gentlemen, my opponent has just demonstrated that science has done nothing for his worldview."

Said Timothy McGrew, chairman of the philosophy department at Western Michigan University, "It is always a shrewd move to paint one's adversary as an enemy of science, and Hitchens rarely let slip an opportunity for good theater. But good theater is not always good reasoning."[15]

So where do most Americans stand on the topic of miracles?

As I began researching this book, my curiosity prompted me to commission a national scientific survey, which was conducted by Barna Research.[16] This is the first place the results have appeared.

Interestingly, half of US adults (51 percent) said they believe that the miracles of the Bible happened as they are described.

Asked whether miracles are possible today, two out of three Americans (67 percent) said yes, with only 15 percent saying no. Young adults were less likely (61 percent) to believe than Boomers (73 percent). Incidentally, Republicans were more likely to believe in modern miracles (74 percent) than Democrats (61 percent).

I was interested in what was generating the skepticism of those who don't think miracles can occur these days. Forty-four percent didn't believe in the supernatural, while 20 percent were convinced that modern science has ruled out the possibility of miracles.

Most of all, I wanted to know how many people have had an experience that they can only explain as being a miracle of God.

As it turns out, nearly two out of five US adults (38 percent) said they have had such an experience—which means that an eye-popping *94,792,000* Americans are convinced that God has performed at least one miracle for them personally.[17] That is an astonishing number!

Even weeding out instances that were actually "coincidences"—as many of those undoubtedly would be—that still leaves a surprising number of seemingly supernatural events.

However, the percentage decreased with education—41 percent of those with a high school diploma said they have had a divine intervention, compared to 29 percent of college graduates. The same was true for income levels, with more skepticism among the wealthy. In terms of ethnicity, more than half of Hispanics and blacks affirmed such an experience, compared to a third of whites.

Unsurprisingly, the number soared to nearly 78 percent among evangelical Christians. Perhaps many of them wouldn't even be believers had they not experienced God in a remarkable way.

Although skeptic Harriet Hall dismissed supernatural reports as being "more common from the uncivilized and uneducated,"[18] a 2004 survey showed that 55 percent of US physicians have seen results in their patients that they would consider miraculous.[19] That's coming from highly educated professionals trained in medicine and working on the front lines of serving the sick and injured.

Three-quarters of the 1,100 doctors surveyed are convinced that miracles can occur today—a percentage that's actually higher than that of the US population in general. So maybe it's not surprising that six out of ten physicians said they pray for their patients individually.[20]

Hitting the Road Again

The big issue, however, is whether belief in supernatural occurrences is based on mistake, misunderstanding, fraud, legend, rumor, wishful thinking, confirmation bias, the placebo effect—or reality.

In other words, does a miracle-performing God actually exist, and has he left his fingerprints all over supernatural events throughout history down to the present age? Is he even available to intervene in *your* life today?

That's what I set out to determine in writing this book. While I'm a committed Christian whose convictions are widely known, I was truly interested in testing the strength of the case for miracles.

"Here we go again," Leslie muttered with a smile when she saw me stuffing clothes into my suitcase.

Yes, I was hitting the road to conduct face-to-face research with leading authorities so I could tap into their lifetime of experience and expertise. That has been the methodology in most of my books: seeking out experts I can cross-examine in digging for truth.

I figured there was no better place to start than to interview the most famous doubter in the country—Dr. Michael Shermer, founder and editor of *Skeptic* magazine.

I zipped my luggage closed and grabbed my boarding pass for Los Angeles. My goal in questioning Shermer was simple: I wanted him to build the strongest possible case *against* miracles. After all, if it's rational to believe in the miraculous, then that case surely should be able to stand up to his challenges.

In the end, I'll ask you to render a verdict on whether or not it does.

PART 1

The Case *against* Miracles

An Interview with Dr. Michael Shermer

CHAPTER 1

The Making of a Skeptic

This was not a place where I would typically hang out. There I was, a committed Christian, sitting at a conference table in the offices of *Skeptic* magazine, inside a two-bedroom wooden house in a residential neighborhood just north of Los Angeles.

Framed covers of the iconoclastic periodical ringed the walls. Busts of Darwin and Einstein perched atop a redbrick fireplace. Crowded shelves teeming with books and snarky trinkets jammed every spare inch of space. There was a bar of "Wash Away Your Sins" soap, promising to reduce guilt by 98.9 percent. The label of a beer bottle acquired on a trip to Utah read, "Polygamy Porter: Why Stop at Just One?"

In a sense, I was visiting the anti-church, a shrine to the science and reason that—in the view of many skeptics, anyway—squeeze out the legitimacy of faith in God.

There was a time when I might have been a writer for this free-thinking journal. But that was years ago, during my atheist era, when I enjoyed nothing more than poking fun at Christians who clung to the teachings of first-century Middle Eastern sheepherders. At that time in my life, I would have relished a pilgrimage to this sanctuary of skepticism.

These days, I'm convinced that science and history—indeed, reason itself—actually support the Christian worldview. My atheism has been turned upside down and inside out, if not miraculously, then unexpectedly and decisively.

Today I came to these offices to meet face-to-face with my polar opposite: someone whose journey has taken him from faith to doubt, turning him from a proselytizer for Jesus into an apologist for disbelief.

In short, a skeptic's skeptic.

After I waited for a few minutes, sixty-one-year-old Michael Shermer, diminutive and wiry, came bounding into the room, fresh from his regular Thursday bicycle ride with two dozen friends. Today he rode fifty miles on his carbon fiber German cycle, which weighs a scant fifteen pounds. The workout was a down payment on the two hundred or so miles he bikes each week.

"It's a little addictive," he concedes with a smile.

Wearing a black T-shirt, black pants, and sandals, Shermer sits down adjacent to me at the conference table and flips up the screen of his laptop. He has a warm handshake and an infectious smile. His graying hair is receding, but he's full of a teenager's energy and enthusiasm.

Shermer seems to check all the boxes of the stereotypical Californian. Exercise enthusiast? Yes, he has even published two books on bicycling. Careful diet? Yes, he eats chicken or fish only once a week. "Rarely red meat," he said. Electric car? Of course: "I haven't been in a gas station in more than a year." Politically, he's liberal on social issues, though conservative fiscally.

Shermer used to live in this 1,062-square-foot house, which was built in 1941 and is surrounded by a tall wooden fence. Now it's the home of his 35,000-circulation *Skeptic* magazine and the Skeptic Society—nonprofit ventures he founded in 1992. Four employees work here; the garage serves as the mailroom. Two other employees live in Canada, publishing a *Skeptic* magazine for kids.

Shermer's office is narrow and lined with posters promoting his various debates, including "Does God Exist?" and "Can Science and Religion Reconcile?" In photos on the wall, he's smiling alongside atheist Richard Dawkins of Oxford and evolutionary biologist Stephen Jay Gould of Harvard.

We pause to take a selfie of ourselves smiling together. He later posts it on Twitter, though I'm doubtful it will end up on his wall.

Both Strange *and* True?

I told Shermer I had sought him out for two reasons. First, I appreciated his reputation as someone wary of religion and yet generally free from the mocking tone employed by some of the more militant anti-theists. Yes, that includes his friend Dawkins, who once encouraged fellow atheists to "ridicule and show contempt" for religious beliefs and sacraments.[1]

In contrast, Shermer likes the approach of Dutch philosopher Baruch Spinoza, who said in 1667, "I have made a ceaseless effort not to ridicule, not to bewail, not to scorn human actions, but to understand them."[2]

Second, I was looking for someone who could present the best possible case against the miraculous, free from emotion and backed with studies and reasoned arguments. "I want your best stuff," I said.

As the interview was about to begin, I glanced over my shoulder. Dangling from a nail was a pair of boxing gloves—*A good sign*, I thought, because I sincerely wanted him to hit me with his strongest objections to miracles.

I made it clear: I was not here to debate him. I didn't fly all the way to California for an argument. I wanted to listen and learn, to dialogue and discuss. I didn't see why the faithful and the faithless couldn't sit down and talk rationally, even about a topic that in its very nature transcends mere rationality. Besides, I wanted to hear Shermer's story directly from him. What could I learn from someone who has taken the opposite path from the one I took?

Certainly I couldn't find a better skeptic than Michael Brant Shermer, whose curriculum vitae goes on for nearly thirty pages. He earned his bachelor's degree in psychology and biology at Pepperdine University, his master's degree in experimental psychology at California State University, and his doctorate in the history of science at Claremont Graduate University. His dissertation was on nineteenth-century British evolutionary thinker Alfred Russel Wallace, who declared himself in 1861 to be "an utter disbeliever in almost all . . . [of] the most sacred truths."[3]

Shermer is a columnist for *Scientific American*, writing under the banner "Skeptic: Viewing the World with a Rational Eye." At Chapman University in Orange, California, Shermer teaches a course on critical thinking, aptly titled Skepticism 101. He has authored more than a dozen books, including *How We Believe, The Science of Good and Evil, Why Darwin Matters, The Believing Brain, The Moral Arc,* and his latest: *Heavens on Earth*.

He has spoken at more than a hundred colleges and universities, including Harvard (three times), Yale, and the Massachusetts Institute of Technology. He is widely published in popular and academic publications (for example, "How to Be Open-Minded without Your Brains Falling Out" in the fall 2002 edition of *Journal of Thought*). He has appeared on numerous television programs and was a producer and cohost of "Exploring the Unknown" on the Fox Family Channel. His TED Talks include one that's titled "Why People Believe Strange Things."

I chuckled when I read the title of that lecture. Surely few things sound stranger to the ears of a skeptic than the idea of a divine Creator intervening in the everyday affairs of human beings.

At issue, however, is whether it's both strange *and* true.[4]

The Interview with Michael B. Shermer, PhD

At the very instant that high school senior Michael Shermer read John 3:16—"For God so loved the world that he gave his one and only Son, that whoever believes in him shall not perish but have eternal life"—and then put his trust in Jesus as his Lord and Savior, a coyote howled outside.

"We wondered whether this was some sort of sign," Shermer told me, a slight smile playing at the corner of his mouth. "Maybe Satan was lamenting that he had lost another soul."

It was a Saturday night in 1971, and Shermer's friend George, a devout Christian, led him to faith in a home in the San Gabriel Mountains of Southern California. Maybe Shermer's motives weren't totally pure at the time—after all, he figured a conversion might help his odds in dating George's sister Joyce. But it was real enough to him, a step of faith that became more solid as time went by.

Shermer recounted the story of his spiritual journey. He was leaning back in his chair, one leg crossed over the other, casually reminiscing as if it all had occurred just recently. On the other hand, I was sitting on the edge of my seat, riveted and weighing each word he spoke. He had gone from being an enthusiastic follower of Jesus to becoming perhaps the world's best-known spiritual skeptic.

"The next day, George and his family took me to a Presbyterian church in Glendale. The pastor was a real intellectual—I liked that. At the end he said, 'If you want to be saved, come on up.' I thought, *Okay, I'll go up.* Maybe doing it in a church would make it more official."

"Did you come from a religious family?"

"Not at all," he said. "My parents divorced when I was four. None of my parents or stepparents were believers. When I announced I was born again, I'm sure they thought it was a little weird. In the words of one of my siblings, I became a Jesus freak."

"What did that involve?"

"I was into it 100 percent. I attended a Bible study at a place called The Barn, where Christian teens and young adults met every Wednesday night. It was very '70s—somebody played the guitar, we sang about Jesus, we all had long hair and wore chains around our necks. Mine was the *ichthys*, the so-called Jesus fish, whose Greek letters represented 'Jesus Christ, Son of God, Savior.' Here—I'll show you."

With a few keystrokes, he pulled up a photograph of him—tanned, bare-chested, and smiling—as he sat in the sunshine with his grandmother on his twenty-first birthday. There, around his neck, hung the necklace.

"For me, the Christian paradigm made sense out of everything," he continued. "If something positive happened, it was God's reward for my good deeds or love of Christ; if something bad happened, well, God works in mysterious ways. It was neat and tidy—everything in its place and a place for everything."

"Did you feel like you were growing spiritually?"

"Absolutely, yeah."

He talked of sharing his faith with family and friends—which elicited a lot of eye-rolls—and even going door to door in a sincere effort to spread the gospel. His atheist friends thought he was obnoxious, but Shermer believed if Christianity were true, he had an obligation to tell others about it, even though the experience made him uncomfortable.

"Did you feel close to God?" I asked.

"Oh, yes."

"You felt his presence in your life?"

"In all that I did. I prayed about everything, from getting a parking space at the YMCA where I worked, to my career choice, to my girlfriend. Everything."

"Back then, if I had tried to talk you out of your faith, how would you have responded?"

He thought for a moment. "Let me put it this way: you would not have been successful."

Shermer enrolled at Pepperdine University, a Church of Christ institution, where he enjoyed the twice-weekly chapel services; courses on the Old and New Testaments, the life of Jesus, and the writings of C. S. Lewis; and living among like-minded Christians. His intention was to study theology.

"I wanted to be a professor of religious studies," he said. "That way, you get the intellectual world of theology and you get tenured at a university, where you're paid to teach and read and think. The life of the mind—that's what attracted me."

"What stopped you?

He chuckled. "To be a professor, I needed a PhD. And to get that, I'd have to learn Hebrew, Greek, Aramaic, and Latin. Well, I could barely get through Spanish class. Foreign languages aren't easy for me. So I switched to psychology, which interested me because I enjoyed science. Still, all the way through graduation I was a Christian."

"And then?"

"And then . . . I slowly lost my faith."

I straightened in my chair. "How?"

"Gradually, on my own, which I think is how it usually happens. I don't think you reason people out of this. As the saying goes, 'You can't reason people out of something they didn't reason their way into in the first place.' I think that's largely true. Not always, but in my case, it was."

The Path toward Skepticism

It was during Shermer's graduate studies in experimental psychology that he began to fall away from his faith, but actually this was the culmination of several steps that started early in his Christian experience.

Indeed, he conceded that "there were problems with my conversion from the beginning," including mixed motives (due to his interest in his friend's sister), his discomfort with sharing Jesus with strangers, and normal sexual urges that created intense conflict and frustration. Deep down on some level, he said he knew there were issues.[5]

He was confused by the response he received when he told a high school friend about his newfound faith. Shermer expected a warm embrace. Instead, when Shermer said, "I found Jesus at the Presbyterian church," his buddy—a Jehovah's Witness—was aghast. "Oh, no," he exclaimed. "Wrong church!"

Said Shermer, "It made me wonder how another religion could be as thoroughly certain they had the truth as I was."

He went to a minister to discuss theological issues: *If we have free will, does this mean God is limited in knowledge or power?* With a Pepperdine professor, he grappled with the problem of evil: *If God is omnibenevolent and omnipotent, then why do bad things happen?*

"To this day, I have not heard an answer to the problem of evil that seems satisfactory," he told me. "As with the problem of free will, most answers involve complicated twists, turns of logic, and semantic wordplay."

At Glendale College, he encouraged his philosophy professor to read a popular Christian book that claimed biblical prophecies pointed to the imminent return of Jesus. But instead of bending his knee to Jesus, the professor sent Shermer a blistering two-page, single-spaced rebuttal to the book. To this day, Shermer still has the letter.

After his undergraduate education, he became unanchored to a community of Christians. "There was no discussion of religion at graduate school. Nobody cared about it," he told me.

"Instead, I saw people who were happy and successful doing their own thing. Then as I studied anthropology, sociology, and social psychology, I could clearly see that religious beliefs are culturally bound. For example, if you're born in America, you're likely to be Christian; if you're born in India, you'll probably be Hindu. So how can we determine which religion is the right one? I began to lose interest in Christianity as I got more fascinated by science. Soon science became my belief system, and evolution my doctrine."

"Was there a time when you took off your *ichthys* necklace?" I asked.

"Yes, after a while I felt hypocritical wearing it because I wasn't sure I really believed this stuff anymore. I didn't throw it down in anger. I didn't declare that I was an atheist. It was just something I did quietly. Frankly, I don't think anyone noticed or cared."

Again he reached over to his laptop and pulled up a photo. "Here's a picture of me from graduate school. This is when I was just coming out—see, no fish necklace."

"What did you replace it with?"

"Later, I began wearing a gold dollar sign. At the time, I was into *Atlas Shrugged*. Now I don't wear anything. I'm neutral."

Still, that wasn't the end of his faith experience. There would be one last attempt to connect with God. In the midst of a profound crisis, there would come a heartfelt plea for a miracle that never materialized.

The Miracle That Didn't Happen

Sometimes tragedy reawakens faith. Pain, as C. S. Lewis observed, can be God's megaphone to rouse the spiritually deaf.[6] But what happens when instead of a miraculous answer to prayer, the tearful petitioner hears only silence from above? The miracle that doesn't happen can be the impetus for faith to dissipate to nothing.

That's what happened to Michael Shermer.

"My college sweetheart was named Maureen, a beautiful and wonderful young woman from Alaska. We met at Pepperdine and were still dating after I finished grad school. She worked for an inventory firm—they would drive in the middle of the night to a company and take inventory while it was closed. One night in the middle of nowhere, the van veered off the highway and rolled over several times. She didn't have her seat belt on—and, *boom*, she broke her back."

I winced. It was heartbreaking. A battered van in the darkness at the bottom of a ravine. The screams, the moans, the confusion, the sirens. Lives changed, dreams broken, futures derailed. It's a grim and gruesome scene, but especially when the person being lifted onto a stretcher is someone you love.

"How did you hear about it?" I asked.

"She called at about five in the morning. I said, 'What's going on?' She said, 'I'm in the hospital.' I was stunned, because she sounded pretty normal. 'What? What happened?' She said, 'I don't know. I can't move.'"

Paralyzed from the waist down, Maureen spent six months at Long Beach Memorial Hospital. "I would visit her almost every day, riding my bike twenty-five miles or so," Shermer said. "It was very upsetting. Why would this happen to such a wonderful young woman?"

I knew what I'd be doing if I were in that situation: as a Christian, I would be praying. But Shermer had already removed his Jesus necklace. Was there still a smidgen of faith left?

"Was there a point where you asked God to heal her?" I asked.

"I did, absolutely. It was one of those all-nighters in the emergency room. Even though I had pretty much checked out of my faith, I figured, *I need to give this a shot and ask God to heal her.* It wasn't like I was putting God to a test. I just felt so bad for her that I'd try anything."

"What was your prayer like?"

"I took a knee and bowed my head. I was as sincere as I had ever been. I asked God to overlook my doubts for the sake of Maureen, to heal her, to breathe life into her. As best I could at that moment, I believed. I *wanted* to believe. If there was a God who was powerful and loving, if there was any justice at all anywhere in the universe, then surely he'd help this precious, caring, compassionate young woman."

I waited for Shermer to continue. For a moment, there was silence. Then I asked, "What happened?"

He shook his head. "Nothing."

I let the word hang in the air before finally asking, "How did you react?"

He shrugged. "I wasn't very surprised. I thought, *Well, there probably is no God. Stuff just happens.* This is the nature of evil. Why do bad things happen to good people? Well, why not? It's the second law of thermodynamics. That's the way the world is."

"Was this the final nail in the coffin of your faith?"

"Yeah, that pretty much did it. I was like, 'Ah, the heck with it.'"

"Were you angry at God?"

"Nothing to be angry at. He's not there. This is just what happens. The good, the bad—it's pretty random."

"Then you think the universe lacks any purpose," I said, more as a statement than a question. Richard Dawkins's well-known declaration came to mind: "The universe we observe has precisely the properties we should expect if there is, at bottom, no design, no purpose, no evil and no good, nothing but blind, pitiless indifference."[7]

Said Shermer, "There is no higher purpose. It's left to us. We must create our own purpose. That's the only meaning we have in this universe."

I looked down at my notes. In the margin I scribbled, "Any credible book on miracles must deal with the ones that never happen."

Then I underlined it.

Twice.[8]

CHAPTER 2

The Knockdown Argument

I paused for a few moments after hearing Michael Shermer's story of how he shed his faith. I felt its emotional punch. The mental image of Shermer pleading for God to heal his paralyzed girlfriend wouldn't go away easily. All the more, his experience wanted me to delve deeper.

I was determined to go after the "why" question: Why is he convinced it's illogical to believe that miracles occur? As I began down that path, I wanted to clarify Shermer's current state of belief—and disbelief.

"How would you classify yourself?" I asked. "Are you an atheist? An agnostic?"

"I'm not a strong atheist who says, 'I know there is no God.' How could you know for sure? The weak atheist says, 'I have no belief in God,' and that's how I live my life. When Thomas Henry Huxley coined the term *agnostic* in 1869, he meant God's existence is unknowable.[1] I think that's correct. Like him, I'd say the God question is insoluble.

"But I prefer *skeptic*," he continued. "I would be utterly surprised if there's a God. And if I did encounter some super-advanced, apparently omniscient and omnipotent being, how would I know it's not just an extraterrestrial intelligence? Given the continual advancement of science and technology, in the future humans will be so powerful and knowledgeable that they might be indistinguishable from a deity."

Skepticism, though, is a slippery term. "Obviously, you're not skeptical about everything," I said. "So how do you define *skeptic*?"

"It's taking a scientific approach to claims. The burden of proof should be on the claimant. The Food and Drug Administration doesn't approve a drug just because you say it works. The burden of proof isn't on them; *you* have to prove your drug works. And it should be like that with all claims."

I said, "You once posed the question, 'How can we tell the difference between what we would *like* to be true and what is *actually* true?' You said the answer is science.[2] I'm sure you don't believe science is the *only* pathway to truth, but what role can science play in guiding us toward what's real and reliable?"

"The history of science since Francis Bacon in the seventeenth century has been to overcome the cognitive biases and psychological and emotional factors that have colored other forms of knowledge—intuition, anecdotal thinking, group thinking, authoritative thinking, and so on. All these methods can be very unreliable."

"Science isn't flawless either," I interjected.

"No, it's not. But it's the most reliable method we have. Why? Because it's a communal process. We have peer review. We have people looking over our shoulders when experiments are done. Other labs either validate or challenge results."

"So there are checks and balances."

"Yes. We need those because we're flawed. There is confirmation bias, hindsight bias, wishful thinking—all these things can influence us. You look at an oar in the water, and it looks bent. The earth doesn't feel like it's moving. The sun appears as if it's rising. Our intuitions are often wrong. Even though there are instances of fraud and embarrassing errors in science, they're almost always caught by other scientists."

I asked Shermer whether he agreed with scientist Jerry Coyne of the University of Chicago, an atheist who said, "It would be a close-minded scientist who would say that miracles are impossible in principle." Coyne added that "to have real confidence in a miracle, one needs evidence—massive, well-documented, and either replicated or independently corroborated evidence from multiple and reliable sources." His conclusion: "No religious miracle even comes close to meeting those standards."[3]

"I'd tend to agree," Shermer replied. "I doubt if there's something supernatural, outside of space and time, that intervenes in our world. But if there were, we would be able to measure its effects. What forces were used? And if it reaches into our environment, then it's part of the natural world, not supernatural."

I cocked my head. "So," I said, "you wouldn't foreclose investigation of seemingly miraculous events?"

"Not at all. Let's check them out as best we can. Let's test them. Bring on the evidence. As Coyne said, we can't rule them out in principle, but I don't think there's sufficient proof of anything miraculous."

Miracles versus Anomalies

I offered Shermer the definition of a miracle formulated by philosopher Richard L. Purtill: "A miracle is an event that is brought about by the power of God that is a temporary exception to the ordinary course of nature for the purpose of showing that God is acting in history."[4]

Shermer nodded. "Let's go with that," he said. "But keep in mind that people use the word *miracle* for a lot of other things. For example, it's used for highly unusual events that simply make you say, 'Wow!' Like the American hockey team that won the Olympics against all odds back in 1980. People called it 'the miracle on ice.'[5]

"So many alleged miracles are just highly improbable events like that," he continued. "If you say the odds against something are a million to one, that event might look miraculous, but actually it would occur pretty often. When you have more than three hundred million people in the country, weird things are going to happen— just enough of them for the evening news."

"Yet," I said, "other incidents aren't merely improbable; they better fit Purtill's definition. For instance, you did a radio show with a pastor who offered examples of several cases in which people were healed after he prayed for them in the name of Jesus. He provided names, dates, witnesses, and medical evaluations. Why don't you find cases like this convincing?"

"First of all, I haven't seen the medical reports myself," he said. "But when you give anecdotes about medical healings, it always seems to be things that might have happened on their own anyway. A tumor went into remission—well, sometimes cancer does go into remission. It's not common, but is it a miracle? I'd say it's a statistical anomaly. It's part of nature, so, no, I wouldn't call it miraculous.

"And by the way, we see remarkable recoveries through the placebo effect, which is when people receive a fake or ineffective treatment, but they get better anyway because they *believe* they're being healed or they *expect* they'll get better. This can be seen when people are asked to subjectively rate their pain. 'How's your migraine today? It's a nine? Okay, we're going to try meditation or prayer.' Now it goes down to a six. Did that really work? I don't know. It could have been wishful thinking. But let's be realistic: you're not going to heal an AIDS patient that way."

"What would it take to convince you?" I asked.

Shermer thought for a moment. "We have all these wounded soldiers coming back from Afghanistan and Iraq. Many of them are amputees. They have Christian families that pray to Jesus, and yet none of them has grown back a limb. Why can't God do that? Certain amphibians can grow back limbs. Why can't God do that?"

"So," I said, "you'd want something unambiguous, out in the open—clear and obvious."

"Yes, growing back a limb would get my attention. That would be more convincing than cancer. It would definitely make the evening news. Of course, I'd want to make sure it wasn't some sort of illusion or magic trick. But assuming it wasn't, I'd say, 'All right, God, here's a roomful of amputees. Get to work!'"

He said the problem with anecdotes about healings and other miracles is that they're just that—anecdotes. "Without corroboration or some sort of physical proof, ten anecdotes are no better than one, and a hundred anecdotes are no better than ten," he said. "We need to study them scientifically. And when we do, guess what? Science doesn't support them. I'm sure you're familiar with STEP."

The Study of the Therapeutic Effects of Intercessory Prayer (STEP), conducted under the auspices of the Harvard Medical School, was a ten-year, $2.4 million clinical trial of the effects of prayer on 1,802 cardiac bypass patients at six hospitals.[6]

Patients undergoing cardiac bypass surgery were broken into three groups. One group was prayed for by intercessors and a second group was not, although nobody in either group knew for sure whether they were being uplifted in prayer. A third group was prayed for after being told they definitely would receive prayer. Then researchers tracked the number of complications from the surgeries.

"The results were very revealing," said Shermer. "There was no difference in the rate of complications for patients who were prayed for and those who were not. Nothing. Zero. And, in fact, those who knew they were being prayed for had *more* complications. This is the best prayer study we have. So when you get beyond anecdotes and use the scientific method, there's no evidence for the miraculous."

I lifted my hand to stop him. "Nevertheless," I said, "these kinds of prayer studies have intrinsic problems. For example, you can't control people praying for themselves or having family and friends who were praying for them."

"That's true," Shermer said. "But you have to admit that this study is the best one we have, and it fails to support all of these anecdotes that claim divine intervention. And it's funded primarily by the Templeton Foundation, which is certainly friendly toward religion and faith."

He gestured toward me. "That's not good for your side, Lee."

"Still," I said, "miracles are a temporary exception to the ordinary course of nature. They're onetime events. Doesn't that make them difficult to investigate scientifically?"

"Yes, it's difficult. But we have to remember that it's okay to say, 'I don't know what happened.' Bodies are super-complex systems. The fact that you don't know why something occurred doesn't mean anything miraculous, supernatural, or paranormal happened. It just means, 'I don't know.'"

A "Knockdown" Argument?

David Hume, then a twenty-three-year-old bookworm, did something radical in 1734: he stepped off his career path, left his native Scotland, and headed to France to live an austere life of thinking and writing. He returned three years later, bearing his three-volume opus, *A Treatise of Human Nature*.

When it was published, though, it failed to garner the attention Hume coveted. Instead, as he would lament years later, it "fell deadborn from the press, without reaching such distinction as even to excite a murmur among the zealots."[7]

Ultimately, after more years of work and rewriting, Hume would emerge as an influential philosopher, economist, and historian, perhaps best known for his skepticism about faith and miracles. He is now regarded as "one of the most important philosophers to write in English."[8]

It was Hume who declared, "A wise man proportions his belief to the evidence"—a phrase Shermer has hailed by saying, "Better words could not be found for a skeptical motto."[9]

Hume devoted Section X of his *Enquiries Concerning the Human Understanding and Concerning the Principles of Morals*, written in 1748, to the topic of miracles. For Hume, miracles were a violation of natural law, yet natural law is always and unalterably uniform. Therefore, no amount of evidence would convince him that God had intervened. Indeed, *any* explanation made more sense than a miracle occurring.

Hume declared that there has never in history been any miracle that has been sufficiently established as being true, having occurred publicly, and having been witnessed and reported by people of unquestioned integrity and reputation.[10]

Scholar Graham H. Twelftree points out that there are different interpretations of the various arguments that Hume sets forth in his works. One is that he was saying miracles are simply impossible. Another is that the evidence against a miracle always exceeds the evidence for it. A third is that the standard of proof to establish a miracle claim is so high that it cannot be met, and hence miracles are irrational. Regardless, Hume immodestly predicted that his case against miracles would provide an everlasting check on superstitious delusions.[11]

When asked why he's personally skeptical about miracles, Shermer invariably invokes Hume.

"His classic argument still stands today: Which is more likely, that the laws of nature be suspended or that the person telling you the story is mistaken or has been deceived?" he said. "Misperceptions are common. People make things up. We have a lot of experience with this. It could be an illusion, a hallucination, a mistake—whatever. All of that is more likely than a miracle."

"So you consider Hume's thinking to be persuasive?" I asked.

"Oh, yeah. I think his treatise against miracles is pretty much a knockdown argument. Everything else is a footnote."

"Why," I asked, "do you think Christians believe in miracles? Are they gullible?"

"It has nothing to do with education or intelligence. When I was a Christian, little things would happen and I'd think, *God caused that*. I'd ignore stuff that didn't fit that pattern. This is confirmation bias: you find confirming evidence for what you already believe, and you ignore the disconfirming evidence.

"The power of expectation is strong," he added. "Take a group of people through an old theatre in London and say, 'This place is haunted.' Take another group through and say, 'We're renovating the theatre; tell us how you feel about the look of the place.' Even if the two groups hear the same noises or see the same shadows, they'll interpret it differently based on what they expect."

"Do you think this kind of expectation affects people at healing services in churches?"

"Much of that is psychological, I'm sure. I don't think the leaders of Pentecostal churches are fraudulent. I think they really believe that the power of God is at work. But when people expect to feel better, often they do. That's the placebo effect. They feel better—for a while. But there's rarely any documentation that these so-called healings are permanent."

"How do you define faith?"

"It's believing something when there's no evidence for it," he said. "If there were evidence, it wouldn't be faith. You don't take the germ theory of disease on faith; you don't believe on faith that HIV causes AIDS. You accept that because there's good evidence for them. I'd say that believing something when there isn't good evidence would be a category of faith."

I was tempted to point out that biblical faith is taking a step in the same direction that the evidence is pointing, which actually is rational and logical. But this wasn't the time for a debate; there was still much ground to cover in his case against miracles.

CHAPTER 3

Myths and Miracles

The Bible records about three dozen miracles performed by Jesus of Nazareth, although the gospel of John says that these are just a sampling of all the wonders he wrought.[1]

"If we open the Gospels at almost any place, we cannot avoid encountering the miracles and the miraculous," observed Graham Twelftree, the noted New Testament professor.[2] Even the liberal Jesus scholar Marcus Borg said, "Despite the difficulty which miracles pose for the modern mind, on historical grounds it is virtually indisputable that Jesus was a healer and exorcist."[3]

I wanted to explore these biblical miracles as I continued my conversation with Shermer. Still feeling stiff from my long flight to California, I stood to stretch my legs and then leaned casually on the back of my chair.

"Let's talk about Jesus," I said. Shermer nodded, apparently eager to do so. "How do you evaluate the credibility of the New Testament accounts of his miracles?"

"I think this, in part, is a reporting problem," he replied.

I gestured for him to elaborate. "How so?"

"Well, how accurate are these stories? People say five hundred witnesses saw the resurrected Jesus, but do we have five hundred sources? No, we have one source that says five hundred people saw him. That's different than five hundred independent sources. How reliable is that one source that gets passed down and passed down—you know, like the telephone game. Decades after the fact, it's written down by proselytizers who have a motive."

He shifted in his seat, sitting up straight as if he were just getting started. "Besides," he added, "they're not thinking of historical accuracy in the way we do today. In ancient times, the point of history wasn't to record what actually occurred; rather, it was to make a point. What Jesus really said and did in sequence wasn't that significant to them. That's why so many details differ.

"It's clear," he continued, "that the gospels are cobbled together, edited, redacted, refined—the whole Bible is like that. All of this goes a long way toward explaining why these particular stories evolved and developed over time as it became more and more important to solidify the Christian faith as the One True Religion rather than one faith among many.

"We're talking four centuries before the church said, 'These are the canonical books, that's it. All these other apocryphal books are out.' Why? What's wrong with the Gospel of Thomas?[4] Or the other ones? To me, they're indistinguishable."

I sat back down and took a sip of water as I pondered my next question. "Do you think other mythologies and mystery religions, like the stories of Osiris and Mithras, influenced the writers of the New Testament?"[5]

"Yes," he answered, "I think there was diffusion across cultures with myths in the Mediterranean world, where there were oral traditions getting passed down."

"If the gospels didn't intend to report actual history," I said, "then what was their purpose?"

"Take the story of Jonah and the whale. Forget whether a person can live inside a whale or not. That's not the point of the story. The point of the story is redemption, starting over. These are homilies. They're myths. In a way, asking if they're true misses the point. The real issue is what they represent. For Christians, it's, 'I get a lot out of the story because it helps me deal with tragedy and pain in my life.' *That's* the point of the story. And by the way, I think atheists miss that too, because their focus is on, 'Did it really happen? We're going to debunk this nonsense. It's trash.' I think everybody is missing the larger picture, the mythic character of it. Myths are important."

"Do you believe Jesus existed?" I asked.

In the back of my mind, I was recalling the cover story on that topic in a 2014 edition of *Skeptic* magazine. Its seemingly reluctant conclusion: based not on the New Testament but on two references by first-century historian Titus Flavius Josephus, Jesus was deemed to be historical, though "barely." Then came this caveat: "Ultimately, however, the historical Jesus is so imbued with mythic characteristics as to render his historicity moot."[6]

"Yes," said Shermer, "I accept that Jesus lived."

"Can we know much about him that's reliable?"

"Details of his life are pretty thin," he responded. "For instance, what was he doing during his childhood?"

I said, "One of the events Christians consider important is the resurrection. The apostle Paul says in First Corinthians 15:17 that if it isn't true, then Christianity crumbles.[7] It seems to me this is a historical issue that can be investigated by skeptics. Did Jesus live? Was he executed? Was he reliably encountered afterward? Aren't those three facts that can lead us to a conclusion?"

"In my opinion, he existed and was crucified," came his reply. "But then there's an ontological leap—was there a miraculous resurrection? You know, sometimes people see or hear voices of their lost loved ones because they want to. They miss them. They've spent decades with the person, and they hear them in the other room: 'Oh, that's right. He's dead. But I heard his voice.' Maybe something like this happened. Or maybe it was a partially concocted story that emerged after decades of thinking, writing, and talking. After all, stories of resurrected deities were not uncommon; they were floating around in the milieu of the day. I can easily see how this could be adopted over a long period of time. And then there's the Jewish problem."

"What do you mean?"

"Culturally, Christians are brothers with Jews. You believe in the same God and much of the same Holy Book. So why don't they accept the resurrection story? Are they just not thinking clearly enough? Have they not examined the evidence properly? You're talking about some really smart people. Even Muslims don't accept it. Allah is supposedly the same God as Yahweh, but they don't think Jesus could have been the Son of God. They think that's not just wrong, but blasphemous."

Shermer wasn't done. "Why do the accounts of his resurrection appearances vary? Why the discrepancies?" he asked. "Again, it's because the details weren't very important. I think the point of the death and resurrection story is destruction and redemption. It's starting over. It's rebuilding. I think the message is that it's up to us to create our own heaven here. The kingdom of God is here. It's now. It's you. It's in your heart. It's up to you to build a better life for you and your family and friends and community. Not in the next life—in *this* life."

"And you think the resurrection was a metaphorical teaching created to make that point?"

"I think it's possible."

"Who do you think Jesus was?" I asked.

"He was probably a moral teacher, fairly advanced for his times. He seemed to be open to women's issues. There's Buddha, Moses, Jesus, Muhammad—they're all great moral teachers who had different roles at different times. No one is above the other. No one is God. Muslims have their own supernatural beliefs—Muhammad went to heaven on a flying white horse. That's no more crazy than rising from the dead. They're equally improbable. Which one is right? Why are 1.2 billion Muslims wrong?"

"But," I said, "why would Jesus have been executed just for being a moral teacher?"

"The Romans were fairly tolerant as long as you paid your taxes and recognized Caesar as God, and I think, in part, that's where Jesus got into trouble—not recognizing Caesar as God," he replied. "People were executed right and left for all kinds of things back then. It's what people did before modern sensibilities."

He paused and then said, "Look, the messiah myth has recirculated through different cultures over the years. The belief in a returning Messiah who offers redemption—that's one of the limited number of responses to the hardships of the human condition. It may be a fictitious narrative, but it represents something deeply meaningful. It's a quest for hope. For purpose. For a second chance. For a new kingdom in this world."

He shook his head. "Not for some imaginary world to come."

The Miracle That Started It All

The granddaddy of all miracles is the creation of the universe from nothing. If Genesis 1:1 is correct when it reads, "In the beginning God created the heavens and the earth," then lesser miracles become more credible. In other words, if God can command an entire universe and even time itself to leap into existence, then walking on water would be like a stroll in the park and a resurrection would be as simple as a snap of the fingers.

"Christians point to cosmology as evidence for the existence of God," I said to Shermer. "Science tells us the universe began to exist at some point in the past, so what could have brought everything

into existence? Whatever it is, it must be powerful, smart, immaterial, timeless or eternal, and so on—all of which are attributes of
God. What's wrong with that argument?"

"Well, first, you can't determine anything about who that God
would be. It could be a committee of gods. It could be some god we
don't even know about. It's not necessarily Yahweh."

"Granted," I said. "But not every argument makes every point."

"Here's the thing: we don't have a consensus in science about
what triggered the Big Bang. And what was there before that? Maybe
there were multiple universes. Maybe a collapsing black hole creates
a singularity that triggers a big bang. So the answer we have at the
moment is, 'We don't know.' To infer that therefore a miracle happened
and that God did it—well, that doesn't really answer the question of
origins. We'd still need to get to the issue of where God came from."

"Christians would say that by definition, 'God is that which
does not need a cause.'"

"Well, why can't I just say the universe is that which does not
need a cause? Why not stop the regress at the big bang and say
that before that, the information is lost? We don't know. Nobody
knows. Christians take the regress one step further back and say,
'God did it.' In that case, I'd go one further step back and ask,
'Where did God come from? Who created him?' Why can't there
be a 'God creator'? A god who makes gods? Maybe there was a
super-intelligent designer that created the intelligent designer who
created this world. People say you've got to stop the causal chain
somewhere, but no, you don't."

He stopped for a minute, taking a swig from a cup of water.
"Look, this is one of those areas where theists have some pretty
good arguments," he said—a concession that frankly surprised me.
"But," he added, "in the end, we can't determine what happened.
It's okay to just say, 'We don't know.'"

"What about the fine-tuning of the universe?" I asked. "Christians stress that the numbers that govern the operation of the universe are calibrated so precisely that they're on a razor's edge. They're convinced that a Creator is the best explanation. Why don't you find this persuasive?"

"It's a good argument," Shermer conceded. "But look—what if there are multiple universes? Then we happen to be in one where the laws of nature are such that they give rise to people like us asking such questions."

"Do you think the concept of a multiverse has some merit?" I asked.

"I'm told by my physicist friends that it's a prediction based on how universes develop. If there are countless other universes with random laws and constants of nature, sooner or later one is going to be hospitable for life—and that's ours. We hit the cosmic lottery. Now, we don't know if there are multiple universes, but it's a more plausible explanation than to say, 'God did it.'"

I interrupted. "Isn't that sort of a 'science of the gaps' argument— 'We don't know, but we trust that science will someday tell us?'"

"It's just that there *is* a gap," he answered. "We may never know. We can't get the information at the moment, and maybe we never will. One of the problems with a multiverse is that, in principle, we can't interact with the other universes, and so getting scientific confirmation isn't likely."

"Still," he said, his tone adamant, "I prefer this hypothesis over the God theory."

Spirituality and Immortality

I know that Shermer occasionally ponders spirituality and the afterlife, even if with humor. He once Tweeted, "I'm in no rush to get there, but being in hell could be interesting." He attached photos of sixty-five celebrity atheists, with the caption: "Fear not hell, for if it exists, you shall find yourself in good company."[8]

"What does spirituality mean for you?" I asked him.

"For me, it's the doors that science has opened to the universe. There's deep time—the almost incomprehensible age of the universe, our earth, our species, and so forth. The numbers are staggering. And the size of the universe—I'm in awe when I visit Mount Wilson and the other great observatories of the world. And, by the way, the cathedrals."

That took me aback. "Cathedrals?"

"Yes, I'm equally awed by cathedrals. The cathedral in Cologne, Germany, where my wife is from, is incredible," he said, referring to the High Cathedral of Saint Peter, a spectacular 515-foot twin-spire monument to Gothic architecture. "It's amazing to stand inside it. Every time we go there, we light a candle."

Now I was thoroughly intrigued. "You light candles? Seriously? Why?"

"Out of respect for the universe, for this world, for this life, and of course for the love my wife and I share. This is it, after all. There's nothing more."

"Does mortality worry you?"

"Not really."

"Can you face it, honestly?"

"Yes, I think so. I'm not particularly concerned about it."

"Do you hope for some sort of immortality?"

"Sure I do. I don't get up every morning and say, 'Oh, I hope I live forever.' But sometimes, yes, I think about it."

"What do you think of the idea of heaven?"

His expression soured. "Boring!" he declared. "Heaven forever? What? What am I supposed to do? Are there tennis courts? It sounds tiresome and intrusive. If you're with an omniscient being, as the skeptic Christopher Hitchens said, it would be like a celestial North Korea. You've got a dictator knowing every one of your thoughts. Hey, my thoughts are private!

"There are a lot of problematic things when you think about it," he added. "Where would I be? What would I do all day? Infinite love—what does that even mean? It's truly inconceivable for a finite being to imagine eternity and infinity. For me, it's so problematic that it's probably not true."

"Do you think there are instances where people, for psychological or moral reasons, ratchet up their skepticism when it comes to God?" I asked.

"Yeah, maybe. Probably."

"What would it take for you to believe God exists?"

"Well, that's a difficult one. I guess if after I died, if I were actually someplace, sentient and conscious, I'd be thinking, *Uh-oh!*"

My eyebrows shot up. "It may be a little too late then."

"I'm not too worried about that, because in my opinion, any god worthy of the title of omniscient, omnipotent, and all-loving surely wouldn't care whether I believe in him or not. I'm more of a works guy. If there's a heaven, I would think getting in would be more based on what you've done, how you've comported yourself, the way you treated other people. Whatever justice system God has set up, it can't be just carrot-and-stick, heaven-and-hell. That's just so primitive."

I said, "What if the entry-level standard of being good is giving your life completely to serving the poor, sacrificing everything, and living a wholly selfless existence? Would you measure up?"

"Well . . . ," he started to say. He paused and then said, "Seriously, I don't think that could be the standard."

I noted that atheist philosopher Bertrand Russell famously said if he died and found himself in front of God, Russell would accuse him of not providing sufficient evidence for his existence. "What would you say if you died and came face-to-face with God?" I asked.

"I would say, 'I used the brain you gave me, and I thought this through. I tried this, I tried that. I really believed, and then I didn't. What did you expect? I did the best I could with the tools you granted me. I have free will. I chose. This is what I chose. I tried to do unto others as I would have them do unto me. Yes, I fell short many times, but I tried to apply the Golden Rule whenever I could.'"

His eyes locked with mine. "Personally," he concluded, "I can't believe that a good God—an all-powerful and loving God—would do anything bad to me for that."

Cracking Open the Door

During the years I was an atheist, there were times I would doubt my doubts. It seemed too simple to attribute everything to random chance. Maybe, just maybe, there was more than the eye could see. An inexplicable coincidence, a glimpse into the intricate complexity of nature, a moment of honest introspection—something would crack open the door to the possibility that a miracle-working Someone might exist.

"Tell me about what has challenged your skepticism," I said.

"Well," he replied with some hesitation, "there was that one incident."

"The one with the transistor radio?"

He nodded. "That's the one."

I had seen his column about it in *Scientific American*. What attracted me was its subtitle, which read, "I just witnessed an event so mysterious that it shook my skepticism."[9]

"That's rather startling," I said.

"Yes," replied Shermer. "I didn't write that subtitle, but I have to admit that this incident really did rock me back on my heels." .

"What happened?"

Shermer proceeded to describe how he and his German fiancée, Jennifer, decided to get married at the Beverly Hills courthouse and then have a celebration at his house.

"She was feeling pretty bad because she was alone. She had been raised by a single mom and her grandfather, whom she loved like a dad. He passed away when she was sixteen, and none of her family or friends were there for the wedding, so she was feeling kind of low.

"Before Jennifer had come to the US, she had shipped some personal items ahead. One was a transistor radio from the 1970s that had deep sentimental value to her. She and her grandfather would often listen to music from it when they were gardening or simply enjoying time together.

"I tried to fix the radio before she arrived, but nothing worked," he said. "I put in new batteries; I checked the wires; I even hit it on the table—nothing. In the end, I threw it in the back of a desk in the bedroom, underneath an old fax machine, and it sat there for months."

As the family gathered after the wedding, Jennifer said, "I really need a moment alone." She was upset and crying. "I miss my grandfather," she said. "I wish he was here."

She and her new husband went into the back bedroom—and suddenly, they heard music. Beautiful, classical, romantic music. But where was it coming from?

"I thought, *Did I leave my cell phone in here?* No, it's not the phone. Was it my laptop? No. Was it from the neighbors? No. It seemed like it was coming from the desk," Shermer told me. "Jennifer shot me a startled look and said, 'That can't be what I think it is, can it?'

"Then she pulled out the drawer. Somehow that little radio had come on—and right then, with perfect timing, it was serenading Jennifer with music, just like it used to do when she was with her grandfather. We sat there in stunned silence for several minutes. Jennifer said with tears in her eyes, 'My grandfather is here with us. I'm not alone.'"

I sat mesmerized by the story. "It was an emotional incident," Shermer continued. "Jennifer felt like she was connected with her grandfather, as if he were right there in the room, right when she needed him the most. The radio played all night and into the next morning—and then it went dead again. To this day, it no longer works."

It was the special timing of the incident that sent tremors through Shermer's skepticism. "What should I make of this?" he said to me. "Was it some sort of divine message? Was her grandfather on some other plane, letting her know everything was all right on this important day? Was it merely a coincidental electronic anomaly? But if it was, how can it be explained? Why did the radio work for just that brief moment—at precisely the right time? It was . . . well, odd."

"Did this incident crack open a door for you?" I asked.

"A little, yeah. Maybe a bit."

He sighed and then added, "I don't know everything. *We* don't know everything. Maybe there's another plane. It's possible. This doesn't prove any of that. It just makes you think, *We should be humble before the universe.*"

"Did you take the radio to an electronics expert to try to find an explanation?" I asked.

"No, because this time I savored the experience more than the explanation. What's important is the emotional meaning it had for Jennifer. And that would be my take-home message about miracles. Don't worry about the mechanics. Did it make you feel better? If so, just take it at that. That's good enough. In our scientific world, sometimes we think we need an excellent answer for everything. Of course, that's fine, but some things you can never explain—and that's okay.

"If it turned out after this life that there is some other plane of existence, I would be very happy about it. I like being conscious. Like most people, I'll be sad when my time is up, because I enjoy life. Maybe it will continue on. I think probably not, but it would be nice to be pleasantly surprised.

"And if God is part of it, I'd welcome that."

PART 2

The Case *for* Miracles

*An Interview with
Dr. Craig S. Keener*

CHAPTER 4

From Skepticism to Belief

It all started as a footnote.

While working on his massive commentary on the book of Acts (yes, *massive*—comprising nearly 4,500 pages over four volumes), Dr. Craig Keener began writing a footnote about the miracles that are found in this New Testament account of the early Christian movement.

He observed that some modern readers discount the historicity of Acts because they dismiss the possibility of miracles, believing that the uniform experience of humankind is that the miraculous simply doesn't occur. But are those claims reasonable?

Keener began researching. And writing. The footnote grew and grew. The more he discovered, the more convinced he became that miracles are more common than a lot of people think and are better documented than many skeptics claim. He wrestled with the arguments against miracles by David Hume; he traveled to Africa to investigate seemingly supernatural healings; he sifted Scripture; he unearthed examples of modern wonders, marvels, visions, and dreams.

Two years later, his book *Miracles* was published—again, an exhaustive scholarly undertaking, so sweeping that it covers two volumes and a staggering 1,172 pages. Scholar Ben Witherington III gushed that it is "perhaps the best book ever written on miracles in this or any age." His comment prompted New Testament professor Craig Blomberg to declare, "The 'perhaps' is unnecessarily cautious." Asked Richard Bauckham of Cambridge University, "So who's afraid of David Hume now?"

Quite a footnote.

✳ ✳ ✳

Driving back to my California hotel, fresh from my stimulating discussion with skeptic Michael Shermer, I thought about Keener's volumes that were sitting on the shelf in my office back home.

Shermer had raised some troubling objections to the idea of the supernatural and whether we can ever be sure that something miraculous has occurred. He was self-assured and almost cocky at times. He dismissed Jesus' purported miracles as the fanciful moralizing of the gospel writers. No apparent miracle, it seemed, could reach the high evidentiary bar he set.

To be honest, I expected nothing less from the editor of *Skeptic* magazine. Still, his critiques demanded answers.

I called a friend to get Craig Keener's email address and then I tapped out a request for an interview. Ever the night owl, Keener sent his reply at three o'clock in the morning. Before long, I found myself flying to Lexington, Kentucky, and then driving twenty minutes to the two-stoplight town of Wilmore—well, okay, *three* stoplights, if you count the one that simply flashes all the time.

Apparently, I mused, lawsuit-happy atheists have yet to discover this hamlet of 1,638 households: its municipal water tower is topped with a giant white cross.

The Interview with Craig S. Keener, PhD

"I'm living proof that God doesn't always perform miracles," Keener said as he greeted me at his modest house in a neighborhood where the scent of burning autumn leaves hung in the air. "I'm still nearsighted and suffering from male pattern baldness—which is spreading!"

He ushered me downstairs to his office, where a cluttered desk was surrounded by twenty-nine file cabinets, each neatly packed with research and other papers—including a collection of the whimsical cartoons he draws for recreation. An elliptical machine stood nearby.

At age fifty-six, Keener is tall and slim (he lists exercise as one of his hobbies), with his graying hair and beard closely cropped. He was wearing a blue knit shirt and jeans; halfway through our afternoon together, he kicked off his shoes and padded around in white socks. His casual and amiable demeanor belies what must be one of the most grueling and productive work schedules imaginable.

I Tweeted a photo of us together, with the caption, "Great time interviewing Craig Keener for a project. While we chatted, he wrote three new books." With Keener's reputation as a prodigious author, I knew that would garner some chuckles.

Just twenty-five years after receiving his doctorate, he has authored twenty-one books, but that only hints at his output. His award-winning four-volume *Acts: An Exegetical Commentary* is some *three million* words in length, densely packed with scholarly insight written with a pastor's heart.

The monumental work stunned academics. Said Gary Burge of Wheaton College, "Keener is a scholar with gifts that come along once every century, and here we see them employed in full force. Words like *encyclopedic*, *magisterial*, and *epic* come to mind . . . Keener has a grasp of the ancient world like few scholars anywhere."

Gregory E. Sterling of Yale Divinity School hailed it as "the most expansive treatment of Acts in modern scholarship." I. Howard Marshall, the eminent New Testament professor from the University of Aberdeen, called it "a remarkable scholarly achievement." To

Darrell L. Bock of Dallas Theological Seminary, it's "a rich gem"; to Samuel Byrskog of Lund University, it's "a gold mine."

That's just the beginning. Keener's curriculum vitae is the size of a small book. His two-volume *Miracles: The Credibility of the New Testament Accounts*, which is 620,000 words in length, is "arguably the best book ever on the subject of miracles," according to noted biblical scholar Craig A. Evans of Houston Baptist University.

When Keener wrote his dissertation at Duke University, where he received his PhD in New Testament and Christian Origins in 1991, it took more than one hundred pages just to list the sources he cited. The dissertation was nearly five hundred pages in total. Today, it takes eighty-five pages to list all of his books, awards, scholarly and popular articles, and lectures from around the world.

A few of Keener's other books include *The Historical Jesus of the Gospels* (add another 831 pages to his total) and commentaries on the gospel of John (with thirty thousand references from ancient sources); Matthew (winning Book of the Year in Biblical Studies from *Christianity Today*); Romans; 1 and 2 Corinthians; and Revelation. His *IVP Bible Background Commentary: New Testament* garnered even more awards.

Now a professor of biblical studies at Asbury Theological Seminary, Keener lives in Wilmore with his wife, Médine, who holds a PhD and teaches French, and their two adopted children from Africa—a son, nineteen, and a daughter, sixteen. Médine was once a refugee for a harrowing eighteen months in the forest of her native Congo. She and Craig tell their story in the book *Impossible Love: The True Story of an African Civil War, Miracles, and Love against All Odds*.

Keener and I settled into chairs facing each other; I set up a digital recorder to capture our conversation. I began by summarizing my interview with Michael Shermer, going over that conversation point by point, which Keener considered with intense interest.

"Dr. Shermer has had a fascinating journey," I commented at the end. "He was a professing Christian but is now a skeptic."

Keener raised an eyebrow. "Quite the opposite from me."

"That's interesting," I said. "Tell me your story."

A Presence and a Purpose

Keener grew up the son of a clothier and an artist in a small Ohio community named after French Catholic Bishop Jean-Baptiste Massillon. Keener clearly fit the dictionary's definition of precocious: at age thirteen, he was reading Plato. By then, he was already calling himself an atheist.

"When I was nine, my mother asked if I believed in life after death," he said. "I told her no. She said she didn't either, and she cited a poll saying that most intellectuals didn't. I felt affirmed, but I also lacked any meaning or purpose in life, which was consistent with my worldview.

"Plato got me thinking about the immortality of the soul. I didn't want to be snuffed out forever. But I thought if immortality were available through God, why would he love me? I was not a loving person. I was entirely selfish, and I knew it.

"Besides, Christianity didn't seem credible. I thought, *If I ever find out there's a God, I would give him everything, but 80 percent of people in this country claim to be Christians, and yet they don't give everything they are to God. They just live like this is the only life.* It seemed to me that most so-called Christians didn't really believe it."

I said, "So even as a teenager, you were wrestling with major spiritual issues."

"That's right. I remember that somewhere along the line, I said, 'If somebody is out there—if there's a God or gods—then please show me.'"

"What happened?"

"When I was fifteen, I was walking home from Latin class, and two fundamentalist Baptists cornered me. They asked me where I would go when I died, and they started telling me how I could be saved in light of the Bible. After going back and forth for a long time, I said, 'Look, guys, I've been humoring you, but you're telling me stuff from the Bible. I don't believe the Bible. I'm an atheist. You've got to give me something other than the Bible.'"

"Did they?"

"It was clear they didn't have anything. So I pressed my big question: 'If there's a God, where did the dinosaur bones come from?'"

I smiled. "You were trying to stump them."

"Yeah. I liked to make fun of Christians. One of them told me, 'The devil put them there to deceive us.' That's when I said, 'This is ridiculous. I'm leaving.' As I turned to walk off, one of them called out, 'You're hardening your heart against God, and every time you do that, it makes it harder for you to repent. Eventually, you'll burn in hell forever.'"

"Well," I said, "there's a good example of friendship evangelism."

"They didn't know friendship evangelism; they didn't know apologetics; and they certainly didn't know paleontology," replied Keener. "Still, as I walked home, I felt convicted by the Holy Spirit. I passed a Catholic church and saw a cross atop the steeple. I knew about the Trinity, and I wondered whether the Trinity was looking down on me. I finally got to my bedroom, where I began arguing back and forth with myself—*This can't be right. But what if it is?* And then I sensed it."

"Sensed what?"

"God's very presence—right there, right then, right in my room. I had been wanting empirical evidence, but instead God gave me something else: the evidence of his presence. So it wasn't apologetics that reached me; my brain had to catch up afterward.

I was simply overwhelmed by the palpable presence of God. It was like Someone was right there in the room with me, and it wasn't something I was generating, because it wasn't what I was necessarily wanting."

I leaned forward, drawn in by his story. "How did you respond?" I asked.

"I said, 'God, those guys on the corner said Jesus died for me and rose again and that's what saves me. If that's what you're saying, I'll accept it. But I don't understand how that works. So if you want to save me, you're going to have to do it yourself.'"

"And did he?"

"All of a sudden, I felt something rushing through my body that I'd never experienced before. I jumped up and said, 'What was that?' I knew God had come into my life. At that moment, I was filled with wonder and worship."

Two days later, Keener walked to a nearby church, where the pastor asked him, "Are you sure you've been saved?" Keener said, "No, I don't know if I did it right." That's when the minister led him in a prayer of repentance and faith.

"This time I felt the same overwhelming sense of God's majesty and greatness and awesomeness," Keener told me. "I felt a kind of joy I'd never experienced before. And for the first time, I understood what my purpose was. What *the* purpose is."

"And what is that?"

"Our purpose is in God—to live for him, to serve him, to worship him." He paused, giving emphasis to one further thought: "Everything is to be built around Jesus."

A Firm and Confident Faith

It didn't take long for young Keener to realize that even children in Sunday school knew more about the Bible than he did, so he crammed to catch up. And catch up he did. He found if he read forty chapters a day, he could read through the New Testament every week and the entire Bible every month.

He turned down a National Merit Scholarship in order to study at a Bible college. After receiving his undergraduate degree in the Bible, he went on to seminary, earning his master's degree in biblical languages and a master of divinity degree. After that he received his doctorate at Duke.

From the beginning, questions swirled in the mind of this onetime doubter, and answers came slowly at first. He would write out each of his objections and then systematically pursue answers, asking God each time for insight and wisdom.

Over the years, especially after he gained access to academic libraries, he emerged with a firm and confident faith, not just based on his personal experience with God but also grounded in history, science, and philosophy.

He said, "I wondered why there were brilliant liberal scholars who questioned the fundamentals of the faith. I'd read their arguments, and I could refute them on paper. But I wondered, *What if they had a chance to reply?* Then when I finally got a chance to engage them, I'd give my best arguments and they'd come back with their answers, and it turned out they were pretty easy to refute. I was perplexed— how could their positions be so weak and yet they believed them?"

"Maybe," I suggested, "it wasn't simply about the evidence or arguments, but a predisposition against the miraculous."

"Well, I remember debating for hours with a professor who was a former Christian. I was frustrated that I couldn't persuade him. A friend who was with me said, 'You've refuted everything he said.' But this professor dismissed every line of evidence I gave. Finally, I asked him, 'If somebody were raised from the dead in front of you, would you believe it?'"

"What was his answer?" I asked.

"He said, 'No.'"

Keener stopped for a moment, as if stunned anew by that reply. "I just shook my head," he said. "Here he was, accusing me of being closed-minded because I'm a Christian, but he very clearly had an anti-supernatural presupposition that was shutting him off from a full consideration of the arguments and evidence."

That was different from Keener's attitude all along. "Even when you were an atheist, it seems to me you were nevertheless receptive to being challenged with something you hadn't considered," I said.

"I like to think I was," came his reply. He shrugged his shoulders. "Shouldn't we all be willing to reevaluate our position based on new evidence?"

For Keener, decades of intense study and reflection have only solidified a faith that came to him initially through—*what*? A miracle?

Yes, it could be argued that the supernatural experience in his bedroom fits the definition of a miraculous occurrence. It was brought about by God's power; it was a temporary exception to the ordinary course of nature; and it showed that God is acting not just in history, but in this fifteen-year-old boy's heart and life—right then, right there.

Could Keener prove that miracle to a skeptic? It was, after all, a personal kind of experience, not witnessed or authenticated by anyone else. And yet it has been confirmed time after time by the radical transformation of his character, values, morality, and priorities—a life devoted to worshiping God with his heart and mind.

And now, decades later, after immersing himself in history and theology, Keener would be the one to write the definitive scholarly tome about the reality of the supernatural in the world today.

"What prompted you to research miracles?" I asked him.

"Well," he replied, "it all started as a footnote to my Acts commentary. Before long, the footnote grew to two hundred pages—and that's when I decided to turn it into a book."

But I wondered if the real impetus reached back to his bedroom some four decades earlier, when the God of Abraham, Isaac, and Jacob deigned to manifest his presence to a precocious teenager who had been reading Plato and debating Baptists on street corners. A young man who had seen a cross atop a steeple and wondered whether there was anyone watching who could guide him Home. A budding atheist who vowed to devote everything to God if he ever encountered him—and who then kept his promise.

Based on Keener's story, the God of miracles supernaturally touched the life of this young but adamant atheist. And now here was Keener as one of the world's foremost scholars describing and defending God's signs and wonders to an increasingly skeptical world.

I pulled out several pages of typewritten questions from my notebook and inched to the edge of my chair. There was much more to ask.

CHAPTER 5

From Hume to Jesus

As professors from various backgrounds were discussing Craig Keener's book *The Historical Jesus of the Gospels* at a scholarly conclave, a member of the left-wing Jesus Seminar stood to address the gathering.

"There are two kinds of scholars: critical scholars and evangelicals," he told the group. "Evangelicals shouldn't even be in the same room with critical scholars, because they're not really critical."

Keener protested that he had followed standard historiographical principles in writing his book. The gospel accounts, he pointed out, are in the genre of ancient biographies, which are normally based on historical events.

"But," countered the scholar, "they have miracles in them!"

His unstated point: if the gospels report that miracles were performed by Jesus, then they simply cannot be taken as historically reliable. Rather, they must be based on legend, mythology, or mistake. Why? Because everyone since David Hume knows that miracles simply don't occur.

I continued my conversation with Keener by saying, "The skeptic Michael Shermer believes the gospel writers didn't even attempt to record actual history. Instead, they tell far-fetched stories about fictional miracles in order to make a moral point."

"Yes, the gospels do make moral points," came Keener's reply, "but that doesn't mean they weren't reporting on historical happenings.

Readers from the middle of the second century through most of the nineteenth century regarded the gospels as biographies of some sort. That view changed in the early 1900s, when some scholars searched for a new classification for them. But now the prevailing assessment has come full circle: today the gospels are widely viewed by scholars as being biographies."

"What does that suggest about them—that they're like modern biographies, which presumably report what actually occurred in a person's life?"

"There are differences between ancient and modern biographies. Ancient biographies weren't as concerned with chronology, for example, or the childhood of the person they were writing about. But like contemporary biographies, ancient biographies were supposed to deal with historical information, not imaginary events that were simply invented to make a point."

"Then we can't legitimately classify the gospels as being mythology," I said.

"Certainly not. The gospel accounts are a far cry from tales in the mythological genre, which tend to deal with the distant past rather than more recent historical individuals. They addressed mythic topics, were set in primeval times, and featured fantastical creatures. No, mythology is a decidedly different genre than the gospels, no question about it."

Keener paused for a moment before resuming. "Think of the opening words of Luke's gospel. He says he 'carefully investigated everything from the beginning' so that he could 'write an orderly account' of what took place with Jesus' life and ministry."

His tone turned more intense. "Those aren't the words of someone bent on manufacturing fairy tales out of thin air in order to teach a lesson. Those are the words of someone who wants to report on the certainty of what took place."

Jesus the Healer and Exorcist

The gospels attribute more than thirty miracles to Jesus. "Walking on water, raising the dead, instantly curing leprosy—you have to admit those are pretty fantastical claims," I said to Keener.

"But look at the way the gospels report them," he replied. "In a sober fashion, with an eye for details. There were eyewitnesses; in fact, often Jesus' miracles were performed before hostile audiences. His opponents didn't dispute that he performed miracles; instead, they simply objected that he did them on the Sabbath. Plus, the gospels were written during the lifetimes of Jesus' contemporaries, who surely would have disputed the facts if they had been made up."

"Okay, maybe these miracle stories aren't myths, but couldn't they be legends—that is, stories that began with a small kernel of truth but grew and grew into more fanciful tales over long periods of time?" I asked.

"Actually, if you drill down to the earliest material about Jesus, you still find him described as a miracle-working healer and exorcist."

"For example . . . ?" I prodded.

"Mark is regarded as the first gospel to be written, and 40 percent of his narrative involves miracles in some way," Keener said. "And there's an acknowledgment of Jesus' miracles in Q, which many scholars believe was a very early source used by Matthew and Luke in writing their gospels. In fact, Q material refers to the Galilean villages of Chorazin and Bethsaida as being judged for not responding to Jesus' extraordinary miracles among them. That's bedrock tradition about Jesus, not some later legend."[1]

He continued. "In another Q account, Jesus tells the followers of John to report back that they had witnessed him performing miraculous feats, including healing the blind, the deaf, the lame, and those with leprosy, and even raising the dead.[2] Further, you see miracles in the material that is unique to Matthew and Luke, as well as in Paul's writing. For instance, Paul appeals to eyewitness knowledge about Jesus' greatest miracle—his resurrection—in a letter he wrote to the church in Corinth.[3] Scholars have dated that tradition to within a few years—or even months—of Jesus' death."[4]

"What about non-Christian sources?"

"The rabbis and the anti-Christian Greek philosopher Celsus are clear that Jesus was a miracle worker. Of course, later non-Christian sources attributed his feats to sorcery, but that's still an acknowledgment that something extraordinary took place. Also, the first-century Jewish historian Josephus wrote that Jesus was a wise man who 'worked startling deeds.'"

"Startling deeds?"

"Yes. What's significant is that this is the same way he describes the miracles associated with the prophet Elisha."

"But isn't that passage in Josephus disputed?" I asked. "Critics charge it was added later by Christians."

"The Jewish historian Geza Vermes of Oxford analyzed the writing style of Josephus and concluded that this particular miracle claim is, indeed, authentic," Keener said.[5] "Frankly, I have to agree with what scholar Raymond Brown said about Jesus, which is that even 'the oldest traditions show him as a healer.'"[6]

"But why did Jesus heal the sick, boss around nature, and cast out demons?" I asked. "Obviously, he wasn't merely trying to prove his divinity, because his disciples later performed miracles—and they certainly weren't deities. What was Jesus' motive?"

"His miracles were a sign of the inbreaking of the kingdom—or the rule—of God," he replied. "They were a taste of the future, when healing will be complete. Jesus said, 'But if I drive out demons by the finger of God, then the kingdom of God has come upon you.'"[7]

These signs were a prelude to the entire restoration, when God will make a new heaven and a new earth. They remind us that a day is coming when there will be no more suffering or pain."

"And they show us something about God's character," I offered.

"Yes, very much so. They show us his power, but also his benevolence and compassion."

In the end, there is no question that reports of supernatural feats by Jesus are inextricably woven into the narrative of his life, even going back to the very earliest sources. Jesus scholars Gerd Theissen and Annette Merz write, "Just as the kingdom of God stands at the center of Jesus' preaching, so healings and exorcisms form the center of his activity."[8]

But were these *actual* miracles, or simply *apparent* miracles? Was Jesus truly tapping into the supernatural, or was he duping gullible and unsophisticated first-century audiences? Just because miracles are reported in an ancient text doesn't necessarily make them true. After all, how can modern, rational people believe that a first-century Nazarene can circumvent nature?

"Belief in miracles is unjustified," scoffed Larry Shapiro, professor of philosophy at the University of Wisconsin–Madison, in his book *The Miracle Myth*. "No one has ever had or currently has good reasons for believing in miracles. The reasons people give for believing in miracles . . . are bad."[9]

David Hume couldn't have said it better.

Presuppositions and Circular Reasoning

Michael Shermer is not alone in considering Hume's case against miracles to be "a knockdown argument." Atheists and agnostics routinely cite Hume when they argue against the possibility of genuine miracles. In fact, Hume scholars point out that modern arguments against the miraculous are often restatements or refor-mulations of Hume's original treatise.[10] Clearly, it's hard to overstate his influence in the controversy over the supernatural.

But is Hume's reputation warranted? Are his arguments as airtight as skeptics believe they are? I couldn't help but smile as I broached this subject with Keener. "If I could summarize what you've written about Hume," I said, "it would be this: *you're not a fan.*"

Keener let out a laugh. "Well, let's be honest: his arguments against miracles are based on presuppositions and circular reason-ing," he said. "Even in his day, he was criticized for recycling old arguments that deists had made against Christianity, without con-sidering the critiques that had already been leveled against them."

"Give me an example of how he used circular reasoning," I said.

Keener thought for a moment. Then he said, "Hume defines *miracle* as a violation of natural law, and he defines *natural law* as being principles that cannot be violated. So he's ruling out the possibility of miracles at the outset. He's assuming that which he's already stated he will prove—which is circular reasoning. In fact, it's an anti-supernatural bias, not a cogent philosophical argument."

"Is he wrong to call miracles a violation of the laws of nature?" I asked.

"Today we understand laws as *describing* the normal pattern of nature, not *prescribing* them. In other words . . ." He turned in his chair to get a ballpoint pen from his desk, holding it up for me to see. "If I drop this pen, the law of gravity tells me it will fall to the floor. But if I were to reach in and grab the pen in midair, I wouldn't be violating the law of gravity; I would merely be intervening. And certainly if God exists, he would have the ability to intervene in the world that he himself created."

Keener tossed the pen back on his desk and turned to face me again. "Hume simply rejects any evidence that contradicts his thesis," he continued. "To him, miracles as violations of nature are more incredible than eyewitnesses are trustworthy, so no evidence can prove persuasive for miracles. In other words, it's fruitless to investigate miracle claims, because no matter how strong your evidence, it cannot prevail. Yes, he does set forth criteria for good evidence, but the bar of proof is set so high that nothing can reach it."

With that, Keener recounted a story about Hume and the influential French scientist and mathematician Blaise Pascal.

"Pascal's niece, Marguerite Perrier, suffered from a severe and long-term fistula in her eye that let out a repulsive odor. At a monastery on March 24, 1656, she was completely healed in a dramatic way, with even bone deterioration vanishing immediately. There was medical and eyewitness evidence; the diocese verified the healing. Even the royal physicians examined her, and the queen herself declared it a healing. In the following months, eighty other miracle claims followed. So here you have miracles that were recent, public, and attested by many witnesses and even physicians—all of which met Hume's criteria for evidence. But ultimately he dismissed all of this as irrelevant."

"Why?"

"On the grounds that miracles simply aren't possible because they violate nature. Now, that's a classic case of circular reasoning."

What's more, Hume felt free to scoff at the entire report about Pascal's niece because these were Jansenists, members of a controversial sect that both Protestants and traditional Catholics opposed.

I asked, "What about Hume's claim that the uniform experience of humankind is that miracles don't happen?"

"That's an assertion, not an argument. What he's saying is, 'Miracles violate the principle that miracles never happen.'[11] Again, notice how circular that is. In addition, his criteria for evaluating miracles are too vague and even contradictory. For instance, he would require any witnesses to be of unquestioned good sense, but then he appears to question the good sense of anyone who claims to have witnessed a miracle.

"Granted, Hume never personally experienced a miracle. But based on that, he extrapolates that the uniform experience of humankind is that miracles don't occur. That's totally unreasonable, especially today, when we've got so many compelling eyewitness reports of miraculous events."

I spoke up. "According to the national survey I commissioned, more than 94 million adults in the US would say they've had an experience that they can only explain as a miracle from God. Globally, that number, based on other surveys, is in the hundreds of millions."

Keener nodded. "That's right."

"But," I cautioned, "that doesn't necessarily mean they were real miracles."

"That's true, and maybe the vast majority are coincidences or anomalies or mistakes or fraud or the placebo effect, or whatever. Certainly those things happen and we need to concede that. But can *all* cases be explained that way?"

He shook his head. "That simply defies reason—and ignores the evidence."

Emperor Hume Has No Clothes

I took a few moments to flip back through my notes for a quick review of what Keener had said so far. Then I commented, "With all the weaknesses in Hume's arguments, it's hard to see how he is still so frequently quoted by skeptics today."

"I agree. Critics have been pointing out the glaring problems with Hume's work ever since he wrote it, and today those critiques are even stronger. Some are downright brutal. A lot of philosophers from various backgrounds are finally declaring that Emperor Hume has no clothes."

Among them is prominent science philosopher John Earman, whose scathing critique, published by Oxford University Press, is titled *Hume's Abject Failure*. His devastating introduction reads:

> It is not simply that Hume's essay does not achieve its goals, but that his goals are ambiguous and confused. Most of Hume's considerations are unoriginal, warmed over versions of arguments that are found in the writings of predecessors and contemporaries. And the parts of "Of Miracles" that set Hume apart do not stand up to scrutiny. Worse still, the essay reveals the weakness and the poverty of Hume's own account of induction and probabilistic reasoning. And to cap it all off, the essay represents the kind of overreaching that gives philosophy a bad name.[12]

What was really behind Hume's screed against miracles? Earman is convinced he was motivated by his animus against organized religion, "which Hume saw as composed of superstitions that have had almost uniformly baneful effects for mankind." He said Hume was driven by a "strong desire to strike a toppling blow against one of the main pillars" of faith, leading him to "claim more than he could deliver."[13]

Incidentally, because of his blistering critique of Hume, some people have questioned whether Earman has a "hidden agenda" of Christian apologetics. He said that although he appreciates much in the Judeo-Christian heritage, he nevertheless finds "nothing attractive, either intellectually or emotionally, in the theological doctrines of Christianity."[14] As one reviewer noted, "His aim is to sketch an epistemology that allows for both the possibility of miracles and a healthy skepticism toward miracle claims—twin goals that many theists also embrace."[15]

David Johnson, who earned his doctorate in philosophy at Princeton University and is a professor at Yeshiva University, agreed that Hume's arguments on miracles are "entirely without merit."[16] In his book, published by Cornell University Press, he said, "The view that there is in Hume's essay . . . any argument or reply or objection that is even superficially good, much less, powerful or devastating, is simply a philosophical myth."[17]

Philosopher and theologian Keith Ward, now retired from his professorship at Oxford University, called Hume's arguments on miracles "exceptionally poor" and said they are only acceptable to those who are "impressed by his general philosophical acuteness—an acuteness that does not carry over into his remarks on miracles."[18]

Ouch.

Extraordinary Claims, Extraordinary Evidence

I gestured toward Keener. "If Hume's approach doesn't work, then how do you think people should look at claims of miracles?" I asked.

Keener leaned forward in his chair. "I think we should look at the evidence with a healthy dose of skepticism but also with an open mind," he began. "Are there eyewitnesses? When we have multiple, independent, and reliable witnesses, this increases the probability that their testimony is accurate. Do the witnesses have a reputation for honesty? Do they have something to gain or lose? Did they have a good opportunity to observe what occurred? Is there corroboration? Are there any medical records? What were the precise circumstances and timing of the event? Are there alternative naturalistic explanations for what happened?"

I pointed out that atheist scientist Jerry Coyne said "massive, well-documented, and either replicated or independently corroborated evidence from multiple and reliable sources" would be needed to have confidence in a miracle.[19]

"Replicable?" Keener replied. "Miracles are one-offs. They are part of history, which can't be repeated. How could we test whether a person was brought back from the dead—shoot him and try again? I don't think so," he said, chuckling. "But aside from that, we do have plenty of cases that meet the standard Coyne is talking about."

"What's the appropriate burden of proof?" I asked. "Many skeptics say extraordinary claims require extraordinary evidence."[20]

"The question is how to define an ambiguous term like *extraordinary*. Skeptics often set the bar infinitely high. I think we need *sufficient* and *credible* evidence, which varies in each case. The standard needs to be reasonable so we're not too credulous but so we don't rule out things at the beginning."

"What standard do you suggest?"

"In civil law, the standard is 'more probable than not.' That's also the standard most historians apply in their work. So I think this is an appropriate benchmark to apply when evaluating miracle claims. Ultimately, of course, people are going to look at events through their own interpretive grid."

"In other words, this really is a worldview issue, isn't it?" I said.

"Certainly. If you give miracles a zero chance of ever occurring, as Hume did, then you're not going to find any. But if you keep an open mind and follow the evidence wherever it leads—well, it might take you to unexpected places."

Pen in hand, I turned to a blank page of my notebook. That's exactly where I wanted to go next.

CHAPTER 6

A Tide of Miracles

A physician picked up Craig Keener's two-volume book on miracles with one goal in mind: to reinforce his highly skeptical worldview.

"I was ready to 'see through' yet another theologian who didn't know much about psychosomatic illnesses, temporary improvements with no long-term follow-up, incorrect medical diagnoses, conversion disorders, faked cures, self-deception, and the like," he said.

But he admitted, "I was blindsided."

After plowing through the philosophical chapters, he came across the thousands of case studies that form the core of Keener's book—reports of extraordinary healings and other incredible events backed up by eyewitnesses and, in many cases, clear-cut corroborating evidence.

"I read them with the critical eye of a skeptic having many years of medical practice under the belt," the doctor said.

Many reports weren't sufficiently documented to convince him. In other instances, he could envision alternative, naturalistic explanations to account for what happened.

But not in all cases. "Not by a long shot," he said. "I found [hundreds of case studies] to be stunning. They couldn't just be dismissed with a knowing answer and a cheery wave of the hand. *With respect to my worldview, I had had the chair pulled out from underneath me.*"[1]

Such is the persuasive power of the evidence for many miraculous claims. It's even enough to win over, well, Keener himself.

A Hermeneutic of Suspicion

"When I was an atheist, of course I didn't believe the miraculous was possible," Keener told me. "But even after I came to faith, I still retained quite a bit of skepticism. As a Christian, I believed in miracles in principle, but I have to admit I doubted the veracity of many claims I would hear."

"Your work as a historian probably influenced you in that regard," I suggested.

"Yes, we're taught to think critically, to demand convincing sources, and almost to use a hermeneutic of suspicion. Academics often take the attitude, 'Doubt all that you can, and then if anything is left at the end, you may accept it—but only tentatively.'"

"There can be a professional risk to investigating this topic, right?"

"No doubt. When I embarked on this project, I was concerned about being labeled a bad scholar because I chose to examine and document these cases. Frankly, it's safer for academics to stay stymied in their skepticism rather than to seek after the truth."

My mind flashed to a professor I had interviewed at a highly respected public university. He told me in detail how he had been incredibly healed of a brain tumor after praying to Jesus. But he wouldn't allow me to publish his story. Why? "I'm up for tenure," he said. "I'm afraid my colleagues would skewer me."

Nevertheless, Keener told me he "tried to maintain intellectual honesty" in his research and to "follow the clues wherever they led." And where did those clues take him?

"Everywhere I looked, I came across miracle claims that better fit a supernatural explanation than a naturalistic conclusion. Pretty soon, there was a tidal wave of examples."

"Such as?"

"Such as . . . ," he repeated, eager to take up the challenge. Keener mentally scrolled through examples from the case studies he had encountered, and he began speaking in a tone that was at once urgent and earnest.

"Cataracts and goiters—instantly and visibly healed," he said. "Paralytics suddenly able to walk. Multiple sclerosis radically cured. Broken bones suddenly mended. Hearing for the deaf. Sight for the blind. Voices restored. Burns disappearing. Massive hemorrhaging stopped. Failing kidneys cured. Rheumatoid arthritis and osteoporosis—gone. Life given back to the dead, even after several hours.

"I have accounts from around the world—China, Mozambique, the Philippines, Nigeria, Argentina, Brazil, Cuba, Ecuador, Indonesia, South Korea, and other countries. Multiple and independent eyewitnesses with reputations for integrity, including physicians. Names, dates, medical documentation in many cases. There's even a peer-reviewed scientific study confirming the healing of the deaf.

"And the timing is usually the most dramatic element—instantaneous results right after prayers to Jesus. Lots of cancer healings too—malignant brain tumors and reticulum-cell sarcoma, for example—but I didn't include most of those in the book, since I knew people would write them off as spontaneous remissions. Still, when the remission happens so quickly and completely after specific prayers, that's very suspicious."

"And your conclusion from all of this is—what?"

"That apart from some sort of divine intervention, many of these phenomena seem inexplicable. In other words, a lot of these cases better fit a supernatural explanation than a natural one."

I asked, "What was the turning point for you?"

His answer turned out to be a very personal one indeed.

The Healing of Thérèse

For years, Keener had heard vague stories about his wife's older sister, Thérèse Magnouha, who had been—what? Revived? Resuscitated? Raised from the dead? It wasn't until Keener flew to Africa and trekked through Congo-Brazzaville that he found out firsthand from eyewitnesses what had actually occurred. It was the family connection that gave this experience an especially profound meaning for him.

"How old was Thérèse when this happened?" I asked.

"She was two. One day her mother went out for a short time to take some food to a neighbor. When she returned, Thérèse was crying—she had been bitten by a snake. Her mother strapped the child to her back so she could run for help, but she quickly discovered that the child had stopped breathing."

There were no clinics or doctors. She carried her child up a mountainous area and back down the other side in order to find a family friend, "Coco" Ngoma Moise. She calculated that Thérèse had stopped breathing for more than three hours.

"Three hours?" I echoed. "Brain damage begins after just six minutes without oxygen."

"That's right. With no medical assistance available, all they could do after arriving was to pray to Jesus. They did—and as they lifted their cries to heaven, Thérèse began breathing again."

"Did she suffer any ill effects?"

"That's the other amazing thing—no. She promptly recovered, and by the next day she was fine. She recently completed a graduate-level seminary degree in preparation for full-time ministry, so there was no brain damage or other problems."

My skepticism kicked in. "Let me guess," I said. "They are part of an exuberant charismatic church where spectacular miraculous claims like this abound."

He shook his head. "No. They're part of a mainline Protestant denomination."

"With no doctors around, was there any way of knowing whether or not she had actually died?" I asked.

"This is a culture where people personally encounter death a lot more than Westerners do. They know what it looks like. Plus, a mother has every reason to grasp at the hope of any breath she could find. But let's say she wasn't clinically dead. Nevertheless, at the very minimum, it would be an astounding recovery, especially given the timing—right after the prayers began."

Because of the family connection, the incident resonated deeply with Keener. But in reading page after page of miracle accounts in his book, it wasn't even among the best attested.

"Of all the cases you examined, what are some of the strongest in terms of witnesses and corroborating evidence?" I asked.

Keener smiled and sat back in his chair. "How long do you have?" he asked.

A Deaf Child Hears

With that, Keener began recounting some of the stories he had investigated. He started with the case of a nine-year-old British girl who was diagnosed with deafness in September 1982, apparently the result of a virus that severely damaged nerves in both of her ears.

"Her case is reported by Dr. R. F. R. Gardner, a well-credentialed physician," Keener said.[2] "What makes this case especially interesting is that there is medical confirmation before the healing and immediately afterward, which is unusual to have."

The child's medical record says she was diagnosed with "untreatable bilateral sensorineural deafness." Her attending physician told her parents there was no cure and nothing he could do to repair her damaged nerves. She was outfitted with hearing aids that did help her hear to some degree.

The girl didn't want to wear hearing aids the rest of her life, so she started to pray that God would heal her. Her family and friends joined her. In fact, her mother said she felt a definite prompting to call out for God's help.

"I kept feeling God was telling me to pray specifically for healing," she said. "Passages kept coming out at me as I read: *If you have faith like children . . . If one among you is ill, lay hands . . . Ask and you shall receive . . . Your faith has made you whole.*"

On March 8, 1983, the girl went to the audiologist because one of her hearing aids had been damaged at school. After being examined and refitted, she was sent home.

The next evening, the child suddenly jumped out of her bed without her hearing aids and came bounding down the stairs. "Mummy, I can hear!" she exclaimed.

Her mother, astonished, tested to see if she could detect noises and words—and she could, even whispers. Her mother called the audiologist, who said, "I don't believe you. It is not possible. All right, if some miracle has happened, I am delighted. Have audiograms done."

The following day, she was tested again, and her audiogram and tympanogram came back fully normal. "I can give no explanation for this," said the audiologist. "I have never seen anything like it in my life."

The girl's doctor ruled out possible medical explanations. After repeated successful audiograms, the dumbfounded consultant's advice to her parents: "Forget she was ever deaf."

In the medical report, the child's ear, nose, and throat (ENT) surgeon used the word "inexplicable" to describe what happened. He wrote, "An audiogram did show her hearing in both ears to be totally and completely normal. I was completely unable to explain this phenomenon but naturally, like her parents, I was absolutely delighted . . . I can think of no rational explanation as to why her hearing returned to normal, there being a severe bilateral sensori-neural loss."[3]

After documenting numerous case studies like this in his book, Gardner concludes, "A belief in the occurrence of cases of miraculous healing today is intellectually acceptable."[4]

He said people who are still skeptical should consider what evidence they would be prepared to accept. "If the answer proves to be, 'None,' then you had better face the fact that you have abandoned logical enquiry."[5]

"One of the Most Hopelessly Ill Patients"

Keener went on to discuss another case, not in his book, for which there's significant documentation. "I've personally interviewed Barbara, who was diagnosed at the Mayo Clinic with progressive multiple sclerosis," Keener said. "I've confirmed the facts with two physicians who treated her. There are numerous independent witnesses to her condition and years of medical records. In fact, two of her doctors were so astounded by her case that they've written about it in books."[6]

One of those physicians, Dr. Harold P. Adolph, a board-certified surgeon who performed twenty-five thousand operations in his career, declared, "Barbara was one of the most hopelessly ill patients I ever saw."

Another physician, Dr. Thomas Marshall, an internist for thirty years until his recent retirement, described Barbara as a budding gymnast in high school, playing flute in the orchestra. But symptoms began appearing: she would trip, bump into walls, and was unable to grasp the rings in gym class.

Eventually, after her condition worsened, the diagnosis of progressive multiple sclerosis was confirmed through spinal taps and other diagnostic tests. After thoroughly examining her case, doctors at the Mayo Clinic agreed with the dire diagnosis.

"The prognosis was not good," Marshall said.

Over the next sixteen years, her condition continued to deteriorate. She spent months in hospitals, often for pneumonia after being unable to breathe. One diaphragm was paralyzed, rendering a lung nonfunctional; the other lung operated at less than 50 percent. A tracheostomy tube was inserted into her neck, with oxygen pumped from canisters in her garage.

She lost control of her urination and bowels; a catheter was inserted into her bladder, and an ileostomy was performed, with a bag attached for her bodily waste. She went legally blind, unable to read and only capable of seeing objects as gray shadows. A feeding tube was inserted into her stomach.

"Her abdomen was swollen grotesquely because the muscles of her intestine did not work," Adolph said.

"She now needed continuous oxygen, and her muscles and joints were becoming contracted and deformed because she could not move or exercise them," Marshall said. "Mayo [Clinic] was her last hope, but they had no recommendations to help stop this progressive wasting disease except to pray for a miracle."

By 1981, she hadn't been able to walk for seven years. She was confined to bed, her body twisted like a pretzel into a fetal position. Her hands were permanently flexed to the point that her fingers nearly touched her wrists. Her feet were locked in a downward position.

Marshall explained to her family that it was just a matter of time before she would die. They agreed not to do any heroics, including CPR or further hospitalization, to keep her alive; this would only prolong the inevitable.

Barbara entered hospice care in her home, with a life expectancy of less than six months.

"This Is Medically Impossible"

One day someone called in Barbara's story to the radio station of the Moody Bible Institute in Chicago. A request was broadcast for listeners to pray fervently for her. Some 450 Christians wrote letters to her church saying they were lifting up Barbara in prayer.

On Pentecost Sunday, 1981, her aunt came over to read her some of the letters in which people offered prayers for her healing. Two girlfriends joined them. Suddenly, during a lull in the conversation, Barbara heard a man's voice speak from behind her—even though there was nobody else in the room.

"The words were clear and articulate and spoken with great authority, but also with great compassion," Marshall wrote.

Said the voice, "My child, get up and walk!"

Seeing that Barbara had become agitated, one of her friends plugged the hole in her neck so she could speak. "I don't know what you're going to think about this," Barbara told them, "but God just told me to get up and walk. I know he really did! Run and get my family. I want them here with us!"

Her friends ran out and yelled for her family. "Come quick; come quick!"

Marshall described what happened next: "Barb felt compelled to do immediately what she was divinely instructed, so she literally jumped out of bed and removed her oxygen. She was standing on legs that had not supported her for years. Her vision was back, and she was no longer short of breath, even without her oxygen. Her contractions were gone, and she could move her feet and hands freely."

Her mother ran into the room and dropped to her knees, feeling Barbara's calves. "You have muscles again!" she exclaimed. Her father came in, hugged her, "and whisked her off for a waltz around the family room," Marshall said.

Everyone moved to the living room to offer a tearful prayer of thanksgiving—although Barbara found it hard to sit still. That evening, there was a worship service at Wheaton Wesleyan Church, where Barbara's family attended. Most of the congregation knew about Barbara's grave condition.

During the service, when the pastor asked if anyone had any announcements, Barbara stepped into the center aisle and casually strolled toward the front, her heart pounding.

"A cacophony of whispers came from all parts of the church," Marshall said. "People started clapping, and then, as if led by a divine conductor, the entire congregation began to sing, 'Amazing grace! How sweet the sound that saved a wretch like me! I once was lost, but now am found; was blind, but now I see!'"

The next day, Barbara came to Marshall's office for an examination. Seeing her in the hallway, walking toward him, "I thought I was seeing an apparition!" he recalled. "No one had ever seen anything like this before."

He told Barbara, "This is medically impossible. But you are now free to go out and live your life."

A chest X-ray that afternoon showed her lungs were already "perfectly normal," with the collapsed lung completely expanded. "The intestine that had been vented to the abdominal wall was reconnected normally," Adolph said. "She was eventually restored to complete health."

Barbara has now lived for thirty-five years with no recurrence of her illness. "She subsequently married a minister and feels her calling in life is to serve others," Marshall said.

Both physicians marvel at her extraordinary recovery. "I have never witnessed anything like this before or since and considered it a rare privilege to observe the hand of God performing a true miracle," Marshall wrote.

Said Adolph, "Both Barbara and I knew who had healed her."

A Broken Ankle That Wasn't

I sat in silence for a while, flabbergasted by Barbara's story. Keener shared my amazement. "When I interviewed Barbara about her case, she was still brimming with excitement, even after all these years," he said.

My mind searched fruitlessly for naturalistic explanations. Could her recovery be written off as some sort of natural remission? If so, why would it suddenly occur after so many years, right when hundreds of people were praying for her? Remissions typically take place over time. Certainly the placebo effect or misdiagnosis or fraud or coincidence or medical mistakes couldn't account for what happened.

Besides, what about the mysterious voice telling her to get up and walk? Or the immediate muscle tone in her atrophied legs? Or the instant and simultaneous healing of her eyesight, lungs, and so on? With so many witnesses of unquestioned integrity and expertise, plus a proliferation of corroborating documentation, her case seemed to meet even the high evidential bar typically set by skeptics.

Absent a presupposition against the miraculous, this did seem to be a clear and compelling example of divine intervention. And Keener was far from finished. He began to rattle off a series of other amazing stories he had documented in his book, including the story of Carl Cocherell.

"In March 2006, on a trip to Missouri, Carl was checking the oil in his car when he stepped down and felt a sharp crack," Keener said. "He fainted from the pain, which was the worst he had ever endured. I have a copy of the radiology report of his X-rays, confirming the fracture. The orthopedist ordered him to stay overnight. During that night, though, Carl experienced a voice from the Lord."

"What did the voice say?" I asked.

"That the ankle was not broken."

I cocked my head. "Despite the X-rays?"

"That's right. The next day the doctor casted his leg and warned he would eventually need months of physical therapy. Back in Michigan, his family doctor ordered more X-rays, and this time the results were radically different."

"How so?"

"There were no breaks or even tissue damage where a break had been. Again, I have the radiology report that says there's no fracture. In fact, the doctor told him, 'You never had a broken ankle.'"

"But," I interjected, "what about the Missouri X-rays?"

Keener calmly continued the narrative. "The doctor looked again at those Missouri X-rays and said, 'Now, *that's* a broken ankle.' But at this point, there was no sign of a break. He removed Carl's cast and sent him home. Carl never had further problems or needed any therapy."

"What do you make of all that?" I asked.

"Personally, I don't see how this could have occurred naturally," Keener said. "Would a sixty-two-year-old man's bone heal so quickly that no sign of a fracture would remain at all? It doesn't seem likely. And, of course, that wouldn't explain how God told him in advance what would happen."

"Can Jesus Heal Me?"

Next Keener brought up Ed Wilkinson, whose education in neuropsychology convinced him that people who rely on faith to cure their ills are merely using religion as a neurosis to avoid dealing with reality.

"Then, in November 1984, his eight-year-old son, Brad, was diagnosed with two holes in his heart. The condition also impaired his lungs. Surgery was scheduled," Keener recounted. "As the surgery got closer, Brad started giving away his toys, not expecting he would survive. One day he asked his dad, 'Am I going to die?'"

"That's quite a question, given the circumstances," I said. "Was his father honest with him?"

"He said not everyone who has heart surgery dies, but it can happen. Then his son asked, 'Can Jesus heal me?'"

"Now, *that's* quite a question," I said.

"His father was aware of how often faith is abused, so he said, 'I'll get back to you on that.'"

"And did he?"

"Yes, a few days later, after some anguished prayers and reading Philippians 4:13,[7] Ed told him that God does heal, but whether or not he would in Brad's case, they still had hope of eternal life in Jesus. After that, a visiting pastor asked Brad, 'Do you believe that Jesus can heal you?' Brad said yes, and the minister prayed for him."[8]

Before surgery at the University of Missouri hospital in Columbia, Missouri, tests confirmed nothing had changed with Brad's condition. The following morning, Brad was taken in for his operation, which was expected to last four hours. But after an hour, the surgeon summoned Ed and showed him two films.

The first film, taken the day before, showed blood leaking from one heart chamber to another. The second film, taken just as surgery started, showed a wall of some sort where the leak had been. The surgeon said there was nothing wrong with Brad's heart, even though the holes were clearly visible the day before. The lungs were also now normal.

"I have not seen this very often," the surgeon said. He explained that a spontaneous closure rarely happens in infants, but it was not supposed to occur in an eight-year-old. "You can count this as a miracle," he said.

The hospital risk manager said firmly, "You can see from the films: this was *not* a misdiagnosis." Added the pulmonologist, "Somebody somewhere must have been praying."

Later, an insurance agent called Ed to complain about the forms he had submitted. "What's a 'spontaneous closure'?" the agent asked.

Replied Ed, "A miracle."

Today, said Keener, Brad is in his thirties with a business and children of his own. He has never had any heart problems since his healing.

A Death, a Prayer, a New Life

Keener continued with the case of Jeff Markin, a fifty-three-year-old auto mechanic who walked into the emergency room at Palm Beach Gardens Hospital in Florida and collapsed from a heart attack on October 20, 2006. For forty minutes, emergency room personnel frantically labored to revive him, shocking him seven times with a defibrillator, but he remained flatlined.

Finally, the supervising cardiologist, Chauncey Crandall, a well-respected, Yale-educated doctor and medical school professor who specialized in complex heart cases, was brought in to examine the body. Markin's face, toes, and fingers had already turned black from the lack of oxygen. His pupils were dilated and fixed. There was no point in trying to resuscitate him. At 8:05 p.m., he was declared dead.

Crandall filled out the final report and turned to leave. But he quickly felt an extraordinary compulsion. "I sensed God was telling me to turn around and pray for the patient," he said later. This seemed foolish, so he tried to ignore it, only to receive a second—and even stronger—divine prompting.

A nurse was already disconnecting the intravenous fluids and sponging the body so it could be taken to the morgue. But Crandall began praying over the corpse: "Father God, I cry out for the soul of this man. If he does not know you as his Lord and Savior, please raise him from the dead right now in Jesus' name."

Crandall told the emergency room doctor to use the paddle to shock the corpse one more time. Seeing nothing to gain, the doctor protested. "I've shocked him again and again. He's dead." But then he complied out of respect for his colleague.

Instantly, the monitor jumped from flatline to a normal heartbeat of about seventy-five beats per minute with a healthy rhythm. "In my more than twenty years as a cardiologist, I have never seen a heartbeat restored so completely and suddenly," Crandall said.

Markin immediately began breathing without any assistance, and the blackness receded from his face, toes, and fingers. The nurse panicked because she feared the patient would be permanently disabled from oxygen deprivation, yet he never displayed any signs of brain damage.[9]

Keener shook his head in wonder. "As you can imagine, this case got a lot of attention in the media," he said. "One medical consultant for a national news program suggested that perhaps Markin's heart had not stopped completely but had gone into a very subtle rhythm for those forty minutes."

"What was Crandall's response?" I asked.

"That he was grasping at straws. The resuscitation couldn't have happened naturally. An electrical shock administered in those circumstances would not normally accomplish anything," Keener said. "The unanimous verdict of those actually present was that Markin was deceased, and that includes Crandall, who is a nationally recognized cardiologist with many years of experience."

Indeed, in light of the circumstances, skeptical explanations seem hollow and forced—and, again, they can't account for the two mysterious urges that prompted Crandall to turn in his tracks and pray for a victim who had already been declared dead. Absent those, Jeff Markin would be in his grave today.

"The critics have to strain at the bounds of plausibility in order to keep their anti-supernatural thesis intact," Keener said.

For me, Acts 26:8 sprang to mind: "Why should any of you consider it incredible that God raises the dead?"

"I Know, It's a Miracle"

I knew Keener could go on for hours talking about the cases he unearthed in his admittedly limited survey of miraculous claims. For example, he has accumulated 350 reports just of people who have been healed of blindness. Here are several cases taken at random from his book:

- A welder named David Dominong suffered extensive third- and fourth-degree burns when he was electrocuted in October 2002. Hospitalized for more than five weeks, he was told it could be five years until he would be able to walk again. He was confined to a wheelchair and considering amputation when he received prayer and was promptly able to walk and run without assistance.

- Dr. Alex Abraham testified to the case of Kuldeep Singh, who had intractable epilepsy to the point where he would lose consciousness during frequent seizures. Ever since Pastor Jarnail Singh prayed that God would heal him fifteen years ago, he has had no more seizures or treatment. Abraham, a neurologist, said the abrupt, permanent, and complete healing of epilepsy this severe is highly unusual.

- Matthew Dawson was hospitalized in Australia with confirmed meningitis in April 2007. He was told he would have to remain under hospital care for weeks or months. But he was abruptly healed at the exact moment his father, on another continent, offered prayers for him.

- Mirtha Venero Boza, a medical doctor in Cuba, reports that her baby granddaughter's hand was severely burned by a hot iron, resulting in swelling and skin peeling off. Less than half an hour after prayer, however, the hand was completely healed without medical intervention, as if it had never been burned.

- Cambridge University professor John Polkinghorne, one of the world's foremost scholars on the intersection of science and faith, provides the account of a woman whose left leg was paralyzed in an injury. Doctors gave up trying to treat her, saying she would be an invalid for life. In 1980, she reluctantly agreed to prayer from an Anglican priest. Though she had no expectation of healing, she had a vision in which she was commanded to rise and walk. Said Polkinghorne, who has doctorates in both science and theology, "From that moment, she was able to walk, jump, and bend down, completely without pain."

- Physician John White reports that a woman with a confirmed diagnosis of tuberculosis of the cervical spine had been unable to walk, but she was instantaneously healed after prayer. He said her doctor "was bewildered to find there was no evidence of disease in her body." Said Keener, "Her illness was certain, her cure permanent, and the witness virtually incontrovertible." Not only was White the doctor who prayed for her, but he later married her.

- Joy Wahnefried, a student at Taylor University in Indiana, suffered from vertical heterophoria, where one eye viewed images at a higher level than the other. This triggered debilitating migraines that could last up to a week. A professor and students prayed for her during three consecutive prayer meetings, and Joy was suddenly healed—her eyesight now 20/20 and her incurable medical condition gone. Her eye doctor said she "can't explain it" and has never seen anything like it in four thousand patients. Keener, who has copies of her before-and-after medical reports, confirmed that she no longer even needs corrective lenses.

- A grapefruit-sized flesh-eating ulcer, with the wound going to the bone, was boring through the calf muscle of a seventy-year-old Florida man. After treatments failed, doctors declared the wound incurable and amputation was scheduled. However, one physician laid his hands on the oozing wound and prayed for healing. Recovery began immediately; within four days, the ulcer was melting away and new skin forming. By the following week, the leg was restored to normal. The doctor's opinion: "It can't happen on its own. Impossible." The patient's wife summed it up: "God's real. God healed his leg."[10]

- University professor Robert Larmer reports that Mary Ellen Fitch was hospitalized with hepatitis B. She was turning yellow; her abdomen bulged with her swollen liver. She was told she would remain in the hospital for months. After a week, though, she had a deep experience with God and committed her condition to him. The next morning, her blood tests were normal. Bewildered doctors repeatedly tested her, with the same results. Years have now passed, and she remains healed.[11]

- The director of a clinic for voice and swallowing disorders reports the case of a fifty-two-year-old man who suffered a severe brain stem stroke in the region of the medulla. Strokes in this location irreversibly damage the ability to swallow. After prayer, though, the man regained his ability to eat and swallow normally. The patient told the startled experts, "I know, it's a miracle." This was the only such recovery the clinic's director had seen in fifteen years.

"A Tide of Miracles"

Page after page, Keener unfolds so many miracle claims that after a while, it's easy to become numb to them. Many of them come from his own circle of acquaintances, which means he's only scratching the surface of the number of supernatural accounts out there. Although the amount of witnesses and documentation varies in the different cases, many of them seem to exceed even the stringent standards suggested by skeptics.

As impressive as those reports are, though, I decided to change the direction of the conversation by bringing up Michael Shermer's question about why we don't see reports of God miraculously regrowing the limbs of amputees. When I posed the challenge to Keener, he considered the issue for a few moments before responding.

"Interestingly, we see many amazing miracles performed by Jesus, including the healing of a withered hand,[12] but we don't see amputated limbs restored," he replied. "While I've heard stories of limbs growing back, I haven't verified or personally examined any of them at this point."

He searched his memory and added, "Douglas Norwood, a pastor in Suriname at the time, does tell of a Christian gathering that was attended by an opponent of the church who had a shriveled arm, paralyzed his whole life. He shouted, 'I defy this Christian God!' With that, suddenly his arm shot up into the air, fully healed. He looked at it and was instantly converted. In fact, this was the beginning of a movement where tens of thousands of people came to faith in Christ in Suriname.

"There's also the case of a Wisconsin man crushed under a semitrailer, destroying most of his small intestine," Keener continued. "He was slowly starving to death because he couldn't digest food. He dropped to 125 pounds from 180. A friend felt God was leading him to fly from New York just to pray for him. When he prayed, the man felt something like an electric jolt go through his body. He was healed; in fact, a medical report says his small intestine had more than doubled in length. A small intestine in an adult can get wider, but it can't get longer."

"That's an example of a body part growing back, but I'm not sure that's what Shermer was getting at," I said. "I think he was saying that he needs to see a more visible healing—something irrefutable."

"We've got plenty of those," Keener said. "For instance, totally blind eyes, white from cataracts, changing color and becoming normal and healthy. That's hard to explain away."

"Still," I said, "a lot of your stories are from Africa, Asia, and other faraway places. Why do so many of these dramatic miracles happen in distant and underdeveloped countries where documentation is particularly difficult?"

"In America, we have a lot of sophisticated medical technology, which is God's gift to us, and we should use it. That's the way he typically brings healing," Keener said. "But in many other places around the world, that's not available, and perhaps God's intervention is the only hope in a lot of instances."

I noted that philosopher J. P. Moreland explained that outbreakings of the supernatural tend to occur in areas where there's leading-edge evangelism into new cultures. In his book *Kingdom Triangle*, Moreland writes, "A major factor in the current revival in the Third World—by some estimates, up to 70 percent of it—is intimately connected to signs and wonders as expressions of the love of the Christian Father-God, the lordship of his Son, and the power of his Spirit and his Kingdom."[13]

Keener agreed. "We've got lots of instances like this," he said. "Some estimate that 90 percent of the growth of the church in China is being fueled by healings. Edmond Tang at the University of Birmingham said, 'This is especially true in the countryside, where medical facilities are often inadequate or non-existent.'"[14]

Intrigued, I asked Keener if he had other examples, which he readily offered.

"Dr. Julia Ma at the Oxford Center for Mission Studies said most converts among the Kankanaey in the northern Philippines came to Christ through the experience of miraculous healings," he said. "A Baptist church in India grew from six members to more than six hundred in just over a year because of healings. In Ethiopia, more than 80 percent of believers surveyed in a Lutheran church attributed their conversions to healings and exorcisms.

"In Brazil, many poor people lack adequate health care, and they're attracted to Christianity when they see healings. Eighty-six percent of Brazilian Pentecostals said they had an experience of divine healing," he added. "In Argentina, healing is by far the primary tool for evangelism and church growth."

I thought of comments by the late Jim Rutz, who used to live close to me when I resided in Colorado. He documented the recent growth of the Christian church worldwide, taking special note of God's supernatural intervention, including accounts of people being brought back from the dead in fifty-two countries.

"Since about the mid-1980s, a tide of miracles has begun to engulf the entire planet," he wrote in his book *Megashift*. "As time goes on, miracles are multiplying like loaves and fishes."[15]

The Miracle Business

Pretty soon, Keener and I began hearing some noises coming from upstairs. "Sounds like Médine has come home from teaching her French class," Keener said. "I'd like for you to meet her."

"Absolutely, I'd love to meet her. *Je voudrais utiliser mon français rudimentaire en parlant avec elle*,"[16] I replied, my accent awkward as usual. "But before we go, let me ask you something else. You set out to accomplish two things with your book. Did you achieve what you had hoped?"

"My first goal involved the New Testament," he replied. "I wanted to show that it's not necessary to dismiss these writings as legendary, fanciful, or inaccurate, just because they report miracles. Today's world is full of firsthand claims from people who say they have witnessed miracles, and there's no reason to suppose the ancient world was any different. If today's accounts can stem from eyewitnesses and potentially report what really happened, then the same is true of the gospels."

Clearly, that goal had been achieved.

"And what was your second goal?" I asked.

"To show that it's rational to consider the possibility of supernatural causation for many of these miracle claims."

"Well, Professor, that's very academic sounding," I said with a grin.

"Okay, let me rephrase it," he said, clearing his throat. "It looks like God is still in the miracle business!"

He stopped for a moment to let that simple declarative sentence hang in the air. Then he added, "At least, that's an entirely reasonable hypothesis from the evidence. Often, the best explanation for what occurred is supernatural, not natural."

"What are some of the implications of this?" I asked.

"Anti-supernaturalism has reigned as an inflexible Western academic premise for far too long. In light of the millions of people around the globe who say they've experienced the miraculous, it's time to take these claims seriously. Let's investigate them and follow the evidence wherever it leads. If even a small fraction prove to be genuine, we have to consider whether God is still divinely intervening in his creation."

I closed my notebook and put my pen in my shirt pocket.

"And you believe he is?" I asked.

Keener's voice was unwavering. This time he answered not merely as a scholar, but also as a relative of the healed Thérèse.

"Yes, I believe he is."

PART 3

Science, Dreams, and Visions

CHAPTER 7

The Science of Miracles

An Interview with Dr. Candy Gunther Brown

That's not good for your side, Lee."

That taunt from skeptic Michael Shermer played in my mind as I drove northward on Interstate 65 the day after my interview with Craig Keener in rural Kentucky.

Shermer was referring to a scientific analysis of prayer's impact on the recovery of cardiac bypass patients. Conducted by the founder of Harvard Medical School's Mind/Body Medical Institute and known as STEP (Study of the Therapeutic Effects of Intercessory Prayer), the decade-long research certainly seemed to have impressive credentials.

Technically, it was a "prospective, randomized, double-blind, parallel group controlled trial"—a so-called "gold standard" in research. It cost $2.4 million and was published in the peer-reviewed *American Heart Journal*.

However, the results were deflating to those who expected confirmation of prayer's miraculous healing power. The study's conclusion: prayer recipients fared no better than those who weren't prayed for.

"Zero. Nothing," was how Shermer crisply summarized what STEP concluded about the effects of prayer. "This is the best prayer study we have," he said. "So when you get beyond anecdotes and use the scientific method, there's no evidence for the miraculous."

When he added, "That's not good for your side, Lee," it was easy to detect a whiff of triumphalism in his voice.

Science, of course, is not the only route to certainty. Believing that science is the sole arbiter of truth is called *scientism*,[1] which is self-refuting. In other words, the sentence, "Science is the only way to know if something is true," is itself not a claim that can be proven by science.

Science aside, my interview with Keener illustrated that corroborated eyewitness testimony, especially when coming from multiple and independent observers who have unquestioned integrity, can go a long way in establishing whether a miracle claim is credible.

Still, there are ways that science and medicine can contribute to the investigation of the supernatural. It's true that miracles can't be analyzed in a test tube; however, it's also true that test tubes can be used to determine whether a virus has suddenly disappeared from the blood of a hepatitis patient immediately after prayer—important corroboration for a claim of a supernatural healing.

In 1997, Harvard paleontologist and evolutionary biologist Stephen Jay Gould, a self-described agnostic, wrote that science and faith occupy "nonoverlapping magisteria." By that, he meant that science deals with the empirical universe, facts, and theories, while religion focuses on questions of moral meaning and value.[2]

Gould's vision was that there ought to be "respectful discourse" and "constant input from both magisteria toward the common goal of wisdom."[3] In other words, science and faith, working side by side, can bring new understandings about our life and world.

While that's a laudable goal, Gould's rigid delineation of the roles of science and faith has been hotly debated. For example, Christianity isn't merely concerned with moral meaning and value; it makes specific factual claims about events—including miracles such as the resurrection—that occurred in history. If those claims aren't actually true, the faith collapses and its moral authority evaporates.

Certainly the use of scientific expertise can help in investigating whether claims of the miraculous are valid or not. Even if science cannot definitively prove God exists or that something supernatural has occurred, it can provide empirical evidence that either supports or undermines miracle accounts.

After all, Jesus wasn't averse to his own miracles being scrutinized. He told eyewitnesses to his miracles to report what they had personally seen,[4] and he instructed a person healed of leprosy to show himself to the priest so he could be examined.[5]

So what is the legitimate role of science in investigating supernatural claims? Equally important, what *can't* it contribute? And is STEP the final word on the efficacy of intercessory prayer? Does this study really establish, as Michael Shermer suggested, that when scientific analysis is applied, there is no persuasive evidence for the miraculous?

Those were some of the questions prompting my nearly two-hundred-mile journey northward from Keener's house to the campus of Indiana University in Bloomington. I checked my watch as I drove my rental car. Still plenty of time to make my appointment with a Harvard-educated scholar who is figuring out ways to use the magisterium of science to investigate the magisterium of faith.

The Interview with Candy Gunther Brown, PhD

Candy Gunther Brown, who earned her undergraduate degree summa cum laude, master's degree, and doctorate at Harvard, is a professor of religious studies at the sprawling Indiana University, which has forty-eight thousand students at its campus fifty miles southwest of Indianapolis.

A scrupulous scholar eager to maintain academic neutrality, Brown takes a nonsectarian approach to religious studies. "I do not assume the existence or nonexistence of a deity or other suprahuman forces," she explains. "What I argue is that people's religious beliefs often have real-world effects that can be studied empirically."[6]

Her books include *Testing Prayer: Science and Healing*, published by Harvard University Press, and *The Healing Gods: Complementary and Alternative Medicine in Christian America*, published by Oxford University Press; and she is the editor of *Global Pentecostal and Charismatic Healing*, also published by Oxford.

Brown has taught a variety of courses at the university, including Religion, Illness, and Healing; Sickness and Health; and Evangelical and Charismatic Christianity in the Americas. She's a popular online writer for the *Huffington Post* and *Psychology Today*, and her peer-reviewed articles have appeared in *Academic Medicine* and numerous other scholarly journals.

What brought me to Indiana was her focus on studying the impact of intercessory prayer on healing. Since the university's campus was bustling with traffic and parking was at a premium, we decided to meet at the nearby house she shares with her husband, Joshua, who's also a professor at the university, specializing in cognitive science and neuroscience.

Wearing her dark hair short and parted on the side, and peering through black-rimmed glasses, Brown is a live wire, bounding with energy, her voice strong and clear from years of lecturing in classrooms. She thinks—and speaks—in a well-organized manner, unfolding her points systematically and with clarity. We chose adjacent wingback chairs in her front sitting room and settled in for our discussion.

"What's your response to skeptics who say science shouldn't investigate prayers for healing?" I asked her. "For example, the textbook

Psychology of Religion says, 'The evidence of the effectiveness of prayers, as they touch events in the material world, remains outside the domain of science. The faithful who want to believe can believe, and the skeptic who chooses not to believe could not be convinced.'"[7]

Replied Brown, "I think that ignores a third category of people, which may be the largest: those who don't have a predetermined conclusion. These people just want to know where the facts point."

"They're open to wherever the evidence leads them," I said.

"Exactly. Let's face it: people get sick, and when they do, they often pray for healing. Whether scientists or medical doctors think this is a good idea or not, it's going to happen. So it only makes sense to find out what occurs when there are prayers for healing. Are they beneficial, whether for natural or supernatural reasons? Or do they cause people to get worse? Policy makers, scientists, physicians, patients—it's relevant to all of them."

"How can science be used to investigate the effects of prayers?"

"In several ways. For one thing, medical records can be compared before and after prayer occurs. Was there a condition that was diagnosed? Do X-rays, blood tests, or other diagnostic procedures show illness or injury? And then was there some resolution of that condition?"

"Of course, you can't prove God healed them, even if their illness disappears," I observed.

"Correct. There may have been medical treatment, or the placebo effect may be involved, or a spontaneous remission. Even diagnostic tests can be open to interpretation. Plus, relapses might occur later," she replied. "On the other hand, if there's no improvement or a worsening of their illness, then we can say a miracle cure definitely *didn't* take place. Science is better at disproving things than proving them."

"Clinical studies can be of help too," I offered.

"I believe so. They're set up for a short-term window of time so we can measure what happens after people pray. Now, there can be complications, such as people outside the study who are praying for people inside the study, or the application of medical treatment, or subsequent relapses. And, of course, everyone brings their own assumptions when they interpret the data, depending on where they are on the spectrum."

"The spectrum?"

"Yes, on one end of the spectrum are those who expect miracles to be very, very likely. They believe God frequently intervenes in nature. They may be quick to conclude, 'God has healed this person through prayer.' But people on the opposite end of the spectrum start with the assumption that miracles *never* happen. If there's a zero likelihood, then regardless of how strong the evidence is, there has to be a more plausible explanation, right? So there is going to be a preconditioning to interpret things depending on where you start off."

The Effects of Intercessory Prayer

I asked Brown for her opinion of the STEP project that Shermer had cited as having shown no impact—or even a slightly harmful effect—on recovering cardiac patients. I anticipated this to be a rather routine conversation, but frankly I ended up thoroughly surprised—even stunned—by what she disclosed.

"Let me start by saying that there have been 'gold standard' studies before and after STEP that reached the opposite conclusion: that the group receiving prayer had *better* outcomes," she said.

"Really?" I asked. "Can you give me some examples?"

"One of the first widely publicized studies was by Dr. Randolph Byrd, published in 1988 in the peer-reviewed *Southern Medical Journal*," she said. "It was a prospective, randomized, double-blinded, controlled study of four hundred subjects."

She explained that born-again Christians, both Catholics and Protestants, were given the patient's first name, condition, and diagnosis. They were instructed to pray to the Judeo-Christian God "for a rapid recovery and for prevention of complications and death, in addition to other areas of prayer they believed to be beneficial to patients."

"What were the results?"

"Patients in the prayer group had less congestive heart failure, fewer cardiac arrests, fewer episodes of pneumonia, were less often intubated and ventilated, and needed less diuretic and antibiotic therapy," she said.

"That's very interesting," I replied. "Do you think this study was scientifically sound?"

"I believe it was. Of course, in any study like this, you can't control for such things as people praying for themselves or other people praying for them outside the study," she said.

"What was the reaction when it came out?"

"The journal got flak from readers who didn't like prayer being studied this way. One doctor wrote in to say the journal had done 'a disservice to the science of medicine and, therefore, to mankind in general.'"

"Well, that's pretty strong!" I said.

She smiled. "I thought so too. The editor wrote back to say Byrd's article had been subjected to the usual peer-review process and was judged to be a properly designed and executed scientific investigation. Then a decade or so later, a replication study by Dr. William S. Harris and colleagues was published in the *Archives of Internal Medicine*."

"Were the results similar?"

"This was a 'gold standard' study of the effects of intercessory prayer on almost a thousand consecutively admitted coronary patients.

Half received prayer; the other half didn't. And again, the group that received prayer had better outcomes than the control group."

"Was there controversy this time as well?"

"Even more, probably because this journal has a higher profile and the article was published in a cultural climate that was more hostile to the idea of prayer being studied scientifically. One critic even cited the biblical injunction against putting God to the test."[8]

I looked back over my notes. "So let me get this straight," I said. "These studies affirmed that the recipients of prayer had better outcomes than those who didn't receive prayer."

Brown nodded. "That's right."

Now I was confused. "Then why do you think STEP reached such a different conclusion?" I asked.

"Ah," she said, "that's where things get very intriguing."

"A Classic New Age Cult"

Brown began dissecting the STEP project by asking me an uncontroversial question. "If you're going to study prayer," she said, "wouldn't it be important who was praying, who they were praying to, and how they were praying?"

That seemed intuitively obvious. "Of course," I replied.

"In the Byrd study, the intercessors were 'born again' Protestants and Catholics, who were active in daily devotional prayer and in fellowship with a local church. They were praying to the 'Judeo-Christian God.'"

That made sense to me. As born-again believers, they would have faith in a personal God who is loving and who possesses the power and inclination to supernaturally intervene in people's lives.

"Yes," I said, "it seems reasonable that if you're studying the effects of Christian prayer, you would want people whose theology is mainstream."

"Exactly. Similarly, in the Harris study, the intercessors were required to believe in a personal God who hears and answers prayers made on behalf of the sick."

Again, that seems entirely appropriate. "What about STEP, which found no beneficial effects of prayer?" I asked.

She shifted in her chair so she was facing me more squarely. "Here's where the difference comes in," she said, as if letting me in on a professional secret. "The only Protestants recruited to participate in the study were from Silent Unity of Lee's Summit, Missouri."

A red flag shot up in my mind. "What?" I blurted out. Truly, I was taken aback—in fact, I was staggered. "Unity isn't genuinely Christian," I said.

"They claim to be Christian—the group's full name is the Unity School of Christianity[9]—but I agree that many Christian scholars wouldn't give them that label," Brown replied. "They trace themselves back to the New Thought movement of the late nineteenth century."

I have studied Christian apologetics, or evidence for the faith, for decades, and I am a professor of Christian thought at a university. Never have I encountered any expert on religious movements who would classify Unity as being traditionally Christian in its theology.

With more than three hundred Unity congregations, a thousand licensed ministers, programs on more than a thousand radio and television stations, and thirty-three million pieces of mail dispatched annually, Unity has been described as "one of the largest metaphysical groups in the United States."[10]

The sect's views on the divinity of Jesus, sin and salvation, the Trinity, the Bible, and just about every cornerstone of Christian doctrine would be unrecognizable to any mainstream Christian.

Reading through Unity's beliefs, I detected a mixture of

Hinduism, Spiritism, Theosophy, Rosicrucianism, and Christian Science, blended with an esoteric species of Christianity. Biblical concepts have been emptied of their historical meaning and refilled with ideas more suited to New Age mysticism or pantheism.

Indeed, Ruth Tucker, an expert on cults and alternative religions, wrote, "Unity's acceptance of non-Christian tenets such as reincarnation and its rejection of various biblical tenets have placed the movement *outside* traditional Christian orthodoxy."[11]

Ron Rhodes, who has a doctorate in systematic theology and has authored sixty books on religious beliefs, wrote, "The Unity School of Christianity may have a Christian sounding name, but it is definitely *not* Christian."[12]

Probe, a respected apologetics organization, calls Unity "a classic New Age cult [that] is not Christian in any aspect of its doctrine or teaching."[13]

How Not to Study Prayer

"What's particularly relevant is Unity's attitude toward prayer and the miraculous," Brown continued. "Unity leaders have long denied that prayer works miracles and have even called petitionary prayers 'useless.'"[14]

Cofounder of the sect, Charles Fillmore, once wrote, "God never performs miracles, if by this is meant a departure from universal law."[15] The other founder, his wife, Myrtle, said, "We do not promise to say a prayer of words and have the saying work a miracle in another individual. Our work is to call attention to the true way of living and to inspire others to want to live in that true way."[16]

The group practices what it calls "affirmative prayer," which involves repeating positive statements, such as, "We are imbued with divinity and are physically healthy."

The sect's website reads, "When most people think of prayer, they think of asking God for something. Not so in Unity. Unity uses 'affirmative prayer.' Rather than begging or beseeching God, this method involves *connecting with the spirit of God within* and asserting positive beliefs about the desired outcome."[17]

Although there is some diversity among those affiliated with Unity, essentially Unity doesn't believe in miracles, doesn't believe in a personal God outside of us who intervenes in people's lives, and doesn't believe it's even appropriate to ask for supernatural help.

I was still shaking my head in disbelief when Brown spoke up again.

"So why do we see different results in STEP?" she asked. "Well, you've got different inclusion criteria. Look who's doing the praying and how they're doing it. It's apples and oranges compared to the Byrd and Harris studies."

I mulled the implications, which are clearly enormous. "This means you can't draw any conclusions about the effectiveness of traditional Christian prayer from STEP," I said.

"That's right," she replied. "None."

With Shermer's comments in the back of my mind, I asked, "Would you consider STEP to be definitive or a final word on prayer research?"

No hesitation from Brown. "Not at all," she said.

I posed one more question along those lines: "In the end, does this study tell us *anything* that's helpful?"

She thought for a few moments. "Well," she said, "it is instructive on how *not* to conduct a study of Christian prayer."

Distant versus Personal Prayer

In addition to her specific critiques of STEP, Brown raised several concerns about the overall approach in these "double-blind" prayer studies.

"First, these studies don't take into consideration that healing seems to be clustered in certain geographical areas," she said, which prompted me to recall J. P. Moreland's observation that miraculous healings often break out in Third World locales where the gospel is making new inroads.

"Second," she continued, "these studies don't recognize that certain people are reputed to have a special 'anointing' or success rate with healing prayer. Third, these studies obscure the presumed role of faith on the part of those offering and receiving prayer. After all, a person receiving prayer can't respond with faith if they don't even know someone is praying for them."

I said, "Basically, you're suggesting that these studies don't reflect the way that prayer is actually practiced, especially among Pentecostals and charismatics who emphasize healing prayer."

"That's right," came her response. "These studies focus on *distant intercessory prayer*—intercessors are given the first name and condition of someone they don't know and told to pray for a complication-free surgery. But when Pentecostals actually pray for healing, they generally get up close to someone they know; they often come in physical contact with them; and they empathize with their sufferings. It's what I call *proximal intercessory prayer*."

As I thought about healings performed by Jesus, this seemed to be his pattern. He often touched those he was about to heal; for instance, Luke 4:40 reads, "At sunset, the people brought to Jesus all who had various kinds of sickness, and laying his hands on each one, he healed them." What's more, the Bible says that the ill should be anointed with oil, which also involves proximity and touching.[18]

"Have any studies looked at the effects of this kind of up-close-and-personal prayer?" I asked.

"Dale Matthews and his team did a prospective, controlled study of the effects of intercessory prayer on patients with rheumatoid arthritis, published in the *Southern Medical Journal* in 2000," she said. "They found no effects for distant intercessory prayer; however, they did find that patients experienced statistically significant improvement with direct-contact prayers, compared with patients who only received medical treatment."

"How was the study set up?" I asked.

"Over a three-day period, subjects received six hours of in-person prayer, plus another six hours of group instruction on the theology of healing prayer," she said. "This particular study didn't clarify whether improvements resulted from the prayer itself, or from attention, touch, social support, counseling, and exchanges of forgiveness that were offered—all of which have been shown to have therapeutic effects."

"That does muddy the waters," I commented.

"Yes. Unfortunately, rheumatoid arthritis is relatively susceptible to psychosomatic improvements."

"So what's the answer?" I asked. "What kind of study can take all of these dynamics into account?"

"I conducted a study that takes these factors into consideration," she replied.

"And the results?" I asked.

"They were fascinating."

Miracles in Mozambique?

To go to a place that is reporting clusters of healing, Brown and her team flew to Mozambique, where reports of miracles abound. Located on the southeast coast of Africa, this desperately poor nation of twenty-five million people underwent a devastating civil war from 1977 to 1992. Slightly half of the country is Christian, 18 percent are Muslims, and the rest have animism beliefs or don't claim any religion at all.[19]

Mozambique fits the four characteristics that Christian author Tim Stafford said are often shared by places where there are outbreaks of the supernatural:

1. There's illiteracy. Miracles show God's power without language.
2. People don't have a framework in their culture for such theological concepts as sin and salvation. "Miracles demand attention even if you don't yet grasp the nature of your problem and God's redemption," Stafford wrote.
3. There's limited medical care, making miracles the only recourse for the afflicted.
4. The spirit world is very real to people, and "a conflict of spiritual powers is out in the open." Miracles are demonstrations of God's power.[20]

To connect with a ministry that reports a high success rate with healing, Brown's team worked with Heidi and Rolland Baker, charismatic missionaries serving in Mozambique for more than twenty years. They have described how healing miracles have accompanied the spread of the gospel there.

Brown focused on the healing of blindness and deafness (or severe vision or hearing problems), which aren't particularly susceptible to psychosomatic healings. Her team used standard tests and technical equipment to determine the person's level of hearing or vision immediately before prayer. After the prayers were concluded, the patient was promptly tested again.

"The length of the prayer varied, from one minute to five or ten minutes usually, but it always involved touching," she said. "For instance, there was a woman who couldn't see a hand in front of her face at a foot away. Heidi Baker put her arms around her; she smiled at her, hugged her, cried, prayed for one minute—and afterward the woman was able to read."

In all there were twenty-four subjects who received prayer. The results? "After prayer, we found highly significant improvements in hearing and statistically significant improvements in vision," Brown told me. "We saw improvement in almost every single subject we tested. Some of the results were quite dramatic."

"For example?"

"We had two subjects whose hearing thresholds were reduced by more than 50 decibels, which is quite a large reduction," she said.

For comparison, 100 decibels is the sound of a nearby motor-cycle or power lawn mower; 80 decibels is the sound of a garbage disposal or food blender; 50 decibels is the sound of a typical conversation at home; and zero decibels is silence.[21]

"Significant visual improvements were measured across the group that was tested for eyesight," Brown added. "In fact, the average improvement in visual acuity was more than tenfold."

The Deaf Hear, the Blind See

Brown mentioned the story of Martine, an elderly blind and deaf woman in the Namuno village. Before prayer, she had no response at 100 decibels in either ear, which meant she couldn't hear a jackhammer if it were being used next to her. After prayer, she responded at 75 decibels in her right ear and 40 decibels in her left ear, which meant she could make out conversations.

After a second prayer, Martine's eyesight improved from 20/400 to 20/80 on the vision chart. This would mean she was legally blind initially, but after prayer was able to see objects from twenty feet away in the same way a person with normal vision can see that object from eighty feet away.[22]

I tried to imagine what it would be like to be on the receiving end of intercession like this. "What was going on during the prayers?" I asked. "What did people feel?"

"It was diverse," Brown said, "but often the recipients reported feeling heat, cold, or even tingling or itching."

In her book, Brown gives an account of Gabriel, who received prayer for his right ear. He said later, "I started to feel heat. And it started to feel like a little ant started to crawl up and down the inner ear, deep down inside . . . [Soon] it was like a whole ant nest was here crawling. And then it became a tingling . . . And then it was very hot, very hot, very hot. And then it suddenly became very cold . . . So exactly the moment that I felt this cold hand on my shoulder, [the intercessor] said, 'Yes, Lord, thank you for your angels. They are here with us helping in this healing.'"[23]

To me, Brown's methodology seemed uncannily simple but intuitively valid. The only thing that changed between the pre-prayer and post-prayer tests was the fact that someone prayed to Jesus for the person to get better. And virtually everyone did improve to one degree or another, often astoundingly so.

"So was this a scientifically sound study?" I asked.

"It was published in a peer-reviewed *Southern Medical Journal*. It was prospectively done. It was rigorous. It was a "within-subjects design"—a standard approach to psychophysical studies published in the flagship *Science* magazine and elsewhere. We had the proper equipment. We had a trained research team. We had statistically significant results. And the validity of the study was evaluated as being scientifically sound by the journal that published it."

I raised my pen. "However," I pointed out, "the number of tested people was pretty small."

"There's a misconception that if you've got a small sample, it's not statistically significant. Actually, that's not true," she replied.

"With a smaller sample, the effects have to be larger and more consistent in order to achieve statistical significance. And our effects were."

Brown and her team then did a replication study in Brazil to check if they would get similar results—and they did. Again, sight and hearing were improved after hands-on prayer was offered in Jesus' name.

In Sao Paulo, for example, a forty-eight-year-old woman named Julia could not see details on faces or read without glasses. "After prayer, she could do both," Brown said. "A thirty-eight-year-old woman in Uberlandia could not count fingers from nine feet away. When she opened her eyes after prayer, she could read the name tag of the person who had been praying for her."

I interrupted. "Could the results be the result of suggestion or a kind of hypnosis?"

"Not likely. A 2004 review article summarized the results of suggestion and hypnosis studies by saying they failed to demonstrate significant improvements in vision or hearing."[24]

"So what's your conclusion?" I asked.

"Our study shows that *something* is going on with Pentecostal and charismatic proximal intercessory prayer," she replied. "This is more than just wishful thinking. It's not fakery; it's not fraud. It's not some televangelist trying to get widows to send in their money. It's not a highly charged atmosphere that plays on people's emotions. *Something* is going on, and it surely warrants further investigation."

In fact, her husband, Joshua, who earned his doctorate at Boston University, is spearheading the Global Medical Research Institute to apply rigorous empirical methods to investigate claims of miraculous healings.

In the meantime, Candy Gunther Brown's work and analysis

have already undermined Shermer's claim that when research is conducted scientifically, it shows "zero" evidence for the miraculous.

Quite the opposite appears to be true. It seems that, upon further study, the evidence *is* good for the Christian side.

CHAPTER 8

Dreams and Visions

An Interview with Missionary Tom Doyle

The brick wall was faded, uneven, and weathered; the imposing wooden door was more than seven feet tall but less than three feet wide, arched at its top and situated in a doorway that was a few feet deep.

The visitor stood outside in the darkness, peering into the warm glow of the Baroque interior—a cavernous room filled with tables overflowing with sumptuous food and chalices of wine. The people inside were ready to enjoy their feast, but they were all waiting as they looked to their left, as if anticipating someone was going to speak before the meal.

Peering in, the visitor saw his friend David sitting at a table not far from the doorway. Surprised, he called out to get David's attention. "I thought we were going to eat together," the visitor said.

David, his gaze never leaving the front of the room, was only able to reply, "You never responded."

As he described the scene to me, my friend Nabeel was staring off to the side, his brow furrowed and his eyes narrowed as if he was reliving the experience. He turned to face me. "That was the whole dream," he said.

My living room was quiet, except for the gentle hum of the air conditioner outside. "And this came after you had asked God for a clear vision?" I asked.

"That's right," he replied. "I called David the next day and asked him what he thought of my dream."

"David was your Christian friend?"

"My *only* Christian friend. I was a devout Muslim; I didn't like to sully myself by associating with too many Christians."

"And what did he tell you?"

"He said there was no need to interpret what I had experienced. All I needed to do was open the Bible to the thirteenth chapter of Luke."

> Then Jesus went through the towns and villages, teaching as he made his way to Jerusalem. Someone asked him, "Lord, are only a few people going to be saved?"
>
> He said to them, "Make every effort to enter through the narrow door, because many, I tell you, will try to enter and will not be able to. Once the owner of the house gets up and closes the door, you will stand outside knocking and pleading, 'Sir, open the door for us.'
>
> "But he will answer, 'I don't know you or where you come from . . .'
>
> "There will be weeping there, and gnashing of teeth, when you see Abraham, Isaac and Jacob and all the prophets in the kingdom of God, but you yourselves thrown out. People will come from east and west and north and south, and will take their places at the feast in the kingdom of God."[1]

"I was standing at the door and it had not yet closed, but it was clear I would not be at this banquet of God—*this heaven*—unless I responded to the invitation," Nabeel said. "The door would be shut for good; the feast would go on without me, forever."

"How did that make you feel?"

He paused before answering. "Chilled. Frightened. Alone. *Desperate.*"

"That passage in Luke—how many times had you read it before that night?"

Nabeel looked surprised by my question. "Not once," he said.

"Never?"

"I had never read *any* of the New Testament before—and yet I saw that passage played out in my dream."

"How do you account for that?"

"I'm a man of science. A medical doctor. I deal with flesh and bones, with evidence and facts and logic. But *this*," he said, searching for the right words, "this was the exact vision I needed. It was a miracle. A miracle that opened the door for me."

Awakening the Muslim World

This dream was pivotal in leading my friend Nabeel Qureshi to faith in Jesus and redirecting his career path from medicine to passionately defending the Christian faith on the global stage.[2] He is just one of countless Muslims who have experienced supernatural visions or dreams—many of them corroborated by outside events—that have brought them out of Islam and into Christianity.

In fact, more Muslims have become Christians in the last couple of decades than in the previous fourteen hundred years since Muhammad, and it's estimated that a quarter to a third of them experienced a dream or vision of Jesus before their salvation experience.[3] If those statistics are accurate, then this phenomenon of Jesus supernaturally appearing to people is one of the most significant spiritual awakenings in the world today.

Christian apologist Ravi Zacharias first brought this worldwide trend to my attention nearly twenty years ago, when I interviewed him for my book *The Case for Faith.*

"I have spoken in many Islamic countries, where it's tough to talk about Jesus," he told me at the time. "Virtually every Muslim who has come to follow Christ has done so, first, because of the love of Christ expressed through a Christian, or second, because of a vision, dream, or some other supernatural intervention. Now, no religion has a more intricate doctrine of angels and visions than Islam, and I think it's extraordinary that God uses that sensitivity to the supernatural world in which he speaks in visions and dreams and reveals himself."[4]

In the Bible, God frequently used dreams and visions to further his plans. From Abraham, Joseph, and Samuel in the Old Testament to Zechariah, John, and Cornelius in the New Testament, there are about two hundred biblical examples of God employing this kind of divine intervention.

Today, reports of these miraculous manifestations seem to cluster among adherents of Islam, from Indonesia to Pakistan to the Gaza Strip. While the experiences are admittedly unique to the individual, in many cases there is authentication, such as Jesus telling the person something in the dream that he or she could not otherwise have known, or two people having an identical dream on the same night.

In addition, the stunning consistency of these experiences across international boundaries suggests that they are more than merely the product of overactive imaginations. A devout Muslim would have no incentive to imagine such an encounter with the Jesus of Christianity, who might lure them into Islamic apostasy and possibly even a death sentence in certain countries.

Why are we seeing these phenomena now? Why would a spate of such manifestations occur today among members of a faith that adamantly denies the crucial theological pillars of Christianity? What does Jesus tell these individuals that so radically rocks their world? And if Jesus can appear in dreams and visions like this, why not manifest himself that way for everyone? Doesn't this phenomenon, in effect, put missionaries out of a job?

I had to admit: these divine interventions didn't fit neatly into my theological framework, which made me all the more anxious to get to the bottom of them.

Leslie and I packed the car and pulled onto the highway for a three-hour drive to Dallas, Texas, where I was scheduled to rendezvous with an author and missionary to the Middle East who is a leading expert on contemporary dreams and visions experienced by Muslims.

The Interview with Tom Doyle, MABS

After graduating from a Christian college (Biola University) and getting a graduate degree (Dallas Theological Seminary), Tom Doyle eagerly dove into his ministry as a pastor for the next twenty years. He served at churches in Dallas, Albuquerque, and Colorado Springs, especially enjoying his role of preaching on Sunday mornings. Then in 1995, Dallas Seminary called and said they were taking some pastors to Israel. Would he be interested in joining them?

"That changed everything for me," Doyle recalls. "I was immediately drawn to the Middle East—hook, line, and sinker."

Over the next twenty years, he became a missionary to the region, eventually leading sixty tours of the Holy Land. Today, he is the founding president of UnCharted, a ministry dedicated to challenging Christians to join the movement of God among Jews and Muslims, as well as to come alongside persecuted believers.

What drew me to Doyle was his authoritative book, *Dreams*

and Visions: Is Jesus Awakening the Muslim World? which he wrote with Greg Webster in 2012. In all, Doyle has authored seven books revolving around his expertise on the Middle East, including *Two Nations under God: Why You Should Care about Israel*; *Breakthrough: The Return of Hope to the Middle East*; *Killing Christians: Living the Faith Where It's Not Safe to Believe*; and *Standing in the Fire: Courageous Christians Living in Frightening Times*.

Doyle, now sixty-two and with his brown hair graying, married his college sweetheart, JoAnn, more than thirty-five years ago, and they have six children and several grandchildren. JoAnn ministers to women in Middle Eastern countries.

Friends who know Doyle call him "the real deal." Said Rob Bugh, senior pastor of Wheaton Bible Church in suburban Chicago, "I have traveled with him overseas and seen firsthand his remarkable love for lost people, displaced people, for Muslims and Jews."[5]

Another one of Doyle's friends, well-known Christian novelist and biographer Jerry Jenkins, said Doyle's personal ministry in the Middle East gives him special authority in discussing trends there. He said Doyle has "the credibility of a man who has the smell of the front lines of the battlefield on his clothes because he was there yesterday and will be back there tomorrow."[6]

Leslie and I had dinner with Tom and JoAnn at a café the night before our interview, chatting for several hours about what grandparents usually obsess over: grandkids. Tom and JoAnn are gregarious, passionate, and empathetic—perfect qualities for missionaries. Pardon the cliché, but in their case it fits so well: their smiles are contagious.

The next morning, JoAnn and Leslie went out for a while to let Tom and me have a private discussion in our hotel room.

"Did you always have an affinity for working with Muslims?"

I began as we sat down, facing each other in (uncomfortable) straight-back chairs.

"No, actually I had a lot of preconceived notions," he replied.

"Prejudices?"

"You could say that."

"What changed your attitude?"

"Shortly after 9/11, I was in Gaza City. A woman in a hijab came running up, grabbed my forearm, and said, 'You're from America, aren't you?' I said, 'Yes, I am.' She said, 'When the buildings came down on 9/11, did you see the video of people in Gaza cheering and celebrating?' I said, 'Yes, I saw that on TV.' She said: 'Not me. I was crying for those people. They didn't deserve to die. That was wrong. I'm very sorry.' She tapped her heart, and then she walked away."

"How did that make you feel?"

"That was the day that God started to create space in my heart for Muslims," he said. "It comes down to this: Are we able to see through Jesus' eyes and not our own? He filters out all the news and prejudice. Once you have his eyes, you see people for who they are—made in his image."

"You're the One! You're the One!"

When I asked Doyle when he became aware of the phenomenon of dreams and visions among Islamic people, he recalled the first time he visited Jerusalem and met with a group of Muslims who had converted to Christianity.

"One of them, Rami, said he had been a fervent Muslim when he started to have dreams about Jesus. He said they were different than anything he had ever experienced. Often dreams are fuzzy or confused, but these were bright and laser focused—and they kept coming."

"What did Jesus tell him?"

"He was a man in a white robe, and he told Rami that he loves him. They were beside a lake, and Rami said he saw himself walking over and embracing Jesus."

"How did you react?" I asked.

Doyle chuckled. "I didn't know if Rami was nuts or what," he replied. "But over and over, from a variety of different people, I started hearing the same basic story: Jesus in a white robe, saying he loves them, saying he died for them, telling them to follow him. It started to snowball—in Iran, Iraq, Syria, all over. There were even ads placed in Egyptian newspapers."

I looked up from my note taking. "What kind of ads?"

"They simply said: 'Have you seen the man in a white robe in your dreams? He has a message for you. Call this number.' In other words, so many Muslims were having these dreams that Christian ministries started placing these ads to reach them."

I asked Doyle if he would give me a typical example of how these dreams play out in someone's life. He chose the story of what happened to Kamal, an underground church planter in Egypt, and a married Muslim mother named Noor.[7]

He explained that Kamal was busy with his work one day, but nevertheless he felt God was leading him to go to the Khan el-Khalili Friday market in Cairo. Frankly, it was the last place he wanted to go—this was right before Muslim prayers, and the market was crowded, noisy, and chaotic. But he went because he felt 100 percent convinced that God had a special assignment for him.

A Muslim woman named Noor, covered head to toe in traditional garb, spotted him from a distance and started yelling, "You're the one! You're the one!" She pushed through the crowd and made a beeline for him. She said, "You were in my dream last night! Those clothes—you were wearing those clothes. For sure, it was you."

Kamal quickly sensed what was motivating her. "Was I with Jesus?" he asked.

"Yes," she replied. "Jesus was with us."

Later she explained, "Jesus walked with me alongside a lake, and he told me how much he loves me. His love was different from anything I've ever experienced. I've never felt so much peace. I didn't want him to leave. I asked this Jesus, 'Why are you visiting me, a poor Muslim mother with eight children?' And all he said was, 'I love you, Noor. I have given everything for you. I died for you.'"

She said that as Jesus turned to leave, he told her, "Ask my friend tomorrow about me. He will tell you all you need in order to understand why I've visited you." She replied to Jesus, "But who is your friend?" Jesus said, "Here is my friend," and he pointed to a person who was behind him in the dream. "He has been walking with us the whole time we've been together."

Now, there in the marketplace, Noor said to Kamal, "Even though you had walked with us around the lake, I hadn't seen anyone but Jesus. I thought I was alone with him. His face was magnificent. I couldn't take my eyes off him. Jesus did not tell me your name, but you were wearing the same clothes you have on right now, and your glasses—they're the same too. I knew I would not forget your smile."

The encounter led to a deep discussion about faith that lasted some three hours. "I have never been loved like I was when Jesus walked with me in that dream," Noor told him. "I felt no fear. For the first time in my life, I felt no shame. Even though he's a man, I wasn't intimidated. I didn't feel threatened. I felt . . . perfect peace."

Kamal explained to her that religion will never bring her that kind of peace. "That's what [Jesus] wants to give you," Kamal told her. "Before he went to the cross, Jesus said, 'Peace I leave with you;

my peace I give you.'[8] You will not—you cannot—find peace like that with anyone else. No one but Jesus even has it to offer."

I was mesmerized by Noor's story. "Did she come to faith in Christ?" I asked Doyle.

"Not on that day," he answered. "She's counting the cost, even as Jesus himself said we should. And the cost to her in Egypt could be very steep. She said she wants to find out all she can about Jesus. There are a lot of people praying for her."[9]

Stopped in His Tracks

Doyle's books are packed with stories like the one about Kamal and Noor, and similar accounts just keep coming. "I could pick up the phone right now and call Syria and ask if our people have any stories about dreams and they would give me three or four new ones," he said. "That's how prevalent they are."

"You don't see a letup, then?" I asked.

"Not at all. Recently I met a guy in Jerusalem who grew up in a refugee camp as a Palestinian," Doyle said. "He hated Israel. He told me his goal in life was to kill as many Jews as he could."

"That's chilling," I said. "So what happened?"

"He was on his way to meet with people who work with Hamas," he said, referring to the terrorist organization. "He didn't know anything about Jesus, but all of a sudden, a man in a white robe was standing in front of him in the street and pointing at him. The man said, 'Omar, this is not the life I have planned for you. You turn around. Go home. I have another plan for you.'"

"What did he do?"

"He turned around and went home. Later that same day, someone was moving into an apartment across the hall from him. He found out the new tenant was a Christian. Omar told him about the experience he had and said, 'What does it mean?' This Christian spent time with him, took him through the Scriptures, and led him to Jesus. Today, Omar is an underground church planter."

The story resonated deeply with me. "So there he was," I said, "on his way to join Hamas and perhaps embark on a life of extremism and terrorism—and yet Jesus literally stopped him in his tracks."

"Absolutely," said Doyle. "We met another guy in Jericho named Osama who was part of the Palestinian Authority. He started having dreams about Jesus. He went to his imam, who told him to read the Qur'an more. But the more he read the Qur'an, the more he had Jesus dreams. The imam told him to get more involved in the mosque, so he did—still, more Jesus dreams. The imam said to make the Hajj to Mecca."

In my mind I could picture this person among the throngs at Mecca, walking around the Kaaba, often called "the house of Allah," a black building in the center of the most sacred mosque in Islam. One of the five pillars of Islam says if a Muslim is able, he should make the Hajj pilgrimage to Mecca once in his lifetime and walk seven times around the Kaaba. More than a million people walk counterclockwise around the Kaaba during this five-day period.

"What happened to him?" I asked.

"You're supposed to look at the Kaaba and say your prayers. Instead, he looked over—and on top of the Kaaba, he saw the Jesus from his dreams."

"That must have startled him!"

"It did!" Doyle replied. "Jesus was looking at him and saying, 'Osama, leave this place. You're going in the wrong direction. Leave and go home.' So he did. Later a Christian friend shared the gospel with him, and he came to faith in Christ. Today, this man has such love for Jesus that you can literally see it on his face."

"That's How Jesus Operates"

One fact seemed clear: most of the people having these dreams were not naturally inclined to imagine a vision of the Jesus of Christianity.

"No way," Doyle said. "Many live in closed countries where they have no prior exposure to images or ideas about the Jesus of the Bible. When Jesus tells them he died for them, that's alien to everything they've learned."

"What does the Qur'an tell them about Jesus?"

"That he's a prophet, but most significantly, the Qur'an says Jesus didn't die on the cross, that Allah does not have a son, and that nobody can bear the sins of another. The very things that Christianity says are essential to faith are explicitly denied in Islamic teachings."

"And so this makes Muslims resistant when you try to initiate a conversation about faith," I said.

"Yes, exactly. A Muslim typically responds by saying the Bible has been corrupted, or Christians worship three gods, or look what happened during the Crusades," Doyle replied. "These are some of the big boulders on the path between them and the real Jesus. But in these high-definition Jesus dreams, they're gently walked around those boulders. They see Jesus for who he is, and now they're motivated to learn more.

"It's interesting," he continued, "that after having a dream or vision, the typical objections that Muslims raise against Christianity disappear. I've never met someone who had a Jesus dream who is still hung up on the deity of Christ or the veracity of the Scriptures. Instantly, they know this: Jesus is more than just a prophet. And they want to know more about him."

I noticed that in Doyle's description of these dreams, he didn't say the Muslim immediately puts his or her trust in Jesus. I said to him, "It seems that people don't go to sleep Muslims, have a Jesus dream, and then wake up as Christians."

"That's right; I've never heard of that happening," Doyle replied. "Usually, the dream points them toward someone who can teach them from the Bible and present the gospel, like Noor in the Cairo marketplace. Or like Omar, who was deterred from meeting with Hamas, went home, and 'coincidentally' found a Christian moving in across the hall," he said, putting the word "coincidentally" in air quotes. "The dreams motivate them to seek the real Jesus and to find the truth in Scripture."

The Jesus they encounter in their dreams, said Doyle, is a perfect antidote to a culture that is based on shame and honor.

"Muslims have felt dishonor and shame ever since Muhammad, but these dreams strike a deep emotional chord because suddenly they feel the opposite," he explained. "They're honored that Jesus would appear to them. They feel love, grace, safety, protection, affirmation, joy, peace—all these emotions they don't receive from Islam. It rocks their world."

"Does Jesus behave in these dreams the same as the Jesus of the gospels?"

"There's a consistency. For example, the Jesus of the New Testament reached out to the marginalized—the Samaritan woman at the well who went through multiple husbands, the blind and crippled, those with leprosy, the hated tax collector Zacchaeus. Today, who's more marginalized than Muslims? Jesus is showing his love for them. That's how Jesus operates."

"Just how similar," I asked Doyle, "are these contemporary dreams to the dreams and visions described in Scripture?"

"I don't want to say they're like what Saul experienced on the road to Damascus," came his response. "But these are earth-shattering experiences to those who have them. They're not like typical dreams—they're exceptionally vibrant. They can't shake them. They sense this love that has been missing from their life—and their response is very understandable: they inevitably want more."

"Take It Up with God"

I gestured toward Doyle. "You were educated at Biola University and Dallas Seminary, both quite conservative evangelical institutions," I said. "Did this dream phenomenon challenge your theology in any way?"

"Well, I was skeptical at first," he said, eliciting a nod from me, since I felt the same way. "I thought, *Lord, why is this happening?* But as I processed it, it began to make sense."

"In what way?"

"The Western world doesn't need dreams and visions—we have easy access to God's Word. But it's estimated that 50 percent of Muslims around the world can't read, so how are we going to get the Scriptures to them? And 86 percent of Muslims don't know a Christian, so who's going to share the gospel with them? In light of these realities, how might God reach them? I believe God is fair—the Bible says, 'Will not the Judge of all the earth do right?'[10] I think he's going to find a way to bring Jesus to them."

"Even in such a dramatic way as this?"

"Sure. I think of Leila, who lived in Baghdad. Her husband was beating her all the time; she thought she would die. One night she said, 'God, I've been crying out to you for months and you do nothing. I keep saying, "God, where are you?" Now I'm going to change one word: "God, *who* are you?" Maybe I've been praying to the wrong God.' That night she had a dream about the Jesus who loves her."

He shrugged his shoulders. "So what should I do with that theologically?" he asked. "It's hard to deny the evidence that something supernatural is happening. Granted, it's the Word of God that leads people to faith, but these dreams plow the hard soil of Muslim hearts so they're receptive to the seed of the gospel."

Doyle let that thought linger for a few moments. Then he continued.

"Put yourself in God's position," he said, pointing toward me. "You want your message to get around the world. Huge numbers of Muslims—whom you love deeply—don't have access to Christians or the Bible. Now, what's your plan B? How would you get their attention—especially in a culture that values dreams? I think we need to look at God's love rather than just automatically thinking we have the correct theology. It's just like our loving God to do something radical to reach them. Extreme times require extreme measures."

Still, I pressed him on this issue. "What would you tell Christians who say, yes, there were a few dreams in the Bible, but that was a different age, a different time, different circumstances—and those things just don't happen today?"

"More than two hundred times there are dreams or visions in the Bible," he replied. "We know there were dreams in the early church, and some spiritual leaders saw that as a vehicle of divine revelation. Obviously, the Word of God is our sole authority— and, interestingly, where do these dreams point people? Toward the Bible."

I said, "A theologian might point out that the canon of Scripture is closed, and this would be extrabiblical revelation that needs to be treated very suspiciously."

"Everything needs to be checked against Scripture. I haven't backed off that one bit. But how many Christians in America might say they've had an impression in a restaurant to go witness to someone sitting nearby? The Spirit leads people that way all the time. So why can't the Spirit lead them through a dream that points them to missionaries and the Bible? Frankly, our theology doesn't determine God's actions."

"And for those who remain skeptical—what would you say to them?"

"What else can I say?" Doyle replied with a sigh. "If they object on some theological grounds, I'd tell them to take it up with God."

As if an afterthought, he added, "Personally, I don't think God has put the supernatural on the shelf."

"Are You Willing to Die for Jesus?"

One way to assess the legitimacy of these dreams is to measure the kind of fruit they bear. In other words, do they lead to a superficial and short-lived faith, or do they result in thorough conversions and a deep commitment to Christ?

"No question—these dreams generally lead to radical life-change," Doyle told me. "A Muslim who comes to faith in the Middle East is exposing himself to possible rejection, beatings, imprisonment, or even death. This isn't for the faint of heart. This isn't casual Christianity."

"It's ironic," I said, "that in America, we see a proliferation of shallow commitments to Christ because of a cultural Christianity that hasn't really revolutionized the person's soul, and yet we're skeptical of how authentic these conversions are in the Middle East, where people face persecution if they pursue their faith."

Doyle agreed. "Before praying with someone to receive Christ, many leaders in the Middle East will ask two questions. First, are you willing to suffer for Jesus? And, second, are you willing to die for Jesus?" he said. "I wish we had those two questions in the New Members classes at churches in America."

"It might thin the ranks a bit," I commented.

"Probably. But even though these Muslims know that following Jesus could very well lead to rejection by their family or even death, they're coming to faith in unprecedented numbers."

"Do you see a way to explain away these dreams and visions naturalistically?"

"It's hard to see how these could be anything but supernatural, given the circumstances," he replied. "How do you explain Kamal feeling an urge from God to go to the Cairo market when he didn't want to, where he meets Noor, a woman who had a dream about him and Jesus the night before?"

"Coincidence?" I ventured.

Doyle couldn't stifle a laugh. "That would take a lot more faith to believe," he quipped.

"But why Noor?" I asked. "Why isn't Jesus appearing in everybody's dreams? He could save missionary agencies a lot of time, money, and effort if he would just appear in the dreams of every non-Christian in the world."

That question prompted a pause from Doyle. "Look, I can't speak for God. All I can do is speculate," he said. "In many parts of the world, the problem isn't a lack of access to the gospel. It's available. So in these locales, the real issue for people is, 'How are you going to respond?'

"We also know that throughout church history, God has focused on different people groups in various eras. There have been great awakenings in Asia, South America, Europe, the United States, and Africa. For whatever reason, today God is reaching out to multiple people groups that have one thing in common: a huge proportion of the people are Muslim. I don't know what he'll do next."

As I chatted with Doyle, I had to confess that I felt a tinge of jealousy toward people who have had Jesus dreams. I've followed Christ for several decades now. I've delved deeply into the Scriptures.

I've felt God's presence, guidance, and power in my life. But to have a vivid and vibrant dream of talking with a white-robed Jesus and hearing his voice offer love, grace, and acceptance—well, I have to admit that would be awesome.

"Do you envy them?" I said to Doyle as we were wrapping up our conversation. "Do you wish Jesus would appear to you in a dream?"

"Wow," he said, just thinking about the prospect. "Who wouldn't want an encounter like that? Yeah, it would be incredible. But I've got the Scriptures to tell me about Jesus; I have his Spirit to affirm and guide me; and I know I'll see him face-to-face someday."

His face looked content. "Yes," he said finally, "that's enough for me."

A Kitchen, a Sandwich, an Angel, a Prophecy

Of the thousands of dreams I had as a youngster, I only carried one of them into adulthood. That's because it was the most dramatic— and puzzling—dream of my early years. I'm still amazed by its clarity and vibrancy, as well as the emotional impact it had on me at the time. While it wasn't an encounter with Jesus, it was a dream in which I spoke with an angel—and received a prophecy that came true some sixteen years later.

When I was about twelve years old, prior to my move into atheism, I dreamed I was making a sandwich for myself in the kitchen when a luminous angel suddenly appeared and started telling me—almost in an offhanded manner—about how wonderful and glorious heaven is. I listened for a while and then said matter-of-factly, "I'm going there"—meaning, of course, at the end of my life.

The angel's reply stunned me. "How do you know?"

How did I know? What kind of question is that? "Well, uh, I've tried to be a good kid," I stammered. "I've tried to do what my parents say. I've tried to behave. I've been to church."

Said the angel, "That doesn't matter."

Now I was staggered. How could it not matter—all my efforts to be compliant, to be dutiful, to live up to the expectations and demands of my parents and teachers. Panic rose in me. I couldn't open my mouth to respond.

The angel let me stew for a few moments. Then he said, "Someday you'll understand." Instantly, he was gone—and I woke up in a sweat. This is the only dream I can recall from my childhood.

Over the years, I came to reject the possibility of the supernatural and even God himself, living as an atheist for a long period of time. But sixteen years after that dream, the angel's prophecy came true.

In a church meeting in a suburban Chicago movie theatre, I heard the message of grace for the first time that I really understood it. I couldn't earn my way to heaven through my behavior—it was all a free gift of God's grace that I needed to receive in repentance and faith.

The moment this clicked for me, a vivid memory came into my mind—it was the angel who had foretold that someday I would understand the gospel. Ultimately, it was this good news that went on to change my life and eternity.

Was my dream a supernatural intervention? Would it qualify as a miracle? I'll leave it to you to make your own judgment. But in a small way, I can relate to some of these stories of dreams and visions coming from the Middle East.

A Dream, a Vision, a Bible, a Baptism

Our world is more knit together than ever before; in fact, the global oil industry has connected the city of Houston, Texas, where I live, to many locales in the Middle East. So perhaps it's not surprising that while I was working on this chapter, I encountered a Jesus dream in the church where I serve as a teaching pastor.

The story involves Rachel, a petite and soft-spoken mother with an olive complexion and a kind and gentle demeanor. She lives with her husband and child in an upscale suburb, where I'm sure her neighbors could scarcely imagine her upbringing as a devout Muslim in a Middle Eastern country where Christianity is forbidden.

When she was twenty-two years old, she was hounded by some personal difficulties. One night before bed she called out to God, "Please send me one of your prophets who will release me from this miserable feeling. I badly need comfort and guidance."

That night she had a dream of being in some sort of movie theatre, where the projector cast an intensely bright light. Suddenly, there was a man—Jesus. "At first, it seemed like a portrait, but the portrait was not still," she said. "He was looking at me with very kind, concerned eyes. It was as if he could feel my pain and my sadness."

She said Jesus spoke to her, but the words weren't as important as the emotion they evoked: a deep and profound sense of relief, comfort, affirmation, and joy. Then his face disappeared. "My eyes opened, but I was sure I was never asleep," she said. "I was in that room with him."

By age thirty, she was married and had moved with her husband to Texas. One day while talking with a neighbor, she blurted out, "I would like to study the Bible." To this day, she's not sure where that comment came from, but eventually, she ended up studying the gospel of John, verse by verse, with a friend who is part of our congregation.

Of course, John's gospel begins with the sweeping affirmation of Jesus not as a mere prophet of Islam but as God himself: "In the beginning was the Word, and the Word was with God, and the Word was God."[11] And John features a revolutionary statement by Jesus that would shake the foundation of Rachel's Islamic training: "I am the way and the truth and the life. No one comes to the Father except through me."[12]

As she began studying the gospel—and before she knew anything about baptism—she had a vision. "I saw a man with a book," she said. "I was standing with him in water. I saw my friend holding my arm, and we were both looking at the man with the book open in his hands. The man was looking into the horizon with tears running down his face, and I knew that this man loves Jesus very much."

The duration of the vision, she said, "was fast and not fast. I could see details, but it only lasted a few minutes." She had never seen the man's face before.

When Easter came, her friend brought her to our church. As they sat in the auditorium waiting for the service to begin, Rachel suddenly saw a man walking down the aisle.

"Over there—that's the man!" she exclaimed. It was the man from her vision—a pastor named Alan, who presides over baptisms at our church. She had never met him before, but there he was, right in front of her.

By the time she closed the last page of John's gospel in her Bible study, Rachel put her trust in Jesus as her forgiver and leader—a joyous occasion in her life, but not one she dared to share with her husband.

So one day when he was out of town, a private baptism was arranged. "We all went into the baptismal pool," she said. There they were: the man who loves Jesus, reading from an open Bible, and her friend at her side—just as foretold.

"The vision was coming true in front of my very eyes," she said. "When the pastor spoke, tears streamed down my face. I asked him to keep me longer under the water so I could feel every moment of it."

A dream. A vision. Tom Doyle's words sprang to mind: "Personally, I don't think God has put the supernatural on the shelf."

PART 4

The Most Spectacular Miracles

CHAPTER 9

The Astonishing
Miracle of Creation

An Interview with Dr. Michael G. Strauss

G eraint Lewis creates universes for a living.

That is, he uses supercomputers to tinker with leptons, quarks, and the four fundamental forces of nature to build exotic simulations of what alternate worlds might look like. He has discovered that it's daunting to pose as a creator, even for someone with a doctorate in astrophysics from the world-renowned Institute of Astronomy at the University of Cambridge.

"Playing with the laws of physics, it turns out, can be catastrophic for life," he wrote. "Often, the catastrophe is boredom. The periodic table disappears, and all the astonishing beauty and utility of chemistry desert us. The galaxies, stars and planets that host and energize life are replaced by lethal black holes or just a thin hydrogen soup, lonely protons drifting through empty space, and a bath of tepid radiation. These are very dull places indeed, and not the kind of place that you'd expect to encounter complex, thinking beings like us."[1]

On the other hand, creating an actual universe from nothing, while fine-tuning it to provide a flourishing habitat for human beings, is a primary job description of God—at least, if the very first verse in the Bible is true: "In the beginning God created the heavens and the earth."[2]

Without a doubt, *creatio ex nihilo* would be the most extraordinary miracle ever performed, persuasively establishing the existence of God and automatically making every other supernatural intervention that much more plausible.[3]

How so? Here's an example. When noted Christian apologist William Lane Craig was a teenager, he doubted the virgin birth. Why? Because it would have necessitated a Y chromosome to be created out of nothing in Mary's ovum, since she didn't possess the genetic material to produce a male child.

"But then," he said, "it occurred to me that if I really do believe in a God who created the universe, then for him to create a Y chromosome would be child's play!"[4]

In short, if God created the laws of nature when he spoke the universe into existence, then it would be easy for him to occasionally intervene in order to perform miracles of all sorts, from the truly astounding (like raising someone from the dead) to the more subtle (like supernaturally encouraging someone in the midst of a struggle).

In my interview with him, skeptic Michael Shermer said he prefers other explanations for the origin and fine-tuning of the universe—and certainly cosmologists and physicists have postulated their fair share of alternate models and theories.

Maybe the universe didn't have a cause. Perhaps there was never an absolute beginning for everything. Possibly there are a multitude of universes, each with randomly selected laws and constants of physics, and so it's not surprising that one of them—ours— happened to hit the habitability jackpot.

Can we ever know for sure whether the universe and its precisely calibrated conditions for life are a cosmic accident or a miracle of staggering proportions? And what about Shermer's objection that if God created the universe, then who created God?

A famous cartoon depicts two scientists chatting at a blackboard. In chalk on the left is a complicated mathematical equation, followed by the words "Then a Miracle Occurs," which leads to another exotic equation on the right. Gesturing toward the miracle reference, one scientist says to the other, "I think you should be more explicit here in step two."

Can Christians be explicit about how the cosmological evidence points toward a supernatural, miracle-working Creator? Or should we shrug our shoulders, as Shermer suggests, and concede, "We don't know" where everything came from?

I was anxious to get knowledgeable responses to Shermer and to build on the scientific evidence that I had compiled for my earlier book *The Case for a Creator*, so I zipped an email to a popular and impressively credentialed professor of physics. The result was a sit-down interview in his house not far from the University of Oklahoma campus in Norman.

The Interview with Michael G. Strauss, PhD

Like Shermer, Michael George Strauss is an ardent bicyclist, riding four miles to his office at the university and then pumping for twenty more miles on a circuitous way home. Asked if he rides for exercise or fun, he replied, "Yes."

Maybe that's one reason he looks so much younger than his nearly sixty years. His brown hair, worn slightly over his ears, is resisting gray, and his unlined face and clear blue eyes give him a fresh, boyish appearance.

Strauss first became interested in science as a youngster, when he lived in Huntsville, Alabama, where NASA built the first stage of the mighty Saturn V rocket that later took astronauts to the moon. There's still enthusiasm in his voice when he says, "They'd light those boosters to test them, and—*wow!*—the whole town would shake!"

Strauss graduated valedictorian from high school and later studied science and theology at Biola University. While pursuing a graduate degree in physics at UCLA, Strauss became fascinated by quantum mechanics and subatomic particles, joining a high-energy physics experimental group doing research at the Stanford Linear Accelerator Center.

Later he received his doctorate in High Energy Physics at UCLA, penning his dissertation on the scintillating topic, "A Study of Lambda Polarization and Phi Spin Alignment in Electron-Positron Annihilation at 29 GeV as a Probe of Color Field Behavior." (I'll give you a moment to process your regret over the fact that he beat you to the topic.)

Strauss joined the faculty of the University of Oklahoma in 1995 and is currently the David Ross Boyd Professor of Physics, having earned several awards for teaching excellence. For fifteen years, he conducted research at the Fermi National Accelerator Center. These days, he performs research at CERN's Large Hadron Collider in Switzerland, smashing protons together to understand, among other things, the properties of the top quark, the fundamental particle with the highest mass.

He collaborated on one of two experiments that used data from the collider to help discover the Higgs boson, the so-called "God particle," in 2012, which was the last unverified part of the Standard Model of particle physics. (The reference to a deity does not reflect any divine characteristics of the particle itself but was coined primarily because it was so difficult to find. Ironically, the particle's namesake, Peter Higgs, is an atheist.[5]) Now Strauss is among those on the hunt for evidence of higher mass Higgs bosons.

Interestingly, Strauss's study of the world's tiniest particles has become more and more relevant to understanding the origin and order of our vast universe itself. This is because when the collider hurls protons together, the resulting energy density is so high that it simulates what the universe was like a trillionth of a second after the big bang, helping lead to new insights into the study of cosmology.

That's what I came to discuss with him: Does the origin and fine-tuning of the universe point to God as the creator of quarks, leptons, Higgs bosons, and other building blocks of nature? We sat down to chat in the front room of his house.

Seeing God in Everyday Nature

"When I go to the lab, I don't expect to see the supernatural," he told me at the outset. "If miracles happened all the time, we wouldn't be able to study the usual way nature works. But just because something works a certain way most of the time with natural laws doesn't mean there can't be exceptions.

"In fact," he continued, "I was just reading an illustration of this.[6] Suppose aliens observed our traffic lights to understand how they work, and they figured out what red, yellow, and green mean. Suddenly, a vehicle with flashing lights and a siren comes screaming through the intersection, breaking all the rules. Does this mean the standard rules are no longer valid because there's an occasional exception? Of course not."

I was about to ask a follow-up question when Strauss jumped in with an interesting theological observation.

"By the way, the Bible says it's through the natural processes of nature that we most commonly see evidence for God, not just through his miracles," he pointed out. "Romans 1:20 tells us that God's invisible qualities are clearly seen—through what? Through what he has made.[7] And Psalm 19:1 says, 'The heavens declare the glory of God; the skies proclaim the work of his hands.' So, frankly, we don't necessarily need miracles to find evidence for God; it's right there, embedded in the natural processes he has created and that we, as scientists, are studying."

It was a good reminder that when protons collide and explode into even tinier particles, scientists are getting a glimpse into the incredible complexity and wonder of God's creativity, just as we detect his supernatural qualities when we watch an awesome thunderstorm sweep through the countryside or gaze at a multitude of stars winking in the night sky.

"Nevertheless," I added, "ambulances might scream through our lives every once in a while. What about you? Have you had an experience that you can only explain as a supernatural intervention of God?"

"Well, *only* is a strong word for a scientist," he began. "So probably not. But there are a lot of things I believe even though I've never personally experienced them. For example, I believe DNA has a helical structure, but I've never seen that myself. When I hear credible people talk about something that can only be explained supernaturally, I don't need to experience it myself to believe something supernatural has occurred."

Implications of an Expanding Universe

Going back to the ancient Greeks, most philosophers and scientists believed the universe is eternal, and that suited a lot of them quite well.

"Many scientists are philosophical naturalists, believing that there's nothing beyond the physical world," Strauss said. "If the universe has always existed, then that's quite consistent with their philosophy. Most of them know that if the universe did, indeed, have a beginning and is continuing to expand, that would have big theological implications."

When Albert Einstein came up with his general theory of relativity in 1915 and applied it to the universe as a whole, he was aghast that it showed the universe should be either growing or collapsing. His solution: add a fudge factor to his equation to "hold back gravity" and thus stabilize the universe—a move he later conceded was the "biggest blunder" of his career.[8]

To this day, the theistic consequences of having a beginning to the universe are readily apparent even to atheists. In his bestseller *A Brief History of Time*, theoretical physicist Stephen Hawking wrote, "So long as the universe had a beginning, we could suppose it had a creator."[9]

I asked Strauss, "What compelled virtually all scientists to conclude that the universe had a beginning—even though some of them had to be dragged kicking and screaming to that conclusion?"

"Back in the 1920s, the Russian mathematician Alexander Friedman and the Belgium astronomer George Lemaître used Einstein's theories to formulate a model showing that the universe was expanding," he said. "So if you play the tape of the universe backward, it shrinks down to . . ."

"The big bang," I offered.

"Yes, that was the term that British astronomer Fred Hoyle came up with. He was an outspoken atheist who was being derogatory and poking fun at the idea, but the term stuck."

In fact, Hoyle was so anxious to get rid of the universe's beginning that he later developed the steady state theory, which conceded that, yes, the universe is expanding, but it is generating its own new matter as it goes and therefore never had a beginning that would require a creator.

His theory did succeed in doing away with a starting point, but it has been universally rejected by cosmologists today because of mounting evidence that the universe did have a beginning more than thirteen billion years ago.

Confirming the Big Bang

I asked Strauss, "What were the scientific discoveries that confirmed the big bang theory?"

"There were three of them," he replied. "First, in 1929, the American astronomer Edwin Hubble discovered the so-called 'red shift' in light coming from distant galaxies, which is the result of galaxies literally flying apart from each other at enormous speeds. So this showed that our universe is rapidly expanding.

"Second, in 1964, Arno Penzias and Robert Wilson measured the cosmic background microwave radiation, which showed that the leftover heat from the big bang was minus 450 degrees Fahrenheit. This is exactly what we would expect if the big bang occurred.

"The third discovery involves the origin of light elements. Heavier elements formed later in stars and were expelled into space by supernovae, but very light elements like hydrogen and helium had to be forged in a much hotter environment like the big bang. When we measure the amount of these two elements in the universe, we find they are precisely what the theory predicted to within one part in ten thousand."

"The case, then, is airtight to you?" I asked.

"Given the evidence, in my opinion not believing in the big bang is like believing the Earth is flat. To me, the data is that strong. The big bang is the origin of everything we know—space, time, matter, and energy."

"Any caveats?"

"Maybe one. We can't measure what happened in the initial split second after the big bang. This is when most scientists believe inflation began, momentarily expanding the universe faster than the speed of light."

I held up my hand. "Whoa, wait a second," I said. "I didn't think anything could go faster than the speed of light."

"Nothing *inside* the universe can, but space itself can actually expand faster than light. So we've lost all information about what happened before inflation started at about a trillionth of a trillionth of a trillionth of a second after the big bang. We need a quantum theory of gravity to describe what occurred, and we don't have that yet."

"Nevertheless," I said, "you believe everything goes back to a beginning?"

"Yes, I think that's clear. Some people like to propose exotic theories for what happened in those microseconds. But cosmologist Lawrence Krauss, who's an outspoken atheist, conceded in a recent debate that the universe probably did begin to exist, even given quantum theories of gravity."[10]

"As more and more discoveries are made, is the evidence for the big bang getting stronger or weaker?"

"Stronger, for sure," he said. "For instance, we've been studying the cosmic background radiation with increasing precision through the Planck satellite, and it's still pointing toward the big bang. Not only does all the evidence confirm that the universe is expanding, but it's actually accelerating.

"In addition, three prominent cosmologists in 2003 formulated what is called the Borde-Guth-Vilenkin theorem,[11] which says that any universe that is expanding, on average, throughout its history, cannot be infinite in the past but must have a beginning. If that theorem is correct, it applies to our universe—regardless of what happened in the microseconds after the big bang."

The Problem of a Cosmic Beginning

William Lane Craig is one of many philosophers who offers various arguments for the existence of God. But if you count the number of articles published in philosophy journals in recent years, you'll find more discussion about Craig's *kalam* cosmological argument than any other contemporary defense of theism. *The Cambridge Companion to Atheism* says, "Theists and atheists alike 'cannot leave Craig's Kalam argument alone.'"[12]

The argument derives its name from the Arabic for "medieval theology,"[13] which is appropriate since it was first formulated by eleventh-century Muslim philosopher Abû Hâmid Muhammad ibn Muhammad al-Ghazâlî. His reasoning is summarized in three steps:

1. Whatever begins to exist has a cause.
2. The universe began to exist.
3. Therefore, the universe has a cause.[14]

I asked Strauss, "What's your assessment of the *kalam* argument?"

"It's extremely strong," he said. "Think about it: Is there anything that comes into existence without a cause behind it? Some scientists say there may be uncaused quantum events, but I think there are good reasons to be skeptical about that.[15] And we know from the evidence that the universe did come into existence. If those two premises of the argument are true, then the conclusion inexorably follows: the universe has a cause."

I said, "Some skeptics, including the late astronomer Carl Sagan, suggest there might be merit to the idea of an oscillating universe, where the universe expands, then crunches back down, and then expands again—on for infinity, without a beginning. Is there evidence to back this up?"

"Not really. Entropy, which is roughly the amount of disorder, would continue to increase from one cycle to the next, meaning each succeeding oscillation would get bigger and bigger. Run the tape backward, and you get smaller and smaller oscillations, until you get to a beginning," Strauss responded. "Besides, this would require that 'dark energy,' which scientists suspect is accelerating the expansion of the universe, would suddenly reverse itself and cause the universe to collapse. That's stretching things beyond credulity."

I said, "Others propose that the universe simply popped out of nothing, from the quantum foam fluctuations of empty space. Make sense?"

"Quantum foam is the space-time fabric of the universe. It's *not* nothing. So if the universe popped out of it, where did the quantum foam come from? You'd have to account for that. Now, quantum fluctuations do allow brief periods of time when virtual particles pop into existence—caused by quantum energy—and then go back out of existence."

"What's the time scale?"

"Trillionths of a second," he said. "So to postulate that something which happens in a trillionth of a second could create an entire universe that lasts billions of years is an extrapolation that seems extremely unreasonable to me. I'll be honest: if this wasn't a way to try to get around God, nobody would have ever thought of it, in my opinion."

"In my interview, the skeptic Michael Shermer said the best answer to how the universe originated is simply, 'We don't know.' He suggested there might be other possible explanations than 'God did it.'"

"Look, we don't live our lives based on obscure possibilities; we live our lives based on probabilities. Is it possible my wife poisoned my cereal this morning? Anything is possible, but not everything is probable," he replied. "The real question is: Given what we observe with the universe, what's the highest probability? Everything tells us there was a real beginning. Everything else is a mere possibility, with no observational or experimental evidence to back it up."

Craig came to a similar conclusion. "In a sense, the history of twentieth-century cosmology can be seen as a series of one failed attempt after another to avoid the absolute beginning predicted by the standard big bang model," he wrote. "This parade of failed theories only serves to *confirm* the prediction of the standard model that the universe began to exist."[16]

Perhaps Alexander Vilenkin, director of the Institute of Cosmology at Tufts University, put it best: "With the proof now in place, cosmologists can no longer hide behind the possibility of a past-eternal universe. There is no escape: they have to face the problem of a cosmic beginning."[17]

Creation of the universe from nothing is an epic miracle, but there's more. Just as the big bang wasn't a haphazard event but a highly ordered phenomenon, the ongoing operation of the universe is an incredibly intricate dance that points toward the existence of a divine Choreographer.

Michael Strauss had much more to say about that, and I was leaning forward in anticipation.

CHAPTER 10

Our Miraculous Universe and Planet

Continuing the Interview with Dr. Michael G. Strauss

The late Christopher Hitchens, author of *God Is Not Great* and one of the most ardent atheists of recent times, was often asked which argument for God's existence is the strongest.

It's a question commonly posed to many skeptics—and Hitchens had a ready response. "I think every one of us picks the fine-tuning one as the most intriguing," he replied.[1]

For University of Oklahoma physics professor Michael G. Strauss, the incredible precision of the universe and our planet is not just intriguing, but it's compelling evidence for a miracle-working Designer.

"Over the last five decades, physicists have discovered that the numbers which govern the operation of the universe are calibrated with mind-boggling precision so intelligent life can exist," he said as we continued our conversation in his home.

"And when I say mind-boggling, I'm not exaggerating," he added with a smile. "Picture a control board with a hundred different dials and knobs, each representing a different parameter of physics. If you turn any of them just slightly to the left or right— *poof!* Intelligent life becomes impossible anywhere in the universe.

"Even just mistakenly bumping into one of those dials could make the world sterile and barren—or even nonexistent," he said. "And that's not only the opinion of Christian scientists. Virtually every scientist agrees the universe is finely tuned—the question is, how did it get this way?[2] I think the most plausible explanation is that the universe was designed by a Creator."

"Can you give me a few examples of the fine-tuning?" I asked.

"Sure," answered Strauss. "One parameter is the amount of matter in the universe. As the universe expands, all matter is attracted to other matter by gravity. If there were too much matter, the universe would collapse on itself before stars and planets could form. If there were too little matter, stars and planets could never coalesce."

"How finely tuned is the amount of matter?"

"It turns out that shortly after the big bang, the amount of matter in the universe was precisely tuned to one part in a trillion trillion trillion trillion trillion," he replied. "That's a ten with sixty zeroes after it! In other words, throw in a dime's worth of extra matter, and the universe wouldn't exist."

A calculation puts the number in perspective: the visible universe is 27.6 billion light-years in diameter. (Each light-year is about six trillion miles.) A single millimeter compared to the diameter of the universe would still be incomprehensibly larger than this one finely tuned parameter![3]

Strauss continued, "British physicist Paul Davies—who's an agnostic—said 'such stunning accuracy is surely one of the great mysteries of cosmology.'"[4]

"How does he try to explain it away?"

"He said cosmic inflation might force the universe to have exactly the right amount of matter."

"Does that make sense?"

"Even if you assume cosmic inflation is a mechanism that works, it doesn't make the fine-tuning problem go away."

"Why not?"

"Here's an illustration. If I tried to pour gasoline into my lawn mower through a really small hole, it would be very difficult. Why? Because the hole is finely tuned. But if I take the same fuel and pour it into a funnel, then I can easily fill the gas tank. Now, does the fact that I have a funnel—a mechanism that works—mean that I've eliminated the fine-tuning problem? No, of course not. If I have a mechanism that works, it also points to a designer."

"So," I summarized, "even if cosmic inflation is true, it merely moves the design issue back one stage."

"Right," Strauss said.

Putting a Zero on Every Particle

Then Strauss offered another fine-tuning example from something he studies in his research—the strength of the strong nuclear force. "This is what holds together the nucleus of atoms," he explained. "Ultimately, it's the strength of this force that produces the periodic table of elements."

I pictured in my mind the colorful periodic table I studied in chemistry class, which displays all naturally occurring elements from atomic numbers 1 (hydrogen) to 94 (plutonium), as well as several heavier elements that have only been synthesized in laboratories or nuclear reactors.

"What happens if you manipulate the strong nuclear force?" I asked.

"If you were to make it just 2 percent stronger while all other constants stayed the same, you'd add a lot more elements to the periodic table, but they would be radioactive and life-destroying.

Plus, you'd have very little hydrogen in the universe—and no hydrogen, no water, no life."

"What if you turned the knob the other way?"

"Decrease the force by a mere 5 percent, and all you'd have would be hydrogen. Again, a dead universe. Another area of my research involves quarks, which make up neutrons and protons. If we change the light quark mass just 2 or 3 percent, there would be no carbon in the universe."

"And no carbon means—what?" I asked.

Strauss gestured at the two of us. "That you and I wouldn't be sitting here."

The examples could go on and on; in fact, entire books have been written about them. Here's another illustration: the ratio of the electromagnetic force to the gravitational force is fine-tuned to one part in ten thousand trillion trillion trillion.

Astrophysicist Hugh Ross said to understand that number, imagine covering a *billion* North American continents with dimes up to the moon—238,000 miles high. Choose one dime at random, paint it red, and put it somewhere in the piles. Blindfold a friend and have him pick out one dime from the billion continents. What are the odds he'd choose the red dime? One in ten thousand trillion trillion trillion.[5]

But the most extreme example I've seen comes from Oxford mathematical physicist Roger Penrose, who partnered with Stephen Hawking to write *The Nature of Space and Time*.

His calculations show that in order to start the universe so it would have the required state of low entropy, the setting would need to be accurate to a precision of one part in ten to the power 10^{125}.

This mind-blowing number, Penrose said, "would be impossible to write out in the usual decimal way, because even if you were able to put a zero on every particle in the universe, there would not even be enough particles to do the job."[6]

Building a Life-Sustaining Planet

These extraordinary cosmic "coincidences" have not escaped secular scientists. "There is, for me, powerful evidence that there is something going on behind it all," said Paul Davies, a professor of physics at Arizona State University. "It seems as though somebody has fine-tuned nature's numbers to make the universe . . . The impression of design is overwhelming."[7]

British cosmologist Edward R. Harrison doesn't hesitate to draw conclusions from the universe's razor-sharp calibration. "Here is the cosmological proof of the existence of God," he said flatly. "The fine-tuning of the universe provides prima facie evidence of deistic design."[8]

And Strauss wasn't done yet. "Not only is our universe precisely calibrated to a breathtaking degree, but our planet is also remarkably and fortuitously situated so life would be possible."

"In what way?" I asked.

"To have a planet like ours where life exists, first you need to be in the right kind of galaxy. There are three types of galaxies: elliptical, spiral, and irregular. You need to be in a spiral galaxy, like we are, because it's the only kind that produces the right heavy elements and has the right radiation levels.

"But you can't live just anywhere in the galaxy," he continued. "If you're too close to the center, there's too much radiation and there's also a black hole, which you want to avoid. If you're too far from the center, you won't have the right heavy elements; you'd lack the oxygen and carbon you'd need. You have to live in the so-called 'Goldilocks Zone,' or the galactic habitable zone, where life could exist."

"Are you referring to intelligent life?" I asked.

"Anything more complex than bacteria," he said.

Then he continued, "To have life, you need a star like our sun.

Our sun is a Class G star that has supported stable planet orbits in the right location for a long time. The star must be in its middle age, so its luminosity is stabilized. It has to be a bachelor star—many stars in the universe are binary, which means two stars orbiting each other, which is bad for stable planetary orbits. Plus, the star should be a third-generation star, like our sun."

"What does that mean?"

"The first generation of stars were made of hydrogen and helium from the big bang. They only lasted a relatively short time. The second generation created heavy elements like carbon, oxygen, silicon, iron, and other things we need. The third generation is made up of stars that have enough material to create rocky planets like Earth and carbon-based life forms."

Strauss paused, but I could tell he wasn't done yet. "There are so many parameters that have to be just right for our planet to support life," he said. "The distance from the sun, the rotation rate, the amount of water, the tilt, the right size so gravity lets gases like methane escape but allows oxygen to stay.

"You need a moon like ours—it's very rare to have just one large moon—in order to stabilize Earth's tilt. As counterintuitive as it sounds, you even need to have tectonic activity, which experts said could be 'the central requirement for life on a planet.'[9] Plate tectonics drives biodiversity, helps avoid a water world without continents, and helps generate the magnetic field. Also, it's nice to have a huge planet like Jupiter nearby to act like a vacuum cleaner by attracting potentially devastating comets and meteors away from you."

"Periodically, newspapers tout the discovery of what astronomers call an 'Earth-like planet,'" I said.

"Yes, but generally all they mean is that it has a similar size as Earth or that it might be positioned to allow surface water. But there's so much more to Earth than those two factors."

"How many conditions have to be met to create an Earth-like planet?" I asked.

"Hugh Ross sets the number at 322," he replied.[10] "So if you run probability calculations, you find that there's a 10^{-304} chance you're going to find another planet that's truly like Earth."

"Still, there are lots of potential candidates out there," I pointed out. "One estimate is there could be more than a billion trillion planets."

"Granted," he said. "So let's factor that number into our probability equation. That still means the odds of having any higher life–supporting planet would be one in a million trillion."

He let that astonishing number sink in. "In science," he said, "we have a phrase for probabilities like that."

"Really? What is it?"

There came a grin. "Ain't gonna happen."

The Multiverse Option

Some scientists, recognizing the obvious design of the universe, have manufactured bizarre explanations for how this uncanny precision could have occurred in a purely naturalistic way.

For instance, John Barrow and Frank Tipler, in their book *The Anthropic Cosmological Principle*, said the universe is clearly designed, which requires intelligence, and intelligence is only possessed by humans. So they hypothesize that humans will continue to evolve until someday they become like gods—*at which point they reach back in time and create the universe themselves!*[11]

"These are two bright scientists, and it's the best they can come up with," Strauss said, shaking his head. "Needless to say, it hasn't gained any traction."

Neither has the idea that our universe is actually a *Matrix*-like simulation being run on a massive computer by some superprogrammer. After all, that still raises the problem of how *his* universe came into existence.

Then there's the idea—mentioned by Michael Shermer in my interview—that black holes lead to the creation of baby universes, which then create more universes through black holes, and so on for eternity. But that leaves open the question of where the first black hole–producing universe came from. Scoffed one scholar, "The physics underlying the idea is speculative, to say the least."[12]

Another hypothesis that quickly evaporated is that the fine-tuning is the result of random happenstance. The odds of that, scientists say, are functionally equivalent to impossible. "The precision is so utterly fantastic, so mathematically breathtaking, that it's just plain silly to think it could have been an accident," William Lane Craig said.[13]

As physicist Robin Collins told me, "If I bet you a thousand dollars that I could flip a coin and get heads fifty times in a row, and then I proceeded to do it, you wouldn't accept that. You'd know that the odds against that are so improbable—about one chance in a million billion—that it's extraordinarily unlikely to happen. The fact that I was able to do it against such monumental odds would be strong evidence to you that the game had been rigged. And the same is true for the fine-tuning of the universe—before you'd conclude that random chance was responsible, you'd conclude that there is strong evidence that the universe was rigged. That is, designed."[14]

So what are the most likely explanations for the fine-tuning? Science philosopher Tim Maudlin, author of *The Metaphysics within Physics*, published by Oxford University Press in 2007, said there are just two plausible alternatives to the universe's apparent design: "It seems that the only reactions are either to embrace a multiverse or a designer."[15]

"Let's talk about the multiverse option," I said to Strauss. "Stephen Hawking talks about M-theory, which would allow for a near infinite number of other universes. If the dials of physics were twirled at random in all of those, sooner or later one universe is going to hit the jackpot and get the right conditions for life."

"First of all," Strauss said, "we don't know if M-theory is correct. It's based on string theory, which is an esoteric concept for which all the equations haven't even been worked out yet. The theory may be untestable and nonfalsifiable, and there's no observational evidence for it, so is it really science?"

Strauss noted that when Hawking proposed the M-theory, science writer John Horgan wrote in *Scientific American*, "M-theory, theorists now realize, comes in an almost infinite number of versions . . . Of course, a theory that predicts everything really doesn't predict anything."[16]

Strauss continued, "Physicists have come up with various ideas for how multiverses could be birthed, but again, there's no observational or experimental evidence for it. In fact, there is likely no way for us to discover something that's beyond our universe. And even if there were multiple universes, the Borde-Guth-Vilenkin theorem says they all must go back to one beginning point, so now we return to the question of who or what created the universe in the first place."

His conclusion? "If you want to believe in one of the multiverse theories, you basically need blind faith."[17]

Similar comments came from John Polkinghorne, former professor of mathematical physics at Cambridge: "The many-universes account is sometimes presented as if it were purely scientific, but in fact a sufficient portfolio of different universes could only be generated by speculative processes that go well beyond what sober science can honestly endorse."[18]

Oxford philosopher Richard Swinburne was blunt: "To postulate a trillion trillion other universes, rather than one God, in order to explain the orderliness of our universe, seems the height of irrationality."[19]

The God Option

Oxford-educated physicist John Leslie, author of the influential book *Universes*, believes that if ours is the only universe—and, again, there's no scientific evidence that any others exist—then the fine-tuning is "genuine evidence . . . *that God is real*."[20]

"I agree," said Strauss. "Let's go back to what I know for a fact as a scientist. I know there's one universe that appears to have a beginning, which is incredibly calibrated in a way that defies naturalistic explanations, and there's a highly improbable planet whose unlikely conditions allow us to exist. To me, all of that begs for a divine explanation."

I raised my hand. "Hold on," I said. "Maybe our universe *isn't* so finely tuned. For instance, why would a creator waste so much space if he wanted to create a habitat for humankind? The universe is unimaginably huge, but it's largely a wasteland that's inhospitable to life."

"Actually, the universe is the smallest it could possibly be and still have life," Strauss replied.

That statement took me aback. "I'd like to hear you explain *that* one," I said.

"If you start with the big bang and your goal is to make a solar system like ours, you have to go through two previous generations of stars. The first generation left behind some of the elements of the periodic table, but lacked the right amounts of carbon, oxygen, and nitrogen to make rocky planets and complex life. Then the second generation of stars formed from the debris of the first generation. When these burned out, they made more heavy elements and scattered them throughout the universe. Our sun coalesced from that debris.

"Now here's my point: this third generation of stars is the first possibility for a solar system like ours to exist. So if you start with the big bang, it takes nine billion years to create a solar system like ours—which is approximately when our solar system formed, 4.5 billion years ago. So if you're God and your purpose is to create Earth suitable for people, and you use these processes, it would take about 13.5 billion years. And during that time, what is the universe doing?"

"Expanding."

"Right, it's getting bigger and bigger. So even though it's incredibly large, this is the youngest, and therefore the smallest, that the universe can be if you want to create one planet that's hospitable for life."

"Okay, now I get it," I replied. "But here's a question that skeptics frequently ask: If this God made the universe, then who made him?"

"Nobody," came the quick reply. "The *kalam* argument doesn't say, 'Whatever *exists* has a cause.' It says, 'Whatever *begins* to exist has a cause.' By definition, God never *began* to exist; he has always existed. He is a necessary, self-existent, eternal being. That's part of the definition of God. Why assume a triangle has three sides? Because that's part of what it means to be a triangle. The real question is: Does the evidence point toward the existence of such a divine being? I believe it does—and not just the evidence of cosmology and physics."

I recalled the words of William Lane Craig in interviews I conducted with him. "This is not special pleading in the case of God," he said.[21] "Atheists themselves used to be very comfortable in maintaining that the universe is eternal and uncaused. The problem is that they can no longer hold that position because of modern evidence that the universe started with the big bang. So they can't legitimately object when I make the same claim about God—he is eternal and he is uncaused."[22]

The Soul of the Artist

I asked Strauss, "If God is the most likely explanation for our universe and planet, then what can we logically deduce about him from the scientific evidence?"

"Several things. First," he said, grabbing a finger as he went through each point, "he must be transcendent, because he exists apart from his creation. Second, he must be immaterial or spirit, since he existed before the physical world. Third, he must be timeless or eternal, since he existed before physical time was created. Fourth, he must be powerful, given the immense energy of the big bang. Fifth, he must be smart, given the fact that the big bang was not some chaotic event but was masterfully finely tuned. Sixth, he must be personal, because a decision had to be made to create. Seventh, he must be creative—I mean, just look at the wonders of the universe. And eighth, he must be caring, because he so purposefully crafted a habitat for us."

"But as Shermer asked, why not a committee of gods? Why just one?"

"The scientific and philosophical principle called Occam's razor says that we shouldn't multiply causes beyond what's necessary to account for all of the phenomena," he said.

"Still, how do we know this creator is the God of Christianity?" I asked.

"All the qualities we've elicited from the evidence are consistent with the God of the Bible," he replied. "If there's just one creator, then that rules out polytheism. Since he's outside of creation, this rules out pantheism. The universe is not cyclical, which violates the tenets of Eastern religions. And the big bang contradicts ancient religious assumptions that the universe is static."

Hugh Ross, who earned his doctorate at the University of Toronto, has pointed to several ways in which the ancient writings in the Bible reflect the findings of contemporary cosmology.

"It is worth noting," Ross said, "that Scripture speaks about the transcendent beginning of physical reality, including time itself (Genesis 1:1; John 1:3; Colossians 1:15–17; Hebrews 11:3); about continual cosmic expansion, or 'stretching out' (Job 9:8; Psalm 104:2; Isaiah 40:22; 45:12; Jeremiah 10:12); about unchanging physical laws (Jeremiah 33:25), one of which is the pervasive law of decay (Ecclesiastes 1:3–11; Romans 8:20–22). These descriptions fly in the face of ancient, enduring, and prevailing assumptions about an eternal, static universe—until the twentieth century."[23]

The rumble of a passing truck interrupted my conversation with Strauss. He stood and asked, "Do you want some water?" He went into the kitchen, filled two glasses, and returned to offer me one. I looked at my watch; because of an appointment that Strauss needed to keep, we were running short on time.

But the purpose of my visit had been fulfilled. Thinking over the case that Strauss had built, the existence of a miracle-working creator—who matches the description of the God of the Bible— had been established beyond a reasonable doubt.

Strauss sat back down and glanced briefly out the window, turning philosophical in our last moments together.

"You know," he said, taking a sip of water, "I'm friends with an artist who says he can look at a piece of art and see the soul of the artist. I can't do that, but I'm a scientist. I can look deeply into the universe and the subatomic world and see the soul of *the* Artist. For instance, I see evidence of his transcendence. So what does that tell me? It tells me that for him, intervening in the world he made is simple. Miracles are trivial. They're easy to do.

"Then I look at the bizarre world of quantum mechanics. Lee, it's so different from anything you or I can imagine. Virtual particles pop in and out of existence; apparently, one particle can be two places at the same time. To me, that's a reflection of Isaiah 55, which says that God's ways are different from our ways. His thoughts are greater than our thoughts.[24]

"The artist looks at a painting and says, 'These brushstrokes tell me about the mood of the painter.' As a physicist, I know that virtual particles inside of protons have a mass that's finely tuned so that I can exist. That tells me something about the mood of the Creator—he's both ingenious and caring. Why else would he cause all of creation to accrue to our benefit?

"Frankly, I look at a painting and say, 'Huh, that's nice.' To me, it's just color on canvas. I can't see the deeper realities that an artist can. But I'm privileged to be a scientist. I can see the nuances and subtleties and intricacies of nature in a way that others can't. And invariably, they point me toward one conclusion: the God hypothesis has no competitors."

CHAPTER 11

The Miracle of the Resurrection

*An Interview with
Detective J. Warner Wallace*

E ven for a decorated cold-case homicide investigator, this was a formidable challenge. J. Warner Wallace had used his considerable detective skills to solve murders that were decades old, but he had never tackled a case that stretched back for two millennia.

What's more, this time he wasn't merely attempting to identify the perpetrator of a long-ago crime; instead, he was trying to determine whether the victim was truly deceased—and whether he defied all naturalistic explanations by rising from the dead three days later.

Quite an assignment for someone who was at the time a hyper-skeptical atheist.

Wallace is the son of a cop and the father of a cop. His dad fought crime in Torrance, California, a residential and high-tech enclave south of Los Angeles. Initially, Wallace resisted the temptation to follow in his father's footsteps. He started out with a career in the arts, earning a degree in design and a master's degree in architecture, but before long the lure of the badge proved too strong.

After doing training through the Los Angeles Sheriff's Department, Wallace joined the force in Torrance, working on the SWAT team and the gang detail and investigating robbery and homicide cases. Later he became a founding member of the department's cold-case homicide unit, assigned to crack murders that nobody else had been able to solve.

His success brought accolades and opportunities. Soon he was being featured on NBC's *Dateline* and news outlets seeking expertise on what it takes to arrest killers who thought they had gotten away with murder.

Through the years, Wallace's street-honed skepticism served him well. "As a cop, if you believe everything people tell you, then you'd never arrest anyone," he said. For him, facts need to be solid; witnesses have to be credible; evidence must be persuasive; corroboration is always crucial; and alibis have to be dismantled. In short, he was the kind of skeptic even Michael Shermer could admire.

Wallace's skepticism as an adolescent cemented him into atheism. His parents divorced when he was young. His father, at his mother's insistence, would drop him off at the Catholic church on Sundays, where he would attend a Latin mass by himself.

"I didn't understand a word, but it didn't matter," he said. "I didn't believe any of it. Plus, I didn't have any Christian role models who could explain why they accepted this stuff."

It wasn't until Wallace was thirty-five that he subjected the gospels to months of painstaking analysis through various investigative techniques, including what detectives call "forensic statement analysis." This skill involves critically analyzing a person's account of events—including word choice and structure—to determine whether he is being truthful or deceptive.[1] Eventually, Wallace became convinced that Christianity is true beyond a reasonable doubt.

"In a sense," he said, "it was my skepticism that led to faith, because it pushed me to question everything, to doubt my own doubts, and to demand answers that could stand up to scrutiny."

The answers ended up convincing him that Jesus, in time and space, actually did conquer his tomb and thereby provide convincing evidence of his divinity. It was that meticulous investigation of the miraculous resurrection that prompted me to jump on a plane and fly to Southern California, where I met with Wallace at his ranch-style house in Orange County.

The Interview with J. Warner Wallace, MTS

"I'm an 'all in' kind of guy," Wallace said to me. "C. S. Lewis said if Christianity isn't true, it's of no importance, but if it is true, nothing is more important—and I agree.[2] That's why I've jumped in with both feet."

After becoming a Christian in 1996, Wallace earned a master's degree in theological studies from Golden Gate Baptist Theological Seminary, served as a youth pastor, and planted a church. Currently, he is an adjunct professor of apologetics at Biola University, is a senior fellow at the Colson Center for Christian Worldview, and teaches at Summit Ministries in Colorado.

I have been a friend of Wallace's for several years, ever since I wrote the foreword to his book *Cold-Case Christianity*, in which he offers ten principles from his detective work that can be used to examine the reliability of the gospels.

His other books include *God's Crime Scene*, in which he examines eight pieces of evidence from the universe that make the case for the existence of God; *Alive*, which focuses on the resurrection; and *Forensic Faith*, which helps readers become better defenders of Christianity. Ever the artist, Wallace creates his own drawings to illustrate his books.

During his two decades of investigative work, Wallace was awarded the Police and Fire Medal of Valor "Sustained Superiority"

Award and the CopsWest Award for solving a 1979 murder. Although now retired from the force, he still consults on cold-case homicides and acts as an investigative consultant for television networks. Wallace and I even did cameo appearances in the motion picture *God's Not Dead 2*, where we testified on the historicity of Jesus in a fictional court case.

Today, this once-doubting atheist travels the country to speak on becoming a "Christian case maker," or someone who can effectively articulate the evidence that backs up the essential claims of the faith.

Wallace is a bundle of crackling energy, speaking in fast, clipped sentences, sometimes verbally machine-gunning others with a flurry of facts. He's constantly taking his eyeglasses off and putting them back on as he speaks, almost using them as a prop. Slender and fit, he looks as though he's still in good enough shape to run down a burglar, although at the same time, his close-cropped silver hair gives him the air of a senior investigator.

I've always appreciated Wallace's no-nonsense, "just give me the facts" exterior, which syncs up well with my own journalistic bent, but I also admire what's underneath—an exceedingly compassionate and gracious heart toward others. I know, because I've been the grateful recipient of his kindness in the past.

Oddly, though, I had never talked at length with Wallace about his journey from atheism to faith. After we sat in his recreation room and chatted for a while about family, I asked, "What prompted you to start checking out the gospels?"

"My wife, Susie, was raised with a cultural Catholicism, so she thought it was important to take the kids to church, and I went along," he explained. "One Sunday, the pastor said, 'Jesus was the smartest guy who ever lived, and our Western culture is grounded in his moral teaching.'"

"How did you react?"

"I thought, *I'm a cop enforcing the penal code, but I know there's a universal moral law above that.* After all, adultery is legal, but it isn't right. So it got me thinking about where that moral code came from. That's why I went out and bought this."

He pulled a red pew Bible from the shelf and handed it to me. "I got this for six bucks," he said.

I flipped it open to a random page and saw that it was very neatly but quite thoroughly marked up. There were homemade tabs, notes in small print in the narrow margins, and color-coded underlining throughout. I went to the gospel of Mark and saw that it was thoroughly annotated.

"I was using forensic statement analysis to analyze the gospels—for instance, here in the gospel of Mark I was looking for the influence of Peter, so that's what one of the colors represents," he explained. "I was nitpicking the details; by the time I was done, I had gone through three Bibles."

"How long did your analysis take?"

"Six months."

"What was your verdict?"

"That the gospels reliably recorded true events," he said. "But that presented a problem for me."

"Why?"

"Because they talk about the resurrection and other miracles," he said. "I could believe the gospels if they said Jesus ate bread, but what if they said the loaf levitated? C'mon, I couldn't believe that. I didn't believe miracles could happen, so I rejected them out of hand."

Getting Past Stubborn Presuppositions

I could relate to the impediment of the supernatural, since it was a stubborn obstruction in my own spiritual investigation. "What changed your mind?" I inquired.

"I asked myself, *Do I believe* anything *supernatural?* And I concluded that, well, yes, even as an atheist, I did believe something extra-natural occurred."

"For instance?"

"The big bang," he replied. "Everything came from nothing. If nature is defined as everything we see in our environment, then there had to be something before that, a first cause that was beyond space, matter, and time. That meant the cause couldn't be spatial, material, or temporal."

I smiled, remembering my conversation with physicist Michael Strauss in the two preceding chapters.

"I realized," Wallace continued, "that if there was something extra-natural that caused the beginning of all space, time, and matter as recorded in Genesis 1:1, then that same cause could accomplish all miracles recorded in the gospels. In other words, if there is a God, then miracles are reasonable, maybe even expected."

"So you got past your presupposition against the miraculous," I said.

"I did. As a detective, I knew presuppositions can derail an investigation. I remember a case in which a woman was found dead in her bed. She was a locally notorious drug addict, and there was drug paraphernalia on her nightstand. The patrol officers got there and didn't even bother to pull down the sheets, since this was so obviously an overdose. But when investigators got there, they pulled down the sheets—and they saw she had been stabbed to death."

He paused as the implications registered with me. "Presuppositions can be impediments to truth," he said. "The resurrection was the most reasonable inference from the evidence, but I was ruling out miracles from the outset."

"What led you to conclude that this first cause of the universe was personal and not just some force?"

"I recognized that there are universal moral laws," he replied. "For example, it's wrong to torture a baby for fun in any culture, anywhere, anytime. And transcendent moral laws are more than simply *truths*—they are obligations between *persons*. If there are objective, transcendent moral obligations, the best explanation for them is an objective, transcendent moral person."

"Okay, you concluded that the gospels contain reliable eyewitness accounts, even of the miraculous," I said. "What came next?"

"I was stuck on the 'why' question: Why did Jesus come, die, and return from the dead? I started analyzing Paul's writings, and I was amazed by his insights into what he called 'natural man' or sinful people. His description fit me in an uncanny way," he replied.

"Plus, the message of grace is so counterintuitive. Every other religion is based on performance, which makes sense because humans love to achieve and compete to get a reward. This message of grace—of unearned forgiveness—didn't sound like it had human origins. It came off as either ridiculous or divine. This doesn't prove anything in and of itself, but it was one more piece of the puzzle."

"In the end, then, it was a cumulative case," I said, a declaration more than a question.

"Bingo," he said crisply. "The totality of the evidence overwhelmed me. When we're trying to solve a homicide, we typically put all the facts on a whiteboard and see if we can make the case. I didn't have to do that here. The case made itself."

The Eyewitness Gospels

As someone who covered criminal justice as a journalist for years, I'm fascinated by how DNA evidence has been used to solve crimes that happened decades earlier. For Wallace, though, DNA hasn't been a factor in any cold case he has solved.

"Typically, we've solved them through the analysis of eyewitness testimony," he said. "And that's the way I tested the gospels."

"Michael Shermer believes they're just moral stories that don't have a historical core to them," I said. "Why are you convinced they're based on eyewitness accounts?"

"There's good evidence that John and Matthew wrote their gospels based on their eyewitness testimony as disciples of Jesus. While Luke wasn't a witness himself, he said he 'carefully investigated everything from the beginning,'[3] presumably by interviewing eyewitnesses. According to Papias, who was the bishop of Hierapolis, Mark was the scribe of the apostle Peter—and my forensic analysis of Mark's gospel bears that out."

"In what ways?"

"Mark treats Peter with the utmost respect and includes details that can best be attributed to Peter," Wallace replied. "Mark also makes a disproportionate number of references to Peter. And unlike the other gospels, Mark's first and last mention of a disciple is Peter, which is an ancient bookending technique where a piece of history is attributed to a particular eyewitness.

"Of course," he continued, "Peter called himself an eyewitness,[4] and John said he was reporting what 'we have seen with our eyes.'[5] In fact, when they were arrested for testifying about the resurrection, they said, 'We cannot help speaking about what we have seen and heard.'[6] Over and over, the apostles identified themselves as 'witnesses of everything he [Jesus] did in the country of the Jews and in Jerusalem.'"[7]

"Nevertheless," I interjected, "you and I both know that eyewitness testimony has been challenged in recent years. In fact, some defendants convicted by eyewitness testimony have been exonerated through new DNA evidence."

"No question—all eyewitness accounts have to be tested for

reliability. In California, judges give jurors more than a dozen factors to weigh in evaluating an eyewitness account," he said. "We can apply these tests to the gospels—for instance, is there any corroboration, did the witnesses have a motive to lie, did their stories change over time? When we do, we find they hold up well."

"How early do you date the gospels?"

"Acts doesn't report several major events that occurred in the AD 60s—including the martyrdoms of Paul, Peter, and James—apparently because it was written before they occurred. We know Luke's gospel came before Acts, and we know Mark was written before Luke, because he uses it as one of his sources. Even before that, Paul confirms the resurrection in material that goes back to within a few years of Jesus' execution.[8] When you consider that Jesus died in AD 30 or 33, the gap shrinks to where it's not a problem."

"So it doesn't bother you that the gospels were passed along verbally before being written down?" I asked.

"Not at all. I've seen witnesses in cold cases say their memories from thirty-five years ago are like it happened yesterday—why? Because not all memories are created the same."

"What do you mean by that?"

"If you asked me what I did on Valentine's Day five years ago, I probably couldn't recall very much. That's because it's only one of many Valentine's Days I've celebrated with Susie. But if you asked me about Valentine's Day of 1988, I can give you a detailed report of what took place."

I cocked my head. "I give up," I said. "Why's that?"

Wallace smiled. "Because that's the day Susie and I got married," he replied. "When witnesses experience something that's unique, unrepeated, and personally important or powerful, they're much more likely to remember it. Of course, many of the disciples' experiences with Jesus met those criteria.

"Can they remember all the times their boat got stuck in a storm?" he asked. "Probably not, but they could remember the time Jesus quieted the squall. And think of the resurrection—as much as anything they experienced, that was unique, unrepeated, and extremely powerful."

Dealing with Gospel Discrepancies

"But what about the conflicts among the various gospel accounts—don't they cast doubt on the reliability of the eyewitness testimony?" I asked.

"Based on my years as a detective, I would expect the four gospels to have variances," he replied. "Think of this: the early believers could have destroyed all but one of the gospels in order to eliminate any differences between them. But they didn't. Why? Because they knew the gospels were true and that they told the story from different perspectives, emphasizing different things."

"The conflicts aren't evidence they were lying?"

"People might assume that if they've never worked with eyewitnesses before. In my experience, eyewitness accounts can be reliable despite discrepancies. Besides, if they meshed too perfectly, it would be evidence of collusion."

That echoed the assessment of Simon Greenleaf of Harvard Law School, one of America's most important legal figures, after he studied the gospels. "There is enough of discrepancy to show that there could have been no previous concert among them," he wrote, "and at the same time such substantial agreement as to show that they all were independent narrators of the same great transaction."[9]

Interestingly, while writing this chapter, I was reading a breakthrough book by New Testament scholar Michael R. Licona, published by Oxford University Press, which offers one innovative way to resolve differences between the gospels.[10] Licona, who earned his doctorate at the University of Pretoria, is a noted resurrection scholar and a colleague of mine at Houston Baptist University.

His research shows that many apparent discrepancies between the gospels can be explained by the standard compositional techniques that Greco-Roman biographers typically used in that era. As Craig Keener pointed out in my interview with him for this book, the gospels fall into the genre of ancient biography.

For example, one common technique, modeled by the historian Plutarch, is called "literary spotlighting." Licona likened this to a theatrical performance where there are multiple actors onstage but the lights go out and a spotlight shines on only one of them.

"You know other actors are on the stage," he said, "but you can't see them because the spotlight is focused on one person."

Applying this to the gospels, he noted that Matthew, Mark, and Luke say multiple women visited Jesus' tomb and discovered it empty. However, John's gospel only mentions Mary Magdalene. Is that a discrepancy that casts doubt on the gospels?

"It seems likely that John is aware of the presence of other women while shining his spotlight on Mary," Licona said. "After all, he reports Mary announcing to Peter and the Beloved Disciple, 'They have taken the Lord from the tomb and we don't know where they have laid him.'[11] Who's the 'we' to whom Mary refers? Probably the other women who were present.

"Then observe what happens next," Licona continued. "In John, Peter and the Beloved Disciple run to the tomb and discover it empty, whereas Luke 24:12 mentions Peter running to the tomb and no mention is made of the beloved disciple. However, just twelve verses later, Luke reports there were more than one who had made the trip to the tomb.[12] These observations strongly suggest Luke and John were employing literary spotlighting in their resurrection narratives."

Based on exhaustive analysis of the gospels, Licona reaches this conclusion: "If what I'm suggesting is correct—that an overwhelming number of Gospel differences are . . . most plausibly accounted for by reading the Gospels in view of their biographical genre—*the tensions resulting from nearly all of the differences disappear.*"[13]

Consequently, he said, the argument that the gospels are historically unreliable due to their differences would be "no longer sustainable."

Gospel Mysteries Solved

Wallace then made the counterintuitive statement that some of the differences between the gospels actually show their cohesion in a way that would be expected if they were based on independent eyewitness accounts.

"I noticed that sometimes one of the gospels would describe an event but leave out a detail that raised a question in my mind—and then this question gets unintentionally answered by another gospel writer," he explained.

"You're referring to what have been described as 'undesigned coincidences,'" I said.

"Right," he replied. "There are more than forty places in the New Testament where we see this kind of unintentional eyewitness support."[14]

"What are some examples?"

"In Matthew's gospel, Jesus encounters Peter, Andrew, James, and John for the first time. They're fishermen mending nets. He says, 'Follow me,' and, sure enough, they spontaneously do.[15] Now, doesn't that seem odd—that they would drop everything and immediately follow this person they've never met?"

"That does create a mystery," I conceded.

"Fortunately, we have Luke's gospel. He says Jesus got into

Peter's boat and preached from it. Then he told Peter to put out his nets, and Peter reluctantly did so, even though they had worked all night and caught nothing. Miraculously, the nets emerged teeming with so many fish that they began to break. In fact, the catch filled two boats. Luke says Peter and the others were astonished and Peter recognized Jesus as Lord."[16]

"All of a sudden," I said, "Matthew's account makes more sense."

"Exactly. When the testimony is put together, we get a complete picture. The disciples heard Jesus preach and saw the miracle of the abundant fish. After they returned to shore, Jesus said to follow him—and they did, based on his revolutionary teachings and his display of supernatural power."

"Have you seen unintentional coincidences in your police work?"

"I've had instances where a witness's account leaves questions unanswered until we find an additional witness later," he said. "This is a common characteristic of true eyewitness accounts."

"What are some other examples?"

"Matthew says during Jesus' trial the chief priests and members of the council struck him and said, 'Prophesy to us, Messiah. Who hit you?'[17] Now, that's a strange request. Couldn't Jesus just look at his attackers and identify them? But when Luke describes the same scene, he mentions one other detail: Jesus was blindfolded. There—" Wallace said, snapping his fingers. "Mystery solved."

"What's your conclusion?" I asked.

"The most reasonable explanation is that the gospels were penned by different eyewitnesses who were just reporting what they saw and unintentionally including these unplanned supporting details," he said.

"So this was one more piece to the puzzle for you," I said.

"One of many. We have archaeology corroborating certain points of the gospels. We have non-Christian accounts outside the

Bible that provide confirmation of key gospel claims. We have students of the apostles who give a consistent account of what the disciples were teaching. And we have a proliferation of ancient manuscripts that help us get back to what the original gospels said."

"Okay then, Mr. Detective. What's your verdict?"

"That the gospels can be messy, that they're filled with idiosyncrasies, that they're each told from a different perspective and have variances between them—just like you'd expect from a collection of eyewitness accounts," he said. "So I became convinced that they constitute reliable testimony to the life, teachings, death, and—yes—the resurrection of Jesus."

Did Jesus Really Die on the Cross?

Ah, the resurrection.

Even skeptics agree with the apostle Paul's assertion that if the resurrection were disproved, then the entire Christian faith would collapse into irrelevancy.[18] Consequently, opponents are constantly minting fresh objections to undermine this central tenet of Christianity. In recent years, for example, agnostic New Testament scholar Bart Ehrman and others have advanced new efforts to cast doubt on whether Jesus died and escaped his grave alive again.

I said to Wallace, "Even if we concede that the gospel accounts are rooted in eyewitness testimony, we're still faced with the issue of whether a miracle the magnitude of the resurrection makes sense. Let me challenge you with some of the most potent objections to Jesus' rising from the dead."

"Shoot," he said, quickly catching himself with a chuckle. "Maybe that's not the best terminology for a cop. Anyway, yes, go ahead."

"It seems to me the two relevant issues are, first, whether Jesus was actually dead from crucifixion and, second, whether he was encountered alive afterward, necessitating an empty tomb," I said.

Wallace folded his arms. "Agreed," he replied.

"So how do we know he was really dead? Is it reasonable that he would succumb that soon? The thieves on either side of him were still alive."

"But the path to the cross for Jesus was dramatically different than the path for the thieves," he said.

"How so?"

"Pilate didn't want to crucify Jesus like the crowd was demanding, so he kind of makes an offer. He says, in effect, 'I'll tell you what I'll do—I'll beat him to within an inch of his life. Will that satisfy you?' Consequently, Jesus was given an especially horrific flogging. That didn't satisfy the crowds, and he was crucified. But he was already in such extremely bad shape that he couldn't even carry his cross."

"These soldiers weren't medical doctors," I said. "Maybe they thought Jesus had died when he hadn't."

"That objection usually comes from people who've never been around dead bodies. As a cop, I've witnessed a lot of autopsies. Let me tell you: dead people aren't like corpses in movies. They look different. They feel different. They get cold; they get rigid; their blood pools. These soldiers knew what death looked like; in fact, they were motivated to make sure he was deceased because they would be executed if a prisoner escaped alive. Plus, the apostle John unwittingly gave us a major clue."

"What's that?"

"He says when Jesus was stabbed with a spear to make sure he was dead, water and blood came out. In those days, nobody understood that. Some early church leaders thought this was a metaphor for baptism or something. Today, we know this is consistent with what we would expect, because the torture would have caused fluid to collect around his heart and lungs. So without even realizing it, John was giving us a corroborating detail."

I reached into my briefcase and removed a copy of the Qur'an, which I placed on the table between us. "Yet," I said, "there are more than a billion Muslims who don't believe Jesus was crucified.[19] Many of them believe that God substituted Judas for Jesus on the cross."

Wallace picked up the Qur'an and paged through it. "Here's the problem," he said, handing it back to me. "This was written six hundred years after Jesus lived. Compare that to the first-century sources that are uniform in reporting that Jesus was dead. Not only do we have the gospel accounts, but we also have five ancient sources *outside* the Bible."[20]

"Still, how can you disprove the claim that God supernaturally switched people on the cross?" I asked.

"That would mean Jesus was being deceptive when he appeared to people afterward. No, that would contradict what we know about his character. And how would you explain him showing the nail holes in his hands and the wound in his side to Thomas?"

"You have no doubt, then, that he was dead."

"No, I don't. When scholars Gary Habermas and Michael Licona surveyed all the scholarly literature on the resurrection going back thirty years, Jesus' death was among the facts that were virtually unanimously accepted," he said.[21]

"Besides," he added, "crucifixion was humiliating—it's not something the early church would have invented. And we have no record of anyone ever surviving a full Roman crucifixion."

Tombs, Ossuaries, and Conspiracies

Even the skeptical Bart Ehrman concedes that Jesus was killed by crucifixion, but he recently wrote a book saying it's "unlikely" that Jesus was buried in a tomb, saying that "what *normally* happened to a criminal's body is that it was left to decompose and serve as food for scavenging animals."[22]

"Of course, if Jesus was never buried, then that would neatly explain why the tomb was unoccupied," I said.

Wallace smiled and pointed toward me. "Seems like your colleague at HBU has answered that pretty thoroughly," he said.

He was referring to Craig Evans, an eminent New Testament scholar on the faculty with me at Houston Baptist University. As part of a book rebutting Ehrman, Evans said Ehrman's description of Roman policy on crucifixion and nonburial is "unnuanced and incomplete."[23]

"It is simply erroneous to assert that the Romans did not permit the burial of the executed, including the crucified," he wrote.[24] "The gospel narratives are completely in step with Jewish practice, which Roman authorities during peacetime respected."[25]

Said Evans, "I conclude that the burial of the body of Jesus in a known tomb, according to Jewish law and custom, is highly probable."[26]

"I'll add one thing," Wallace said to me. "An ossuary with the remains of a crucifixion victim was discovered in 1968, with part of an iron spike still in his heel bone. This is evidence that at least some crucifixion victims were buried, as the earliest account of Jesus' death tells us he was."[27]

Ironically, one of Ehrman's own colleagues at the University of North Carolina at Chapel Hill, a Jewish archaeologist named Jodi Magness, affirmed, "The Gospel accounts describing Jesus' removal from the cross and burial are consistent with archaeological evidence and with Jewish law."[28]

Whatever occurred nearly two thousand years ago, there's little dispute that the disciples *believed* the once-dead Jesus appeared to them alive. Not only do the four gospels report this, but there's confirmation from students of the apostles (Clement and Polycarp), as well as in an early creed of the church found in 1 Corinthians 15:3–8 and a speech by Peter in Acts 2.

"You've broken a lot of conspiracy cases as a cop," I said. "Do you see any way these people could have been lying about this?"

"For a conspiracy to succeed, you need the smallest number of coconspirators; holding the lie for the shortest period of time; with excellent communication between them so they can make sure their stories line up; with close familial relationships, if possible; and with little or no pressure applied to those who are telling the lie. Those criteria don't fit the resurrection witnesses.

"On top of that," he added, "they had no motive to be deceitful. In fact, we have at least seven ancient sources that tell us the disciples were willing to suffer and even die for their conviction that they encountered the risen Jesus."[29]

"But," I interjected, "research has shown that history is murky on what actually happened to some of them."[30]

"True, but what's important is their *willingness* to die. That's well established. They knew the truth about what occurred, and my experience is that people aren't willing to suffer or die for what they know is a lie.

"Even more importantly, there isn't a single ancient document or claim in which any of the eyewitnesses ever recanted their statement. Think about that for a minute. We have ancient accounts in which second-, third-, or fourth-generation Christians were forced to recant, but *no* record of an eyewitness ever disavowing their testimony. I think that helps establish the truthfulness of the eyewitnesses."

From One Miracle to Another

I tried another approach. "I'm sure you've seen cases where people close to a murder victim are so full of grief that it colors their recollections about what happened," I said.

"To some degree," he replied. "But I sense where you're going with this: Did the sorrow of the disciples cause them to have a vision of the risen Jesus? That's a different matter altogether."

"Why?"

"First, groups don't have hallucinations, and the earliest report of the resurrection said five hundred people saw him. Second, Jesus was encountered on numerous occasions and by a number of different groups. The vision theory doesn't seem likely in those varying circumstances. And I can think of at least one person who *wasn't* inclined toward a vision."

"Paul?"

"Yeah, he was as skeptical as, well, Michael Shermer."

"What if one of the disciples—maybe Peter—experienced a vision due to his sorrow and then convinced the others that Jesus had returned? As you know, Peter had a strong personality and could be persuasive."

"I've had murder cases where one emphatic witness persuaded others that something happened," Wallace conceded. "Inevitably, the persuader has all the details in their most robust form, while the others tend to generalize because they didn't actually see the event for themselves. But this theory can't account for the numerous, divergent, and separate group sightings of Jesus, which are described with a lot of specificity. Also, Peter wasn't the first to see the risen Jesus."

"Good point," I said.

"I'll add one last point," said Wallace. "With all these theories of visions or hallucinations, the body is still in the tomb."

I asked Wallace, "What happened when you finally concluded that none of the escape hatches would let you avoid the conclusion that the resurrection really happened?"

"I remember being in church one Sunday, though I can't recall what the pastor was saying," he said. "I leaned over and whispered to Susie that I was a believer."

"As easy as that?"

He chuckled. "Not that easy," he said. "Yes, the evidence broke through my philosophical naturalism, and the gospels passed all the tests we use to evaluate eyewitness accounts. So I came to believe *that* Jesus is who he claimed to be. But then there was another step—believing *in* Jesus as my forgiver and leader."

"How did that happen?"

"The more I understood the true nature of Jesus, the more *my* true nature was exposed—and I didn't like what I saw. Being a cop had led me to lose faith in people. My heart had shriveled. To me, everyone was a liar capable of depraved behavior. I saw myself as superior to everyone else. I was cynical, cocky, and distant."

Honestly, I was surprised by his description of himself. I have only known Wallace as a warm, sincere, and generous person—but then, I've only known him since he has been a follower of Jesus.

"It sounds like a cliché," Wallace continued, "but coming to faith in Christ changed me drastically over time. As someone forgiven much, I learned to forgive others. After receiving God's grace, I was better able to show compassion. Now my life is consumed with letting others know that faith in Christ isn't just a subjective emotion, but it's grounded in the truth of the resurrection."

I thought of the words of the apostle Paul, himself a hardened law enforcer who was transformed after encountering the risen Jesus: "Therefore, if anyone is in Christ, the new creation has come: The old has gone, the new is here!"[31]

Why Don't Jews Accept the Resurrection?

After we finished our interview, Wallace gave me a tour of his study, its walls festooned with commendations he received as a detective, mementos from his years on the police force, and family photos, including one showing three generations of cops together: his dad, him, and his son.

"One last thing," I said before I turned off my recorder. "Shermer asked why Jewish people, who share much of the same holy book as Christians, don't accept the resurrection. Any ideas?"

Wallace leaned against the desk where he tapes his podcasts and spent a few moments organizing his thoughts.

"There are probably three reasons people reject this," he said. "The first is rational. Of course, everyone expresses their rejection in rational terms, because it feels good to say they're too smart for this. But I wonder how many Jewish people have conducted their own in-depth analysis of the issues. Some synagogues hold counter-missionary seminars to argue against Christianity, and people merely accept what they say without checking it out themselves.

"Second, there's an emotional reason. In Jewish families, there are barriers of culture and tradition. Christians see Jesus as the fulfillment of Jewish prophecies, but when a Jewish person comes to faith in Christ it's often viewed as a betrayal or abdication of their Jewish identity. The fear of rejection can be an impediment.

"The third reason people reject it is volitional. The Jewish people are proud of having followed the laws of God; in fact, they added six hundred more laws, which the devout have tried to scrupulously adhere to.

"Humans love works-based systems because they can measure their progress and compare themselves favorably with others. It's hard to accept a grace-based system that says, 'The laws were there to demonstrate your need for forgiveness, because they can never be totally obeyed.' A lot of people don't want to accept that."

My mind drifted to my Jewish friends who took the time to research the issues for themselves and came to faith in Christ. I thought of Louis Lapides, a soldier who returned disillusioned from Vietnam. Prodded by a street evangelist, he went on a quest to find Jesus in the Jewish scriptures—which he did, through the ancient prophecies about the Messiah that Jesus fulfilled against all odds.[32]

And the late Stan Telchin, a feisty businessman who set out to expose the "cult" of Christianity after his daughter went away to college and received *Yeshua* (Jesus) as her Messiah. His investigation led him and his wife to the resurrected Jesus, and he later became a pastor.[33]

As with Wallace, the miracle of the resurrection led these Jewish friends to a second miracle that's just as extraordinary, just as jaw-dropping, just as worship-inducing. In each of their lives, they exchanged their sin for God's grace; they experienced a profound spiritual rebirth; and they were changed in ways that were simply inexplicable in mere human terms.

That's the enduring power of the miracle of the resurrection. Over and over to this day, in my own experience and in the experiences of countless others, the resurrection miracle begets personal miracles of forgiveness, redemption, and new life.

PART 5

Difficulties with Miracles

CHAPTER 12

Embarrassed by the Supernatural

An Interview with Dr. Roger E. Olson

The request was simple: "Tell us about your journey to faith."

I was in a conference room, surrounded by my pastor, several of the church's elders, and a college professor of theology, being interviewed for ordination as a minister of the gospel. I had left my journalism career, taking a 60 percent pay cut, and joined the staff of a large congregation in suburban Chicago. Being ordained was a next step.

I had no hesitation in sharing the story of how I went from being an atheistic journalist at the *Chicago Tribune* to becoming a committed follower of Jesus. I knew my account of how I used my journalism and legal training to investigate the scientific and historical evidence for Christianity would resonate with everyone in the room.

After all, this was a church filled with successful people living in upscale suburbia—thinkers, achievers, leaders, influencers. They would certainly relate to how God used logic and reason to lead me to conclude that the resurrection is an actual historical event that proved Jesus is the unique Son of God.

But I was wrestling with how much I should tell about the rest of my story. For example, should I mention the influential dream that I described in the chapter on dreams and visions, in which an angel appeared to me when I was a youngster and gave me a prophecy that came true sixteen years later? How would they react if I described something supernatural like that, a seemingly bizarre event that went beyond normal reason and evidence?

Of course, everyone in the room believed in a miracle-working God. Each one of them would affirm that God is sovereign and can intervene at any time to make his presence known and achieve his purposes.

Still, would they think less of me if I began chattering about dreams and angels and personal prophecies? Would that be a step too far? Would mouths fall open if I made the claim that my dream was an actual encounter with a messenger from the Almighty? Where is the line between sheer irrationality and a reasonable belief that God has intervened miraculously in my life?

In the end, I did tell them about the dream with the angel—and they weren't shocked or disturbed by it. My ordination was conferred without controversy. Nevertheless, I have always remembered the discomfort I felt in deciding whether to share that part of my story. In fact, to this day I almost never refer to the dream in public settings.

That's why my interest was piqued by a theologian's blog post titled "Embarrassed by the Supernatural." Without even reading it, I could relate to the sense that in twenty-first-century America, even Christians like myself often hesitate to talk openly about divine interventions in our lives.

We don't want to be seen as being weird or outside the main-stream. We don't want to be lumped with televangelists and flamboyant faith healers. We want to be respectable and accepted by people in our secular culture. The result? In our churches and even in our prayers, sometimes we subconsciously hold back from fully embracing the God who still performs the miraculous.

I noticed that the author of the blog was a professor at Baylor

University in Waco, Texas, just a few hours from my home. A phone call yielded an appointment, and in quick order I was once again hitting the road.

The Interview with Roger E. Olson, PhD

Roger E. Olson grew up in the strict but loving home of a Pentecostal pastor, where there was no television, no movies, and no dancing. He enjoyed going to church services ("They were never boring"), and he even toted his Bible to class when he was in high school. "The kids would laugh at me, but that didn't matter," he said. "My friends weren't at school; they were at church."

While earning his master's degree at Rice University in Houston, where he later received his doctorate in religious studies, Olson shifted to a more mainline church culture, serving as a youth minister at a Presbyterian church.

Today, Olson is the Foy Valentine Professor of Christian Theology of Ethics at George W. Truett Theological Seminary of Baylor University. He describes himself as being "passionately evangelical," which he defines with a smile as "a God-fearing, Bible-believing, Jesus-loving Christian."

In scholarly circles, he's known as an ardent Arminian[1] who spars frequently (and effectively) with Calvinists over their theological distinctives; in fact, one of his books, *Against Calvinism*, is paired with the counterpoint *For Calvinism* by Reformed theologian Michael Horton.

However, Olson doesn't fit neatly on the conservative-liberal theological spectrum. I like to call him "theologically feisty," since he has authored such books as *How to Be Evangelical without Being Conservative*, *Reclaiming Pietism*, *Reformed and Always Reforming*, and *Counterfeit Christianity*.

His scholarly works, several of which have won significant awards, include *20th-Century Theology* (coauthored with the late Stanley J. Grenz), *The Story of Christian Theology, The Westminster Handbook to Evangelical Theology, Arminian Theology: Myths and Realities, The Essentials of Christian Thought*, and *The Mosaic of Christian Belief.*

On a popular level, Olson has long been a contributing editor for *Christianity Today*, and he authors a popular *Patheos* blog on his "evangelical Arminian theological musings," where he weaves thoughtful and sometimes quite personal observations about faith and life.

Olson and I met in the hotel where I was staying in Waco, a city of 135,000 along the Brazos River halfway between Dallas and Austin. Waco (named for an Indian tribe) is a vibrant university community that's still trying to live down its reputation for the "Waco siege," in which seventy-four members of the Branch Davidian cult perished in a fire after a fifty-day standoff with federal agents in 1993.

The bespectacled Olson is short (five foot four), an enthusiastic jogger (four days a week) and a weight lifter. He wears his salt-and-pepper hair combed back and sports a trim mustache that's also graying.

Coincidentally, we were born just a few days apart in 1952. He and Becky, married for almost forty-five years, have two daughters, a grandson, and a granddaughter. Olson is active in Calvary Baptist Church, a congregation of the Cooperative Baptist Fellowship.

I was drawn to the fact that Olson has experience in different Christian circles that have varying degrees of openness to God's supernatural activity in today's world. He was a Pentecostal until the age of twenty-five, even teaching for a while at Oral Roberts University. His brief foray into a Presbyterian church gave him a mainline perspective. Later he became a Baptist, serving on the faculty of the mainstream evangelical Bethel College (now Bethel University) in Minnesota, before joining Baylor in 1999.

I figured he would be a good source of wisdom from a variety of relevant perspectives—and I wasn't disappointed.

"As If God Were Not Here"

More than thirty years ago, two respected Christian thinkers—Stanley Hauerwas, professor of theological ethics at the Duke University Divinity School, and William H. Willimon, professor of Christian ministry at Duke—wrote a bracing indictment of mainline Protestant churches in America.

The title of the piece in the *Christian Century* was convicting enough: "Embarrassed by God's Presence."[2] After nearly three pages of largely gentlemanly prose, they were blunt in their bottom-line assessment: "The central problem for our church, its theology, and its ethics is that it is simply atheistic."[3]

Yes, you read that quote correctly. They were accusing mainline churches of conducting their business as if God didn't really matter. "We endow pensions for our clergy and devise strategies for church growth," they wrote, "*as if God were not here.*"[4]

How does this godless presupposition affect the church? "Our Sunday worship is immoral and indifferent (if not rather silly) unless we really believe that God is present in our gathering and in the world, and that our listening to the story, our service to others and our breaking of bread are dangerous attempts to let God be God."[5]

I referenced the article to Olson as he settled into a green couch. "Granted, they were being hyperbolic to make a point," he said. "But the grain of truth in their argument helped raise awareness of the prevailing secularity of modern Western Christianity. I've seen it in some of the churches where I've been active through the years."

"In what way?"

"Years ago, I noticed that churches were tending not to think biblically or theologically about the way they ran their operations.

Decisions seemed secular to me, as if they were being made in the boardroom of a corporation. They'd ask, 'Will this fit into our budget?' regardless of any faith that more funding could come in. They wanted predictability. And fear of lawsuits meant lawyers were gaining more and more say-so in churches and Christian organizations."

"You'd agree with Hauerwas and Willimon, then?"

"In essence, yes, though I might not put it as strongly. The situation varies from one denomination to another, but I agree that American religion in general has become secularized. That is, a lot of churches don't really believe that God intervenes or guides, except through what we might call human wisdom and reason."

I pointed out that American evangelicals like to pride themselves on resisting the secularism of our culture—but Olson wasn't buying it.

"My point is that American evangelical Christianity has accommodated to modernity's rationalism and naturalism," he said. "The truth is, they don't really expect God to do anything except in their interior spiritual lives. They pay lip service to the supernatural, whereas the Bible itself is saturated with it."

"Can you give me an example?" I asked.

"We still hold on to the idea that God can change people, but mostly we mean God will help them turn over a new leaf rather than a radical transformation. When that kind of radical rebirth does happen, we go, 'Wow! We didn't really know that could still occur! I wish it would happen more often.' But then we sink back into not really expecting it to occur again. After all, we don't want to get too fanatical.

"You see," he continued, "there's a certain unpredictability with the Holy Spirit, and we mainstream evangelicals have come to love predictability. We don't want any big surprises. We don't want to open the door to something that will really shock us, because we can't control it."

"And we're a bit afraid of it?"

"We are, absolutely. Many evangelicals are not convinced in the depth of their soul that God is still supernaturally active. They don't make room for that kind of activity in their church or in their life."

"Still," I said, "balance is important."

"True. I've been in churches where the opposite attitude prevailed and people thought miracles were an everyday occurrence. Everything became a miracle. That's another danger too; it takes away the specialness. To me, the book of Acts is the best guide."

I mentally scrolled through Acts, which unfolds the story of the early church. The apostles seemed to go around expecting that when Jesus and his resurrection were proclaimed, something supernatural might very well occur. But that's not true today, Olson said.

"All we expect to happen these days when we proclaim Jesus and the resurrection is that people will nicely nod and say, 'Oh, we agree with that.' Then they go home and live as if that's not really true, because they don't expect miracles to happen anymore. They don't expect God to do things that are inexplicable. It would make their life unpredictable."

"That's a sad perspective for a Christian," I said.

"It should be, yes. But I think a lot of people are happier living with predictability than really expecting that God will do unusual things in their lives. They hear of supernatural activity and miracles happening in Africa, and they say, 'Well, praise God,' but the unsaid part is, *I'm really glad it doesn't happen here. That would be scary. That would be threatening.*"

"Why Are We Whispering?"

Olson's point was clear: whether they recognize it or not, many American evangelicals have relegated the supernatural and miraculous to the past (biblical times) and elsewhere (mission fields) rather than seeing them as an ever-present possibility in their lives.

"This is obvious from the way we react when someone gets sick," he said. "Of course, we pray for them, but what do we ask? That God would comfort them in the midst of their suffering. That God would guide the hands of surgeons. That God would give doctors wisdom and discernment. What's missing?"

"Asking God to supernaturally heal them."

"Precisely," he replied. "The Bible says to pray for their healing, lay hands on them, and anoint them with oil, but mainstream evangelicals tend to look down their noses at churches that do that. They suspect those churches are cultic or discourage ill people to seek medical treatment. What's more, they avoid any mention of demons, and they shun exorcism as primitive and superstitious— unless Jesus did it."

Olson's remarks prompted me to think back to 2012, when Leslie found me unconscious on our bedroom floor. I was rushed by ambulance to the hospital, where a doctor told me after I awoke, "You're one step away from a coma, two steps away from dying."

I was suffering from severe hyponatremia, a precipitous decrease in blood sodium, which was causing my brain cells to absorb water and expand within the restricted confines of my skull. The prognosis if untreated: mental confusion, hallucinations, seizures, coma, and death.

While I underwent urgent treatment for several days, a succession of friends came by to pray for me. Many of them did exactly as Olson said: they prayed for wisdom for the physicians and for my strength—both of which I greatly appreciated—but very few came out and asked God, in a direct, bold, and straightforward way, to supernaturally heal me.[6]

Continued Olson, "A lot of mainstream evangelicals have bought into the notion that 'prayer doesn't change things; it changes me.' They don't realize it, but they're adopting the teachings of Friedrich Schleiermacher, the father of modern theological liberalism, who denigrated petitionary prayer as something that children do because they don't know any better."

Olson mentioned an encounter he had with a Baptist pastor and his wife, who is a medical doctor.

"I was telling them about my own physical healing, even though I'm often reluctant to share that story even with evangelicals because they look skeptical when I do it. Then the pastor lowered his voice and said quietly, 'You know, my daughter was very sick, and I anointed her with oil and prayed fervently for her and she was healed—it was absolutely supernatural.' And I thought, *Why are we whispering?*"

I chuckled. "Seems like he should be shouting about this."

"Well," said Olson, "that illustrates the problem. Then he conceded to me that his church probably wouldn't respond favorably to his story."

"We Are Desperate to Fit In"

I asked Olson if there's one word that could summarize why a lot of evangelical Christians seem embarrassed by the supernatural. He gave it some thought and then said, "Respectability."

"Why that word?" I asked.

"Evangelicals in general are trying to live down our past," he replied. "We're very aware of Hollywood's version of us—the oddball preacher, the phony faith healer, the hyperemotional revivalist, the money-grubbing hypocrite. We want to run from those depictions. We want our neighbors to see us as normal people who are not very different from them. We are desperate to fit in."

"So," I said, "we divorce ourselves from the supernatural, since it seems odd to the world."

"That's right. We want to show that we're cultured and refined, that we're not gullible or superstitious, that we're not like the over-the-top fanatics that our neighbors see on television. In fact," he added, "my experience is that the richer and more educated evangelicals become, the less likely they are to really expect miracles to happen."

"Why is that? Too sophisticated?"

"I could almost predict by the brand of cars in the parking lot what the church believes. The more prosperous and educated we are, the more likely we are to substitute our own cleverness and accomplishments for the power of prayer. That's the seductive power of prosperity—it makes us less reliant on God. We think we've got everything under control."

Then he added an observation that resonated deeply: "Many evangelicals don't really believe in the supernatural until the doctor says, 'You have a terminal illness.'"

I could remember lying in my hospital bed, told that I could be facing death, and suddenly feeling desperately vulnerable and much more dependent on God to rescue me. No question about it— times like that strip away our self-sufficiency and leave us frantic for God's direct supernatural touch.

"Before a moment like that occurs," Olson continued, "many people don't make room in their life for God to do anything supernatural. Oh, sure, they believe in God; they love Jesus. But he's an image much more than a living reality."

Olson's observations spurred me to reflect once more on the national poll that I commissioned for this book. Sure enough, the data shows that the greater a person's education and income, the less likely they believe that God has supernaturally intervened in their life.

Asked if they ever had an experience only explainable as a miracle of God, 41 percent of those with a high school education said yes, compared with 29 percent of college graduates. More than

43 percent of people earning less than fifty thousand dollars a year said they've had such an experience, compared with 29 percent of those with incomes of a hundred thousand dollars or more.

"The richer we get, the more education we attain, the less comfortable we are with the miraculous," Olson said. "We don't feel we need it, really. We're getting along just fine. After all, we're successful."

Trickle-Down Theology

Ever the historian of theology, Olson has a theory about how the evangelical subculture has become more secularized and less open to the supernatural. "I call it the trickle-down theory of theology," he said. "In other words, we're influenced by thinkers in the past who we've never even heard of."

"Do you mean people like Schleiermacher, who you mentioned earlier?"

"Yes, he's the father of liberal theology who died in 1834. He was to Christianity what Copernicus was to astronomy, Newton was to physics, Freud was to psychology, and Darwin was to biology. By that I mean he was *the* trailblazer, the one thinker who subsequent theologians cannot ignore."

Olson went on. "He and Baruch Spinoza were instrumental in the growth of methodological naturalism, which says the proper way to conduct any serious inquiry is to focus on naturalistic explanations to account for a phenomenon, thereby excluding miracles."

"This is the typical worldview of science," I observed.

"Correct, it flourishes in the scientific academy. But Schleiermacher then introduced a naturalistic view of the whole world into the stream of Protestant theology. He said that to believe in miracles is to question God, because it's implying that God didn't know what he was doing when he set up the world as a closed system."

"So he denied the possibility of miracles?" I asked.

"It's very doubtful whether he believed in miracles. He said if one did occur, it must have been part of God's universal plan from the outset and already built into the universe. In other words, it was determined to happen ahead of time. It couldn't be a response to something new that happens, and so it's not really supernatural."

"Did he deny the miracle of the resurrection?"

"Yes, he did. He didn't even believe Jesus was God incarnate in any traditional sense. He tried to make all of Christianity based on experience, but not supernatural experience. So faith is internalized."

"How has this trickled down to churches today?"

"Even in many Baptist churches, by and large, people internalize God and their relationship with him. That means God acts on our consciousness and inner life, but not on the outer world. Inside is where God is at; science can explain everything outside. So religion is reduced to two spheres: spirituality and ethics."

"What's missing?" I asked, knowing full well how he would answer.

"The book of Acts!" he declared. "The supernatural. And this has trickled down to us without us being aware of it. Frankly, most mainline evangelicals don't really miss the miraculous dimension of faith because they grew up without it. They're used to religion focusing primarily on our devotional life, and maybe evangelism and morality."

Though I didn't want to confess it, I said, "I see some of that in my own life."

"Me too," he replied.

"Really?"

"Oh, absolutely."

"How so?"

"I had a deeply profound experience in which God spoke to

me. I didn't audibly hear his voice, but what he told me was crystal clear. It wasn't what I wanted to hear, but I did what he said, and remarkable things happened. Yet when that experience occurred, I was utterly shocked. If I hadn't grown up in a church where it's normal for a Christian to hear from God, I don't know how I would have reacted. I might have said, 'Well, that was just a brain hiccup.'"

I asked, "What about Bible-believing theologians who say miracles have ceased?"

"There are two kinds of cessationists," he explained. "One kind says God no longer offers a spiritual gift of healing; the other kind says miracles themselves have ceased. In other words, once the Bible was written and the early church took root in the Roman Empire, miracles were no longer needed and God stopped doing them."

"What's your reaction to that?"

"Bewilderment. I know miracles have happened to me, so that can't be right. If God is omnipotent—which he is—then it makes sense to me that he's going to continue to act."

Caught by an Angel

Olson's reference to supernatural interventions in his own life prompted me to ask about a physical healing that he received as a child.

"My mother died of heart damage from rheumatic fever at age thirty-two, when I was two and a half years old," he began. "At age ten, I contracted strep throat and was very, very sick. My family believed in God's healing through prayer, and doctors were a last resort, but they took me to an osteopath, who wrote a prescription for penicillin."

"Did it cure your strep throat?"

"It might have, except my stepmother threw the prescription away."

"Wow, seriously?"

"She said, 'I don't think you really need this.' Well, a week later, I developed rheumatic fever, just like my mother. I was sick and in and out of hospitals for three months. Rheumatic fever attacks the valves of your heart; most patients eventually need heart-valve replacement surgery, which didn't exist when my mother died."

"I assume your family and church prayed for you."

"Yes, I remember the elders of the church coming to the house, laying hands on me, anointing me with oil, and praying for me. And this was not a perfunctory prayer. Later I went for my weekly checkup, and the doctor said, 'I don't hear any heart murmur.'"

"You had one before this?"

"Yeah—in fact, the doctor had called it 'impressive.' Now he said, 'I don't hear anything, and your blood test for inflammation is normal.'"

"Was he surprised?"

"Very much so, but he chalked it up to the care I had received. Nevertheless, today I have zero heart-valve damage. I go to the cardiologist every year to check, and he always says the same thing: 'You don't have a rheumatic heart.'"

"You believe that God healed you?"

"Absolutely. I don't know what else to call it."

"Still, it's scary to think of your stepmother throwing away the prescription for the antibiotic that could have averted the rheumatic fever in the first place," I said.

"I don't think the best approach is to say, 'God will heal me, so I'm just going to pray.' Usually God works through natural means. He expects us to make use of the gifts he has provided to us, such as medication and technology. Otherwise, it would be like expecting manna to fall from heaven when there's a grocery store down the block."

I smiled. "That's a good analogy."

"The best approach," he concluded, "is to merge both prayer and medicine."

The congregation of his father's Pentecostal church had no problem accepting Olson's healing as being a miraculous gift from God. For them, the supernatural was an ever-present element in their lives.

"I remember one incident where a little boy in our church, probably ten years old, accidently opened the door and fell out of the family car while it was driving down the road," Olson recalled. "When they rushed to pick him up, they thought he would be dead, but instead he was just standing there. They said, 'What happened?' He said, 'Well, didn't you see the man? He caught me.'"

Olson cleared his throat and then slowly removed his wire-rim glasses. He pulled a handkerchief from his pocket and wiped his eyes.

"I'm a little emotional, because I miss this," he said. "I really do. There's no doubt in my mind that an angel caught him."

He replaced his glasses and continued. "I remember when I was teaching at Oral Roberts University, and my car broke down. I didn't have enough money to fix it. Then a colleague—who had no idea about my car—came to me, gave me a check for five hundred dollars, and said, 'God told me to give this to you.' It was what I needed to fix the car."

I said, "I had a very similar experience, except I was on the giving end of the money."

"Well, to me, this should be normal in the Christian life," he replied, putting the handkerchief back into his pocket. "I've been away from it for so long that sometimes it just hurts."

"This Is Not Our Christianity"

Olson's classes at Baylor attract students from around the globe, including Third World countries where Christianity and its attitude toward the supernatural look quite different than in the United States.

"When these African and Asian students see Western evangelicalism for the first time, what's their assessment?" I asked.

"They have to be coaxed to give it," Olson said. "But when they do, it's total dismay."

"How so?"

"They say, 'This is not our Christianity. Our Christianity in Africa is surrounded by spiritual warfare. We can't brush it off as superstition. God really intervenes and does amazing things, but we don't see that here. We think it's your prosperity, individualism, materialism, and a lack of belief in the spiritual world,' by which they mean the supernatural."

Olson told me about the time he invited a Catholic priest from Nigeria to address his class. "He didn't want to talk about Catholic doctrine," Olson said. "He wanted to talk about miracles. For an hour and twenty minutes, he talked about God's supernatural actions in Nigeria."

"How did the students react?"

"They were in awe. They couldn't believe it."

"Did it light a fire in the students?"

"For sure."

"Some people say the reason miracles proliferate in Africa and other places in the Third World is because that's the leading edge of the gospel," I said.

"Yes, Benjamin Warfield first made that argument in a book called *Counterfeit Miracles* in the early twentieth century," he replied.

"What do you think of that claim?"

His reply was unvarnished. "It's nonsense."

"Really?" I replied.

"We need the supernatural as much as they do in China.

America is still a mission field. I suspect that real Christianity is a minority, even among people who call themselves Christian. Too often, we think we only need apologetics, evidence, debates, and arguments to spread the gospel here rather than to see God do a supernatural work. So Warfield came up with this explanation that miracles don't happen in the enlightened Western societies because we're already Christianized. Well, I respectfully dissent."

I moved on to another reason that many Christians are uncomfortable with the supernatural. "Not all people who are prayed for recover their health," I said. "Maybe that's a reason why our churches don't pursue those prayers—they don't want to be embarrassed if an answer doesn't come. How do we explain it when God *doesn't* heal someone?"

"We don't," came his response. "I believe God is sovereign and not arbitrary. He knows what he's doing. When he doesn't answer our prayers as we want, there may be particularities about the situation that we just don't understand. The apostle Paul talks about having a thorn in the flesh that God never healed despite prayers."

I noted that it's common in some Pentecostal circles to blame the patient's lack of faith for why God didn't heal them.

"That's simply harmful," he said. "When my mother died, a woman who had been associated with a healing evangelist told my father that it was because my parents didn't follow God's call to the mission field."

"Yikes, that's harsh," I said.

"Fortunately, my dad shrugged it off and said, 'That's nuts.' But those kinds of ill-informed statements can be very hurtful. We have to move away from trying to explain why a particular individual wasn't healed. That's God's business. All we know is that he asked us to pray for their healing, and we have to be obedient."

"That can be challenging," I said.

"Yes," he replied. "But let's face it: the Christian life is a challenge."

Gentle Whispers of God

Not all miracles are spectacular healings of incurable diseases. Not every supernatural intervention is as earth-shattering as someone rising from the dead. More often, God speaks in gentle whispers, or he orchestrates everyday events in a way that sends a message of encouragement, correction, or hope to someone who desperately needs it.

Many Christians experience these subtle and inaudible "leadings" or "impressions" from God, but they're often reluctant to talk about them for fear of the skeptical reaction they'll receive—and so they keep quiet, embarrassed by the supernatural.

Why did my friend Bill Hybels, the influential leader of Willow Creek Community Church outside Chicago, wait thirty-five years before writing a book about these Holy Spirit nudgings? "Because of the controversy this subject tends to arouse," he explained.[7]

"When I make public reference to the whispers of God, I barely make it off the stage before half a dozen people approach to remind me that ax murderers often defend their homicides by claiming, 'God told me to do it,'" Hybels said. "Conservative Christians question my orthodoxy when I describe my experiences . . . and secularists either are humored or quietly tell their spouses that Hybels has lost his marbles. Or both."[8]

Yet Hybels has found that these subtle but very real communications from our transcendent God are among the most exhilarating aspects of the Christian life.

"Without a hint of exaggeration," he said, "I can boldly declare that God's low-volume whispers have saved me from a life of sure boredom and self-destruction. They have redirected my path, rescued me from temptations, and reenergized me during some of my deepest moments of despair. They inspire me to live my life at what boaters call 'wide-open throttle'—full on!"[9]

When I asked Olson for his opinion about whether God still speaks to his followers, his answer was quick and unabashed. "No question," he said. "I continue to believe that God speaks to his people today, although I'll concede that sometimes I find myself feeling pretty alone on this."

In one of his blog posts, Olson described how he walked away from a medical examination deeply troubled and discouraged. The doctor had found a problem and raised the specter that surgery might be required.

The next day, an old hymn began running through Olson's mind, even though he hadn't heard the song since childhood. The words kept playing over and over, like a broken record, serving as background noise all week.

"It's a hymn of comfort and assurance—of God's presence whatever happens," he said. "Being a good Baptist, I simply thought it was my own mind's way of handling the emotional distress I was experiencing."

That Sunday, Olson went to his wife's church, where he noticed that the first hymn to be sung was #220, which was "Crown Him with Many Crowns." Olson reached for the hymnal from the rack in front of him and turned to #220—but that wasn't the song he found there. Instead, he found the hymn that had been running through his mind all week.

"Then I noticed that the hymnal I grabbed was not the church's hymnal, which doesn't even contain that hymn," he wrote. "It even had a different church's name embossed in gold letters on the front. I have never seen that hymnal before; it didn't belong there. I have no idea how it got there."

Indeed, it was the only one of those hymnals in the sanctuary—and it just happened to be in the rack directly in front of where Olson sat down.

"So, what to make of that?" Olson asked. "Sheer coincidence? Possibly. Is it simply magical thinking to believe this was God sending me a message that the hymn was from him? Possibly. My Baptist half says, 'It's just a coincidence; don't make more of it.' My Pentecostal half says, 'That's unbelief; accept it as from God.'"

Often Christians object to the legitimacy of these "God things" because they say people don't need God to speak anymore. After all, they insist, the canon of Scripture is complete, and today God chooses to speak through preachers to communicate messages based on those biblical teachings.

"Personally, I find that absurd," Olson said. "If God was gracious enough to give personal guidance, comfort, and correction to individuals and groups 'back then,' why would he stop?"

The idea that God now only uses pastors to communicate his messages "is hardly consistent with Baptist belief in the priesthood of believers," Olson said. "It's a form of clericalism."

He did add cautions. "By God speaking outside of Scripture today, I do not mean with the same inspiration and authority as in Scripture," he said. "Everything must be tested against the Bible to determine its validity."

While Olson is aware that skeptics label these "God things" as "magical thinking," what troubles him is that many Christians have the same attitude. "They pay lip service to God's contemporary 'speaking,' but immediately turn around and, when confronted with an example, call it magical thinking."

Regarding the hymnal incident, Olson said, "I can't state with certainty that what happened to me was truly a 'God thing.' Maybe it was; maybe it wasn't. Maybe it was just a very strange coincidence. I believe coincidences happen, but some are just too coincidental not to stop and consider whether they are more."

He capped his thoughts with a question worth pondering: "If there is a God who cares not only *about* us but *for* us, why *wouldn't* he do such things?"

Like Olson, Hybels, and many others, I believe he does do "God things" like that—even to the point of dispatching an angel in a dream to assure a spiritually confused youngster that someday he would understand his amazing grace.

Something to celebrate, I'd say—rather than feel embarrassed about.

CHAPTER 13

When Miracles *Don't* Happen

An Interview with Dr. Douglas R. Groothuis

Every day my wife, Leslie, is in pain. When traditional medical treatments failed, she tried acupuncture, deep massage, diet supplements, and other alternative therapies. While some brought temporary relief, none of them stopped the chronic muscle throbbing that assaults her over and over again.

There is no known cure for fibromyalgia, a neurobiological disorder that affects the way pain signals are processed in the central nervous system. And so year after year, decade after decade, she copes as best she can with the discomfort, the soreness, the aching.

Let me tell you something else about Leslie: she is a wholly devoted follower of Jesus, a woman of prayer and spiritual depth whose persistent intercession with God was, in my view, the most influential factor in bringing me to faith in Christ. She devours the Bible daily; she consumes a steady diet of Christian resources; and her compassion for the hurting and spiritually confused is boundless. She is simply the finest and most devout person I have ever known.

Have we prayed for relief from her pain? *Continually.* Have we beseeched God for her healing? *Often and fervently.* Have we seen any improvement? *Quite the opposite.*

Could I give you half a dozen theological reasons that there's suffering in this sin-scarred world? Absolutely. I'm a Christian apologist who gives lectures on that topic. But this is *my* Leslie. This is *my* wife. This is *her* pain and suffering. And that makes this starkly personal.

While researching this book, I came across inspiring examples of how God miraculously restored sight to the blind, hearing to the deaf, and life to the deceased. I vicariously celebrated with each recipient of God's tangible expression of grace.

But after I wrote each story, I asked, *Why no miracle for Leslie?* Yes, I know God promises to cause good to emerge from our suffering if we're devoted to him. *But why no miracle for Leslie?* Yes, I understand that suffering produces perseverance and sharpens our character. *But why no miracle for Leslie?* Yes, I am aware that there will be no more tears in heaven. *But why no miracle for Leslie?* Every day my wife is in pain. She needs a miracle.

When Michael Shermer described how prayers for his paralyzed girlfriend seemed to rise unheard into the ether, I could empathize with his lament. Although my faith endures, I can understand why his waned. Maybe you can too, because you've been imploring God to meet an urgent need in your life—with no miracle forthcoming.

This chapter is for you—and Leslie and Michael. And me.

✧   ✧   ✧

Sometimes Leslie experiences "fibro fog," a mental cloudiness or forgetfulness that's endemic with fibromyalgia sufferers. That's what my friend Douglas Groothuis thought was happening with his wife, Rebecca, who had been diagnosed with fibromyalgia several years earlier.

Then one day, she went to the same beauty salon where she had been going for years—but she couldn't find her way home. Becky was missing for several hours; Doug finally had to seek help from the police. Clearly, this went beyond mere absentmindedness.

Thus began a descent into dementia for Becky, who was later diagnosed with a progressive, incurable, and invariably fatal brain disease. In a dark irony, this onetime Mensa member who wrote and edited books with such elegance and flair now struggles to find the right word for common household objects.

Humanly speaking, there is no hope. Death is as certain as the slow and inevitable deterioration of her ability to speak, to think, to plan, and to perform the simplest of tasks. So as committed Christians, Doug and Becky have earnestly sought divine help— and yet, all the while, she continues to gradually lose her mind.

The Interview with Douglas R. Groothuis, PhD

Groothuis (pronounced GRŌTE-hice) grew up as an only child in Alaska. His father, an activist in the labor movement, died in an airplane crash when Groothuis was eleven. That tragedy was formative in a lot of ways, contributing to his drive for achievement, as he tried to earn the acceptance of a father who was no longer in his life, and fueling his naturally melancholy temperament. He found solace in books and became an aficionado of jazz music.

His original goal of becoming a journalist was thwarted when he failed a typing test in college, unable to peck out twenty-five words a minute on a manual typewriter. He soon found that his inquisitive personality, his passion for learning, and his attraction to deep issues gave him a flair for philosophy.

Although taught as a youngster to believe in God, he began delving into Eastern mysticism when he attended the University of Northern Colorado in Greeley. His brief foray into atheism was stymied every time he would look at the grandeur of the Rocky

Mountains. Finally, through some Christians he encountered and books he read, including *The Sickness unto Death* by Danish philosopher Søren Kierkegaard, he came to faith in Christ and was baptized at age nineteen.

Groothuis went on to earn his doctorate in philosophy at the University of Oregon, while retaining a journalist's taut writing style. He served as a campus pastor for a dozen years before joining the faculty of Denver Seminary in 1993.

Since then he has published thirteen books, including *Unmasking the New Age, Deceived by the Light, Truth Decay, The Soul in Cyberspace, Jesus in the Age of Controversy,* and *Philosophy in Seven Sentences.* His 752-page *Christian Apologetics* is a comprehensive and lucidly written survey of the evidence for Christian theism. His interests are truly encyclopedic—from history, psychology, and sociology to art, poetry, and theology.

Along the way, he has taught at a secular college, debated atheists, and contributed to such books as *The History of Science and Religion in the Western Tradition* and *The Encyclopedia of Empiricism.* For years, he blogged under the banner *The Constructive Curmudgeon,* whose title was a nod to both his melancholic personality and his deft sense of humor. (He quipped, "I once read a book called *Against Happiness*—and I enjoyed it.")

And then there's the book he never wanted to write. His crushingly honest memoir *Walking through Twilight* chronicles his wife Becky's affliction with primary progressive aphasia.[1] This memoir is, without exaggeration, a masterpiece.

"This is a hard book to read—like watching the news and learning about war, poverty, and famine," said Kelly M. Kapic, professor of theological studies at Covenant College. "We would rather look away, ignore, and pretend." And philosopher J. P. Moreland said he had never read a book like this. "There are no cheap Christian slogans, no slapping of a Bible verse as a Band-Aid on a near-mortal wound, no simplistic happily-ever-after," he wrote. "But there is hope. Hope built on deep reflection about Christianity, suffering, and the meaning of life."

Groothuis, approaching his sixtieth birthday and wearing an unruly beard, had not yet written this book when we met for an interview in his cramped and book-lined office in Littleton, Colorado.

In fact, I later learned that he nearly canceled our meeting because of the difficulty of talking about what he and his spouse were going through. But he agreed to proceed if it might benefit others who are also waiting—apparently in vain—for a miracle to rescue them from their own painful plight.

The Post-Hume Era

Dressed casually as if for a morning stroll, Groothuis turned around in his office chair to face me. He looks young for his age, though some lines are freshly etched on his face. His brown hair looked like it had been combed with his fingers.

I began our discussion by noting that he is coeditor of the scholarly book *In Defense of Natural Theology: A Post-Humean Assessment,*[2] which systematically dismantles David Hume's arguments against God and miracles—a case that Michael Shermer considered a "knockdown" of Christianity.

"Hume's arguments were long considered sacrosanct and impenetrable, but the tide shifted in recent years due to the vigorous resurgence of Christian philosophy," Groothuis told me. "The solvent of critical thinking and affirmative evidence for theism has pretty much dissolved Hume's case. Personally, I find his arguments unconvincing. His criticisms end up either begging the question or not carefully considering the New Testament evidence."

"So it's rational to believe in miracles?" I asked.

"Yes," he replied. "When you consider the strong evidence for a creator and designer—for instance, the cosmological and fine-tuning arguments—then miracles are certainly possible. Beyond that, you can look at the compelling historical evidence for miracle claims and see that miraculous events are actual. If there's a supernatural Creator, then certainly he could intervene in history—and Christianity sticks out its neck by basing everything on the miraculous resurrection of Jesus."

"Speaking of the resurrection, this miracle brings hope to those who are going through suffering," I observed. "A philosopher once told me that if God can take the very worst thing that could ever happen in the universe—the death of his Son on a cross—and turn it into the very best thing ever to happen in the universe—the opening of heaven for all who follow him—then he is able to take our difficult circumstances and draw good from them."[3]

"There's truth to that. I often go back to Genesis 50:20, where Joseph says to his brothers who betrayed him, 'You intended to harm me, but God intended it for good.' We may not know what good God is achieving in the short run, but given the credibility of Christianity and my forty years of experience as a Christian, I am justified in believing there can be significance and purpose in suffering."

"Yet," I said, "often that's small comfort in the midst of our pain."

"We can't read the mind of God," came his reply. "We're not privy to why he chooses to work a miracle in some cases and not others. Yes, it can be agonizing when you've prayed and fasted for the healing of a loved one and God seems to have said no or to wait until eternity."

And that brought us to Becky.

The Story of Rebecca

"Tell me about Rebecca," I said. "Where did you meet?"

"We were both in our late twenties and part of a campus ministry in Eugene, Oregon. She was a writer and an editor, and I was a campus minister."

"How would you describe her?"

"Serious, maybe a bit melancholic like me. Shy, sharp, bookish, insightful, an excellent sense of humor, attractive. A pianist and singer. We were interested in the same things, especially apologetics and the relationship of Christianity to culture and art."

"She was especially good with words," I commented, having perused some of her writing. Through the years, she wrote and edited several books on marriage and gender issues, including *The Feminist Bogeywoman*; *Women Caught in the Conflict: The Culture War between Traditionalism and Feminism*; *Discovering Biblical Equality*; and *Good News for Women: A Biblical Picture of Gender Equality*.

"Absolutely, she was an elegant writer and a sharp editor. I remember she marked one short paragraph in an article I was writing and wrote in the margin, 'One grammatical error and two clichés.'" The memory prompted a smile. "That was the worst I ever got, though. But she always improved what I wrote."

"What did she add?"

"Clarity. The perfect word. The right turn of a phrase. She loved language. She could write magnificent sentences that flowed for sixty words or more."

"How long after you met did you get married?"

"Only about a year."

"And how much later did the health problems emerge?"

"She was in her thirties when she was diagnosed with fibromyalgia," he replied. "It was a fairly new diagnosis back then—some doctors didn't know what to make of it. We tried alternate therapies, but nothing helped very much."

I nodded, having gone through the same process with Leslie, starting in the days when skeptical doctors thought the illness was more psychological than physical.

"Over time," he continued, "she began experiencing forgetfulness and confusion. At that point, we didn't know if it was the early stages of dementia or what. The most troubling event was when she went to the hair salon—which she had visited dozens of times—and couldn't find her way home. I had to file a missing person report with the police. It was a horrible evening."

"Were there other episodes like that?"

"She went to the dentist, and when she got in the car afterward, she didn't know how to start it. I went and found that the car had been in gear. She once asked me, 'How do you work the windshield wipers on our car?' At that point, we had owned that car for ten years. She had increasing difficulty working on the computer—in fact, I bought her a new one that was simpler to use, but she never figured it out. I ended up giving it away.

"We thought that all of this was fibro fog, but it was getting worse. A neurologist believed it was depression mimicking dementia and treated her for a year, but there was no improvement. In fact, she got worse."

Sliding into Dementia

Then the day after Valentine's Day in 2014, Groothuis rushed Becky to the emergency room for acute depression. "She basically couldn't get out of bed. She couldn't talk," he said, pursing his lips at the recollection. "The psychiatrist put her in the behavioral health unit of a hospital across town. They strapped her down and took her away on a stretcher—she looked so forlorn."

"How long was she hospitalized?"

"Five weeks in total. I visited her virtually every day. It was incredibly sad to see her in that psychiatric unit, wandering aimlessly, muddled and confused. At the end, she wasn't even able to sign the release papers. They diagnosed her with primary progressive aphasia."

"I've never heard of that," I said.

"It's pretty rare. Aphasia is the difficulty in finding words, especially nouns—tragic because of her love of language," he said. "Just this morning, she came downstairs upset because she couldn't find a hairbrush and she couldn't think of the word for it. She would gesture and point to her hair. I said, 'Hairbrush?' She said, 'Yes.' The other day she didn't know what the telephone was or how to work it."

"The condition is progressive, is that right?"

"Yes, it begins in the frontal lobe of the brain and moves backward, which is the opposite of Alzheimer's. You lose your use of words and then your executive functions—the ability to analyze and perform tasks. The particular cruelty of this disease is that you slowly lose your mind—and you're aware of it slipping away."

"I'm so sorry," was all I could muster.

Groothuis acknowledged my sympathy with a nod and then continued. "Alzheimer's patients can generally speak to the end, even though they might not know what they're saying. But with this illness, words fail from the beginning. Typically, people die within five to ten years of onset."

"So day by day, you're seeing deterioration," I said.

"Unfortunately, yes. Now we have a caretaker who lives with us; she and Becky live upstairs in our house. Becky can still tie her shoelaces, since that's an automatic function, but many times her shoes are on the wrong feet. For the most part, I can figure out what she's trying to say, and I find myself completing her sentences. When she's upset, though, she can be unintelligible. It's so unnatural that this woman who adored language no longer has a single book in her bedroom."

I didn't know how to respond. Sadness settled like a dark cloud. For a few moments, Groothuis didn't speak. When he resumed, his voice tender, he said, "I always marveled at her mind. She was smarter than I am. I remember cleaning out some papers and finding her membership card from Mensa, the society for certified geniuses. I held it—and I cried. Her signature at the bottom was in her beautiful handwriting—but today, she can't write a word. She doesn't know how to use a pen."

"We live in a disposable society, where divorce is common," I said. "Yet you have maintained your Christian commitment in a way that's countercultural."

He shrugged. "I guess it is. But I'm no hero. The decision to stay married and to be supportive of my wife was settled when we exchanged our wedding vows—for better, for worse, in sickness and in health. Of course, that turned out to be more profound than either of us thought."

The Marks of Tears

I've known Groothuis for many years, and so I felt the liberty to be candid. "You look exhausted," I said to him.

"I *am* exhausted," he said. "This is a daily struggle. Many years ago, a colleague's wife was suffering from cancer, and she said to him, 'I didn't know the human body could bear so much pain.' Well, I didn't know a soul could endure so much emotional anguish. I'm becoming an expert on suffering." With a weak smile, he added, "I wish God had picked someone else."

"As a philosopher, though, you're uniquely equipped to reflect on many of the deep issues all of this raises," I said.

"On the intellectual level, I suppose that's true," he replied. "But much of what we're going through is just visceral. I've never cried so much as I have in the last few years. Even in public. Sometimes when my glasses are smudged, I take them off and see that they're the marks of tears.

"One day Becky and I were lounging on the bed, just enjoying some quiet moments together, and I started to weep. I was feeling melancholy over what we've lost. She said to me, quite sweetly, 'Tell me what's wrong.' I said, 'It is everything.' She laughed a little, but it seemed appropriate—an acknowledgment that, yes, *everything* was an apt word. This dementia has spread its tentacles to every aspect of our life."

"When Becky despairs, what do you say to her?"

"What can I say? I can't tell her it's going to get better in this life. That wouldn't be honest, and we're committed to avoiding clichés and too-easy answers," he replied. "So I tell her to take it one day at a time, to look for the good things in life, to remember that God loves her. I say, 'Think of the future, of the world without tears, without a curse, when you'll have a perfect resurrection body and you'll be face-to-face with God.'"

"Does that help her?"

"It does. In fact, just this morning I said to her, 'In the long run, everything will be all right.' She asked, 'What do you mean?' I said, 'The new heaven and the new earth.'"

"How did she respond?"

"Big smile. We have hope, but it's deferred," he replied. "Recently Becky and I were having dinner, and I felt moved to offer a toast."

"A toast?" I said. "To what?"

"To the source of our hope," he said. "To the afterlife."

To Lament but Not Sin

"How has all of this affected your relationship with God?" I asked.

He exhaled deeply. "I've learned to lament," he said. "Sixty of the psalms are laments. There's lament in Ecclesiastes and Job. Jesus laments over the unbelief of Jerusalem. On the cross, his lament came as the cry, 'My God, my God, why have you forsaken me?'[4] If Jesus can lament and not sin, then I suppose we can. And just as his lament was answered by his resurrection, so ours will be too.

"Look—God's good world has been broken by sin, and it's morally and spiritually right to lament the loss of a true good. I'm grateful for the lament we see in Scripture—it's God helping us learn how to suffer well."

"Suffer well?" I echoed. "Sounds oxymoronic."

"That phrase can take people aback. They say, 'Suffering can't be done well; it's bad.' No, you can suffer well when you admit your grief, when you pray despite not feeling like you want to, when you're honest with God, and when you don't paper over your emotions."

"That's messy, no doubt."

"Very. And I haven't always suffered well. I've gone over the line at times. I've told God that I hated him for what was happening. That was a heartfelt expression of my grief at the time, but I don't want to impugn God. He, too, bears scars—the scars of your sins and mine. Jesus suffered far more than you and I ever will.

"I never questioned whether God exists, but I confess that there were times when I questioned his goodness. There's a book called *Hating God*, in which Bernard Schweizer named a new religion—*misotheism*.[5] These are people who admit God exists, but they hate him and refuse to worship him. Ivan in *The Brothers Karamazov* is a misotheist, who expounds his hatred for God after recounting case after case of human suffering."

"How do you get beyond those emotions?"

"In the end, I know too much to think that God isn't perfectly good," he replied. "I'm grateful he allows us to vent our frustration. Read Ecclesiastes or the psalms of lament—they are startlingly honest. For me, I found that there's a practice that helps put everything into perspective."

"What's that?"

"When I'm angry at God, when I'm distressed and anguished and seething at my circumstances, I think of Christ hanging on the cross for me. This brings me back to spiritual sanity. He endured the torture of the crucifixion out of his love for me. He didn't have to do that. He chose to. So he doesn't just sympathize with us in our suffering; he empathizes with us. Ultimately, I find comfort in that."

"As a philosopher, you're accustomed to giving intellectual answers when people ask why there's suffering in the world," I said. "If you were to step back and offer a strictly cerebral response to someone in your situation, what would you say?"

"I look at it in terms of the worldview possibilities," he replied. "Atheism doesn't give a sufficient answer—under that philosophy, the world is meaningless and there's no purpose for life. Islam believes in a personal God, but not in a savior. Pantheism doesn't have a God who cares about the plight of people.

"Compare Jesus with Buddha. The first of the four noble truths of Buddhism is suffering. It's not that there is suffering in a good world, but life *is* suffering. The Buddha's answer is to escape the world and enter nirvana through a change of consciousness—to depersonalize yourself and sort of float out of the world. There's no resurrection, no redemption, no savior.

"Christianity is so different. Think of Jesus at the tomb of Lazarus. Jesus weeps; he identifies with the suffering of Lazarus's sisters. They're angry—'Why, Jesus, didn't you come earlier? You could have healed him, and he wouldn't have died.' That's pretty impious, but what does Jesus do? He restores Lazarus to life.[6] For us, the message is clear: there is a future; there is hope; there is resurrection; there will be a new body in a world without tears."

"Still," I said, "evil is a challenge for Christianity too, because God is all-good and all-powerful, and yet there's so much suffering."

"Christianity has the best explanation for evil and suffering because of the fall of humanity. Ever since then, the world has been plagued by death, decay, and disappointment. But because Christ experienced the worst of the world and triumphed over it and is now at the right hand of the Father, I know there will be a resurrection, and my wife and I will live in the new heaven and the new earth. Granted, God has not dealt with suffering and evil completely, but we have the assurance that he *will*. You see, there's a difference between meaningless suffering and inscrutable suffering."

"What's that?"

"*Meaningless suffering* means that suffering is simply there. It doesn't achieve a greater good; it has no purpose. *Inscrutable suffering* means we don't know what the purpose is, but we have reason to believe that God is providential, loving, and all-powerful. Our suffering may seem meaningless to us, but it's not. Here's the point: God uses evil to produce a greater good that could not be achieved otherwise—though we may not understand how, given our finite intelligence and our fallible nature.

"In other words, we have a framework of knowledge about the truth of Christianity, but within that framework are pockets of ignorance. God is infinite and unlimited in power and knowledge and wisdom, and we are not. We should expect that certain things will be obscure for us."

The Prayer of Relinquishment

"Do you still pray for a miracle?" I asked. "Do you continue to ask God to supernaturally heal Becky?"

"For a long time, we prayed and fasted and prayed some more. We sought out those gifted in healing and spiritual deliverance. We read all the books on healing and tried to follow their advice. But these days, I only pray for a miracle every once in a while. Sometimes I come up behind Becky when she's eating and hug her. I touch her head and I ask, 'God, will you go in there and fix this?' Part of her brain is dying, and it's terrible. But, no, I don't pray for a miracle much anymore."

To be frank, that surprised me. "Then what do you pray for?"

"I pray for wisdom in dealing with all the complications of being a caretaker. I pray for her spiritual well-being and for ways to give her some meaning and happiness."

"So you've lost hope of a healing?" I asked.

"There's a verse in Ecclesiastes that says there's a time to give up.[7] After we got the diagnosis, I didn't give up on God, I didn't give up on Becky, but after a while, I essentially gave up on her being healed. We dropped all the exotic remedies and alternative doctors and I've tried to support her as best we can for this sad journey. The Swiss psychiatrist Paul Tournier said that wisdom is knowing when to resist and when to surrender."[8]

"Were you tempted to give up on Christianity?"

"No, I think of the time when some disciples departed from Jesus because of his hard teachings, and he asked the Twelve, 'You do not want to leave too, do you?' Peter said, 'Lord, to whom shall we go? You have the words of eternal life.'[9] I'm not sure Peter understood Jesus' teaching that day, but he trusted him because of his character and miracles. I ponder that a lot. I know too much to turn back from being a Christian. It's like the words in that old hymn, 'I have decided to follow Jesus; no turning back, no turning back.'"

"Do you feel like if you were God, you would definitely heal Becky?"

"That's fallacious thinking. God is perfect, and he acts accordingly. If I were God, I'd be perfect—and therefore I'd act in the very same way he does. We might not understand why he does what he does, but it's folly to think we'd do things better."

I scratched my head. "It's vexing, though, that God performs healings in some circumstances but not others."

"Yes. You feel lonely. You feel empty. But God gets the glory one way or the other. He gets the glory when somebody is miraculously healed, and he also gets the glory when someone develops faithfulness and character through suffering."

"But shouldn't we *always* be praying for God's miraculous intervention?" I asked. "To give up seems . . ." I searched for the right word, not wanting to sound harsh. "Well, it seems a little . . . unspiritual."

To my relief, he wasn't offended. "Not at all," he said. "Remember, I'm not giving up on my faith. I'm not walking away from God. I'm not leaving Becky, and I'm not abandoning hope. But sometimes the most appropriate step when your pleas for healing aren't being answered is to pray a prayer of relinquishment."

Catherine Marshall talks about this species of prayer in her book *Adventures in Prayer*. "There is a crucial difference here between *acceptance* and *resignation*," she writes. "There is no resignation in the Prayer of Relinquishment. Resignation says, 'This is my situation, and I resign myself and settle down to it.' Resignation lies down in the dust of a godless universe and steels itself for the worst. Acceptance says, 'True, this is my situation at the moment. I'll look unblinkingly at the reality of it. But I'll also open my hands to accept willingly whatever a loving Father sends.' Thus acceptance never slams the door on hope."[10]

Said Groothuis, "At Gethsemane, Jesus asked the Father to rescue him from the fate of the cross, but his final prayer was one of relinquishment. He surrendered when he could have escaped. He put himself totally in his Father's hands—whatever his Father had in store for him was what he wanted for himself. And when healing isn't coming, sometimes we have to say, 'Lord, whatever you have in store for me is what I want,' as difficult as that might be at the time. In a sense, it's a prayer of obedience, of submission, of trust, of faith."

I later learned that in the prayer that Marshall models, she suggests confessing if we've had a demanding attitude or elevated our personal desires to the point of idolatry or tried to manipulate or bargain with God to do our bidding. "I want to trust you, Father," she prays. "My spirit knows that these verities are forever trustworthy even when I *feel* nothing: that you are there . . . that you love me . . . that you alone know what is best for me. . . . So now, by an act of my will, I relinquish this to you. I will accept your will, whatever that may be."[11]

I asked Groothuis, "How has praying a prayer of relinquishment changed your attitude toward healing?"

He reflected for a minute, stroking his beard. "Rather than feeling like I'm always beating God with my fists," he said, "now I feel more like I'm resting in his arms."

I asked, "When you hear stories of other people being healed, how does that make you feel? Joyful? Jealous?"

"Honestly, both. I try to rejoice with those who experience a miracle, but it's hard not to say, 'Why not Becky?' But I don't comprehend all of God's ways. God never gave Job a specific reason for why he allowed his suffering; instead, he revealed his own greatness and power and asked Job to trust him in that light. The best I can do is trust in God's love and faithfulness—and, as far as I'm able, to smelt meaning out of suffering."

A Hope Well Placed

By definition, miracles are outside the normal course of events. They're a supernatural exception to the way the world usually works. Though they're more common than we may think, they're still relatively rare—which means that for most people, a sudden and complete healing isn't going to happen. But that doesn't mean God is absent. It doesn't imply that we are cast adrift to face our struggles on our own.

"There's a line we should walk," said Groothuis. "We shouldn't be Pollyannaish. We shouldn't blithely pretend everything's okay when it isn't. If someone asks how I'm doing, I don't answer with a smile, 'Dementia is consuming Becky, but no big deal—God will fix her eventually.' That's not being authentic. That's not allowing for grief. That's not giving space for lament.

"On the other hand, God *will* fix her eventually. And Scripture promises in Romans 8:28 that God can—and will—cause good to emerge from the difficulties of life, if we're faithful to him. That sounds like a cliché because at times that verse is casually tossed around in a flippant way. Yes, it's difficult in the midst of our circumstances to *feel* that, but let's not forget something."

"Like what?"

"That it's true!" he declared. "In this world or the next, in one way or another, I do have faith that God will bring some good out of Becky's tragic circumstances. The apostle Paul knew that hope is refined through tribulation.[12] Jesus said, 'Blessed are those who mourn,'[13] so I know that God will lift up those who suffer. I trust that what is to come will be better than what is now."

"So our hope is well placed," I said.

"Absolutely. Time after time, when I begin to lose sight of that, I go back to apologetics—to the clear and compelling reasons to have confidence that God exists, that Jesus is his unique Son, that the resurrection actually occurred, and therefore his promises to us—promises of hope and eventual healing—are true. I look back over decades of my own personal experiences with God, and I can see how he has blessed me in so many ways.

"Although it has been hard, God has allowed me to see the world through tears, which is maybe the most authentic way to experience it. Mourning has taught me lessons I would never have learned otherwise."

I glanced around his office, which was bursting with books. There on Colorado's Front Range, overlooking the magnificent Rocky Mountains, Groothuis still stands in the classroom, teaching the next generation of church leaders how to love God with all their heart, with all their soul, with all their strength—and, yes, with all their mind too.[14]

His considerable reservoir of knowledge is now topped off with life experiences nobody would wish for themselves, but which have given him new depth, new understanding, new empathy. Unable to rescue Becky, Groothuis has invited God to refine *him*.

"This campus is so beautiful," I said. "I can imagine you walking to class and someone calling out, 'Hey, Professor Groothuis, how are you doing?' What would you tell them?"

"Well, of course, I'd tell them the truth."

"Which is . . . ?"

"That I'm hanging by a thread," he said. "But, fortunately, the thread is knit by God."

Reaching Your Verdict

Adrian Holloway felt trepidation. No, make that *reluctance*. He was standing in front of more than four thousand people in a British stadium. For the first time, he was going to offer a public prayer asking God to heal the sick.

Like mine, Holloway's background was in journalism, where he honed a skeptical outlook. He came to faith as a teenager, and when he was later challenged by doubters, he used his history degree from the University of Durham to fully satisfy himself that the resurrection of Jesus rests on solid ground.

After a successful career covering soccer matches for newspapers, radio, and television, he left it all to spend his life spreading Christ's message of hope and grace throughout his native England and beyond.

But publicly praying for healings? He wasn't comfortable doing that. His faith was more cerebral than emotional. Besides, surely God would want a purer, holier vessel than him for such a sacred task. And what if nobody was healed? If they were already ill, this might bring even further disappointment. He couldn't bear that thought.

Sure, he had scoured the Scriptures to assure himself that God is still active in healing the afflicted. But that was a theological exercise. Now, here was the real thing.

The scene was a soccer stadium called Meadow Lane in Nottingham. It was the middle of the summer in 2005. Spiritually curious people had come to hear Holloway talk about what happens *after* people die, and he certainly felt confident explaining what the Bible says about that—sin, redemption, forgiveness, eternity. But praying for God to heal people *before* heaven? He had never done that in a setting like this. Yes, *reluctance* would be a good description of his demeanor.

He drew a breath. He offered the prayer. At the end, he said, "If you've been healed, come and tell us." With that out of the way, he went on to his evangelistic talk. "I had no idea what would happen," he told me.

Instantly in the crowd, something did happen to a sixteen-year-old girl named Abbi. She knew she had been healed. For a decade, she had suffered from a life-threatening allergy to a protein that would spark anaphylactic shock if she ate an apple or touched rubber. Three times she had to be resuscitated at the hospital. She took medication daily and carried an emergency response kit wherever she went. Her life was severely inhibited, typically anchoring her to home.

Abbi was so confident of her instant healing that she immediately put a latex wristband on her forearm. No reaction. She ate a slice of her cousin's apple. No reaction. Frantic, her disapproving friends stood ready to call an ambulance if needed.

At the conclusion of the event, Abbi came onto the stage, carrying two of her syringes and an apple. As far as anyone could tell, she had been immediately and totally healed.

This was not some adrenaline-driven emotional response that would fade; a year later she would report, "I am totally well now. I haven't had a single hive, a single itch, a single tingle. Nothing . . . I am Abbi. I am not the girl with the allergy. I'm free."

And so, in a sense, was Holloway. From that time forward, he felt freed to offer prayers of healing wherever he went. God has answered many times.

There's Annie, whose heart condition called postural orthostatic tachycardia syndrome caused her to suffer fainting spells, and who burst into tears as her symptoms instantly disappeared after she received prayer in the name of Jesus. Medical tests confirmed the healing; a year passed and she was still well—and by then pregnant. "I'm a completely different person now!" she exclaimed.

Hannah lacked any hearing in one ear since birth; she was as profoundly deaf in that ear as doctors had ever seen. After prayer, there was complete and spontaneous healing; said the audiologist later, "To go from being absolutely deaf to perfect hearing is something that cannot be explained."

Edie was confined to a wheelchair for fifteen years from multiple sclerosis, couldn't speak without mechanical assistance, and needed around-the-clock medical care, yet she was restored to health after prayer. Holloway has a letter from her physician: "I was astonished at her recovery, which appears to be full and unexplained."

The examples go on and on. Holloway checks out stories as best he can, confirming the character of the person, obtaining medical documentation when available, and recording people's accounts on video.

"My main take-away is—*Wow!*" Holloway exuded in a conversation with me. "*This* is the power of God."

"How has this experience changed your life?" I asked.

He thought for a moment. "It has strengthened my confidence in the integrity and reliability of the Bible and God's willingness to act today," he replied. "It shows God's compassion—this is immediate evidence of his care for the person he has just healed. And over and over he has used these demonstrations of his power to open hearts to the gospel."

Holloway has reached his verdict in the case for miracles: God is still supernaturally restoring life and health to the ailing—and every effort on our part to control it or harness it or predict it or fully understand it invariably ends in frustration.

"The truth is, there's great celebration at the moment someone very ill realizes they have been instantaneously made whole," he said. "But still, churches have funerals. Not all are healed."

When the Miracle Isn't Yours

I first came across Holloway, a gregarious, balding, and self-effacing father of four girls, when I heard him debate American skeptic Michael Shermer about miracles on a British radio program.

Shermer may not have come away convinced—as far as I'm aware, he hasn't shut down *Skeptic* magazine—but I suspect lots of listeners concluded from Holloway's documented cases that God is still up to something supernatural in the lives of the hurting.

Naturally, Shermer raised the question of why many people remain sick despite intercessory prayer. It didn't come off as a debater's ploy to score points. For me, as the husband of a chronically ill wife, it's a thoroughly legitimate issue.

"Even Jesus didn't heal automatically," Holloway explained to me. "When Jesus was in Nazareth, Matthew's gospel says, 'He did not do many miracles there because of their lack of faith.'[1] The disciples were given authority to heal in Matthew 10, and yet seven chapters later, they failed to heal an epileptic boy.[2] Paul didn't heal everyone; the Bible says he left Trophimus sick in Miletus,[3] and Paul himself was never relieved of his 'thorn in the flesh.'[4] So there are biblical reasons that we shouldn't be surprised when everyone isn't healed in each and every instance."

Nevertheless, the emotional punch of this issue still stings. The other day I came across a guest blog from someone who speaks with personal authority on miracles that haven't happened.[5]

Tricia Lott Williford's husband died unexpectedly after a twelve-hour illness, leaving her a widowed single mom with two children not yet in kindergarten. The author of *And Life Comes Back: A Wife's Story of Love, Loss, and Hope Reclaimed* frequently deals with the issue of personal heartache and unanswered prayers. Here, she was writing with unvarnished honesty.

"When God gives to other people in a way he hasn't given to you, it's easy to feel left out, and it's hard to want to hear how good he has been to other people," she said.

She quoted Nancy Guthrie as saying, "Some claim that strong faith is defined by throwing our energies into begging God for a miracle that will take away our suffering and then believing without doubting that he will do it. But faith is not measured by our ability to manipulate God to get what *we want*; it is measured by our willingness to submit to what *he wants*.[6]

"The truth is," continued Williford, "there's no formula we can count on for when Jesus says yes and when he says no. That's the catch with sovereignty: *He gets to decide yes, no, if, when, and how*. We can't figure out what he'll decide, and we can't base our own confidence on his favor. We can, however, base our confidence on his faithfulness.

"Miracles are temporary, but the word of Jesus, his teachings—they bring eternal life. Real life. Your faith in him, your belief that he is real, even when the miracle isn't yours, even when he doesn't say yes to you—this is what brings eternal life."

Though Williford has now been blessed with a new marriage, she finds that others are helped when she speaks about some of her struggles along the way. She has discovered that our ability to endure hardship is nearly limitless—if we have the confidence to live in hope.

Her advice to those who suffer: "Saying to God, 'Lord, I don't trust you, but I want to,' is the beginning of hope when the miracle isn't yours."

Finding Common Ground

I reclined in my easy chair after wrapping up the last of my travel and research for this book. File folders, textbooks, yellow legal pads, and stacks of interview transcripts were strewn on the floor of my family room, having outgrown my cluttered office. Cup of coffee in hand, I was reflecting on this journey of discovery into the miraculous and the supernatural.

I thought fondly of my interview with Michael Shermer nearly a year earlier. Though we disagree on much, neither of us let that stand in the way of a cordial relationship. He's an easy guy to like. I was glad to have given him every opportunity to build the case against miracles—and I did, indeed, identify some common ground.

For instance, Shermer's magazine published a seven-page article by a retired physician named Harriet Hall in which she sought to refute the possibility of divine intervention in the world.[7] While there's much in the piece to dispute, I also found myself agreeing with some of her assertions.

For instance, she says spontaneous remissions occur. *Granted.* She says there are charlatans in the world. *Unfortunately, yes.* She says sometimes blood tests are in error, X-rays are misinterpreted, and diagnoses are wrong. *Absolutely.* She says coincidences happen. *Definitely.*

She says some people have a motivation to lie. *Undoubtedly.* She says even honest people can misperceive things. *Certainly.* She says memories can falter. *Indeed.* She says people who are only apparently dead can revive. *Unquestionably.* She says any quack can supply testimonials that his snake oil works. *Sure.*

All of that is accurate, but does it explain away all of the accounts of miracles? *Sorry, no.* Believing in miracles doesn't necessitate endorsing every supernatural claim that gets splashed across the front page of supermarket tabloids.

Hall said eyewitnesses are "notoriously unreliable." Yes, there can be problems with some eyewitnesses, but I would hazard to guess that if Hall's spouse were murdered, she would want any eyewitnesses to testify in court against his assailant.

All her point does is emphasize that it's important to test eyewitness accounts by considering the witness's character, motives, biases, and opportunity to see what occurred—and to seek corroboration and documentation wherever possible.

This is simply standard practice for lawyers, judges, journalists, detectives, historians, juries, and others who are authentically trying to pursue truth.

Persuaded by the Evidence

Ultimately, the case *against* miracles falls short. In fact, its very foundation has been eroded by the "abject failure" of philosopher David Hume to debunk the miraculous—to borrow a phrase from the title of the devastating Oxford-published critique of his writings.[8] Hume's supposed "knockdown" argument against miracles was, in the end, knocked down itself.

What's more, Craig Keener's voluminous study of miracles is compelling in its depth and scope. I found myself agreeing with the skeptical physician who admitted that while there might be possible naturalistic explanations for some of the miracle accounts reported by Keener, that's not true of all of them. *Not by a long shot.*

Actually, I was impressed by so many astounding instances of supernatural intervention in which there were multiple, reliable eyewitnesses; medical documentation; and a lack of motivation to deceive.

As for the clinical study that Shermer so confidently touted—the one that showed no effect of intercessory prayer on healing—well, it has been decisively undermined.

Candy Gunther Brown revealed that the people doing the praying in the project were part of a non-Christian sect that doesn't even believe in the possibility of divine intervention. Thus, the ten-year, $2.4 million study tells us nothing about the effect of authentic Christian prayer on healing.

On the contrary, Brown's own peer-reviewed research shows instant improvements in eyesight and hearing after hands-on prayer by sincere followers of Jesus. Other peer-reviewed studies also show prayer to have a positive impact on healing. More and more, researchers are taking the case for miracles from anecdote to data.

The extraordinary dreams among Muslims, as reported by missionary Tom Doyle, clearly go beyond mere coincidence because they are validated by an external and independent source or event. For instance, many dreams were later authenticated when the dreamer encountered specific individuals he or she had only seen in their earlier vision. That's not just happenstance; something peculiar was going on.

Something supernatural, you might say.

On a fundamental level, I found myself ever more convinced

that the origin and fine-tuning of the universe, which physicist Michael Strauss described in his interview, point powerfully toward the existence of a supernatural Creator.

And I am persuaded that the facts of history, cited by detective J. Warner Wallace, establish convincingly that Jesus of Nazareth not only claimed to be the unique Son of God, but then proved it by returning from the dead.

In fact, the resurrection goes beyond confirming the existence of the divine. The torture, death, and empty tomb of Christ also answer the question of *why* God would want to intervene in individual lives through his miraculous touch.

The willingness of Jesus to endure the crucifixion tells us that God is motivated to take extraordinary action to rescue individuals from the consequences of their wayward life. And if he loves individuals *that* much, then it's reasonable to believe there would be times when he would choose to use one hand to hold back the forces of nature while using his other hand to miraculously heal someone who is suffering.

Reaching Your Verdict

As a former atheist myself, I'm always interested in what it would take for a skeptic to concede that a miracle had occurred. In our interview, Michael Shermer suggested that a human regrowing an amputated limb might be persuasive to him.

Harriet Hall doesn't find even that to be sufficient. After all, she said, "an advance in science might conceivably give us enough control over our DNA to do what lizards and starfish do."

So where does Hall set the bar of belief? How about this? she asks: "What if a chicken started speaking English, learned to read, and beat a grandmaster in chess?"

Something like that, she said, could cause her to "provisionally conclude" that something "outside the ordinary course of events" had happened, something that seemed "impossible to explain without appealing to supernatural forces." Even then, however, she couldn't quite bring herself to utter the word *miracle*.

I chuckled as I read that. Certainly I could understand the temptation to set the evidential bar comically high—to say, in a sense, *Miracles are impossible, period. Now, go ahead and try to make your case.*

The Bible talks about our human tendency to suppress the truth and walk the other way from God, and I've seen this play out in my own life. When I was an atheist, I didn't *want* Christianity to be true. I was living an immoral, drunken, and narcissistic lifestyle—and I enjoyed it.

When Leslie came to faith in Jesus, her character and values began to change for the better. While that was intriguing, I wanted the old Leslie back. I figured if I could disprove that Jesus returned from the dead, maybe I could debunk Christianity.

As I unleashed my curiosity on this pivotal event of the faith, I knew I would be wasting my time if I approached the investigation with a biased perspective, my conclusion already reached in advance.

If my journalism training taught me anything, it was to keep an open mind as I pursued answers. Only the worst hacks abide by the motto, "Don't let the facts stand in the way of a good story." In law school, I learned how to evaluate evidence and testimony to determine whether they are solid or shaky.

Here's what surprised me: Christianity *invites* investigation. The apostle Paul said if you can show that the miracle of the resurrection is mythology, make-believe, a mistake, a legend, or a fairy tale, then you are justified to abandon the faith.[9] When the gospels report supernatural events, they aren't introduced with, "Once upon a time . . ." Rather, they're reported in sober language, with specificity and within a historical context that can be checked out.

After nearly two years of research, I came to my own verdict about miracles: they're often credible and convincing, and they contribute powerfully to the cumulative case for Christ. Compelled by the facts, I joined Leslie in following Jesus—and the word *miracle* isn't far off in describing the way God has revolutionized my life as a result.

As for the time I invested in studying the evidence for this particular book, it was certainly well spent. In the end, my confidence in a miracle-working God has been deepened and strengthened. As a court of appeals would say, *The verdict is affirmed.*

If Christianity is true, though, this means Shermer's reliance on a merit-based system of salvation would be tragically misplaced. I remember him saying in our interview that he didn't think God would judge him harshly if he tried, however imperfectly, to live by the Golden Rule.

I recall asking him, "What if the entry-level standard of being good is giving your life completely to serving the poor, sacrificing everything, and living a wholly selfless existence? Would you measure up?"

"Well . . . ," he replied hesitantly. "Seriously, I don't think that could be the standard."

Actually, the standard is even greater than that—it's perfection. That's something none of us can attain through our efforts. Thankfully, God's provision is *grace*—a free gift of forgiveness and eternal life to all who receive it in repentance and faith.[10] That's what Jesus' death and resurrection were all about: paying the penalty we deserve for our failures and wrongdoing, and then rising to give us new life with him—forever.[11]

It's the most valuable miracle of all.

Each of us must make our own decision to receive or decline his gift. As you reflect on the contents of this book, I trust that you will keep an open mind and a receptive heart. It's my hope that you will be encouraged by this promise from the book of Proverbs:

> If you scream for insight
>> and call loudly for understanding,
> if you pursue it like you would money,
>> and search it out as you would hidden treasure,
> then the LORD will be awesome to you,
>> and you will come into possession of the
>> knowledge of God.[12]

Acknowledgments

Although one name is credited on the cover, this book has many "coauthors" who contributed significantly to its content and production. I am profoundly thankful for each of their roles in shaping this manuscript and getting the final product into your hands.

As always, my friend Mark Mittelberg offered key guidance and astute editing on the project from start to finish. Before any of my manuscripts go to the publisher, Mark is there to sift through them and offer valuable input.

John Sloan, the Zondervan editor for all of my *Case* series titles, was a constant source of encouragement and sage wisdom throughout the research and writing of this book. He has made strategic suggestions that have improved each volume in the series.

I am thankful too for the entire staff at Zondervan, especially Dirk Buursma, my new copy editor; Tom Dean and the marketing and sales teams; Zondervan trade publisher David Morris; and the dedicated folks who designed, produced, and publicized this book.

My wife, Leslie, deserves special commendation for tolerating my absences as I traveled the country to seek out experts on miracles. And speaking of the authorities I interviewed, thanks to each of them for sharing their expertise and personal stories. In the end, a writer is no better than the sources he consults.

Most of all, I am grateful to the God of miracles, who gave a drunken and narcissistic newspaper editor new life and a new purpose: to tell the world there is hope through Jesus. I can't help but think that I'm Exhibit A in the case for miracles.

Meet Lee Strobel

Atheist-turned-Christian Lee Strobel, the former award-winning legal editor of the *Chicago Tribune*, is a *New York Times* best-selling author of more than twenty books. He formerly taught First Amendment law at Roosevelt University and currently serves as professor of Christian thought at Houston Baptist University.

Lee was educated at the University of Missouri (Bachelor of Journalism degree) and Yale Law School (Master of Studies in Law degree). He was a journalist for fourteen years at the *Chicago Tribune* and other newspapers, winning Illinois' highest honor for public service journalism from United Press International. He also led a team that won UPI's top award for investigative reporting in Illinois.

After examining the evidence for Jesus, Lee became a Christian in 1981. He subsequently became a teaching pastor at two of America's most influential churches and hosted the national network TV program *Faith under Fire*. Now he is a teaching pastor at Woodlands Church in Texas.

Lee has won national awards for his books *The Case for Christ, The Case for Faith, The Case for a Creator,* and *The Case for Grace.* In 2017, his spiritual journey was depicted in a major motion picture, *The Case for Christ,* which ranks among the top twenty faith-based films at the box office.

Lee and Leslie have been married for forty-five years. Their daughter, Alison, is a novelist. Their son, Kyle, is a professor of spiritual theology at the Talbot School of Theology at Biola University.

Recommended Resources
for Further Investigation

Miracles

Belmonte, Kevin. *Miraculous: A Fascinating History of Signs, Wonders, and Miracles*. Nashville: Thomas Nelson, 2012.

Brown, Candy Gunther. *Testing Prayer*. Cambridge, MA: Harvard University Press, 2012.

Earman, John. *Hume's Abject Failure: The Argument against Miracles*. New York: Oxford University Press, 2000.

Geivett, R. Douglas, and Gary R. Habermas. *In Defense of Miracles: A Comprehensive Case for God's Action in History*. Downers Grove, IL: InterVarsity, 1997.

Grudem, Wayne A., ed. *Are Miraculous Gifts for Today? Four Views*. Grand Rapids: Zondervan, 1996.

Keener, Craig S. *Miracles: The Credibility of the New Testament Accounts*. 2 vols. Grand Rapids: Baker Academic, 2011.

Larmer, Robert A. *Dialogues on Miracle*. Eugene, OR: Wipf & Stock, 2015.

———. *The Legitimacy of Miracle*. Lanham, MD: Lexington Books, 2014.

Lennox, John C. *Miracles: Is Belief in the Supernatural Irrational?* Cambridge, MA: Veritas Forum, 2013.

Lewis, C. S. *Miracles: A Preliminary Study*. New York: HarperOne, 2001.

Metaxas, Eric. *Miracles: What They Are, Why They Happen, and How They Can Change Your Life*. New York: Dutton, 2014.

Stafford, Tim. *Miracles: A Journalist Looks at Modern-Day Experiences of God's Power*. Minneapolis: Bethany House, 2012.

Strobel, Lee. *The Case for Faith*. Grand Rapids: Zondervan, 2000.

Twelftree, Graham H. *Jesus the Miracle Worker: A Historical and Theological Study*. Downers Grove, IL: InterVarsity, 1999.

———. *Paul and the Miraculous: A Historical Reconstruction*. Grand Rapids: Baker Academic, 2013.

The Gospels and the Resurrection

Bauckham, Richard. *Jesus and the Eyewitnesses: The Gospels as Eyewitness Testimony*. Grand Rapids: Eerdmans, 2008.

Blomberg, Craig L. *Can We Still Believe the Bible? An Evangelical Engagement with Contemporary Questions*. Grand Rapids: Brazos Press, 2014.

———. *The Historical Reliability of the Gospels*. 2nd ed. Downers Grove, IL: InterVarsity Academic, 2007.

Copan, Paul, and Ronald K. Tacelli, eds. *Jesus' Resurrection: Fact or Figment? A Debate between William Lane Craig and Gerd Lüdemann*. Downers Grove, IL: InterVarsity Academic, 2000.

Craig, William Lane. *The Son Rises: Historical Evidence for the Resurrection of Jesus*. Eugene, OR: Wipf & Stock, 2000.

Evans, Craig A. *Fabricating Jesus: How Modern Scholars Distort the Gospels*. Downers Grove, IL: InterVarsity, 2006.

Evans, Craig A., and N. T. Wright. *Jesus, the Final Days: What Really Happened*. Louisville, KY: John Knox Press, 2009.

Habermas, Gary R., and Michael R. Licona. *The Case for the Resurrection of Jesus*. Grand Rapids: Kregel, 2004.

Habermas, Gary R., and Antony Flew. *Did the Resurrection Happen? A Conversation with Gary Habermas and Antony Flew*. Downers Grove, IL: InterVarsity, 2009.

Keener, Craig S. *The Historical Jesus of the Gospels*. Grand Rapids: Eerdmans, 2009.

Köstenberger, Andreas J., and Justin Taylor. *The Final Days of Jesus*. Wheaton, IL: Crossway, 2014.

Licona, Michael R. *The Resurrection of Jesus: A New Historiographical Approach*. Downers Grove, IL: IVP Academic, 2010.

———. *Why Are There Differences in the Gospels? What We Can Learn from Ancient Biography*. Oxford: Oxford University Press, 2017.

McDowell, Josh, and Sean McDowell. *Evidence That Demands a Verdict: Life-Changing Truth for a Skeptical World.* Updated and expanded ed. Nashville: Thomas Nelson, 2017.

Roberts, Mark D. *Can We Trust the Gospels? Investigating the Reliability of Matthew, Mark, Luke, and John.* Wheaton, IL: Crossway, 2007.

Strobel, Lee. *The Case for Christ.* Updated and expanded ed. Grand Rapids: Zondervan, 2016.

———. *In Defense of Jesus* (formerly *The Case for the Real Jesus*). Grand Rapids: Zondervan, 2016.

Swinburne, Richard. *The Resurrection of God Incarnate.* Oxford: Oxford Press, 2003.

Wallace, J. Warner. *Cold-Case Christianity: A Homicide Detective Investigates the Claims of the Gospel.* Colorado Springs: David C Cook, 2013.

Wright, N. T. *The Resurrection of the Son of God.* Minneapolis: Fortress, 2003.

Origin and Fine-Tuning of Our Universe and Planet

Bussey, Peter. *Signposts to God: How Modern Physics and Astronomy Point the Way to Belief.* Downers Grove, IL: IVP Academic, 2016.

Craig, William Lane. *Reasonable Faith: Christian Truth and Apologetics.* 3rd ed. Wheaton, IL: Crossway, 2008.

Dembski, William A. *Mere Creation: Science, Faith, and Intelligent Design.* Downers Grove, IL: InterVarsity, 1998.

Gonzalez, Guillermo, and Jay Wesley Richards. *The Privileged Planet: How Our Place in the Cosmos Is Designed for Discovery.* Washington, DC: Regnery, 2004.

Lewis, Geraint F., and Luke A. Barnes. *A Fortunate Universe: Life in a Finely Tuned Cosmos.* Cambridge: Cambridge University Press, 2016.

Ross, Hugh. *Improbable Planet: How Earth Became Humanity's Home.* Grand Rapids: Baker, 2016.

———. *Why the Universe Is the Way It Is.* Grand Rapids: Baker, 2008.

Strobel, Lee. *The Case for a Creator.* Grand Rapids: Zondervan, 2004.

Wallace, J. Warner. *God's Crime Scene: A Cold-Case Detective Examines the Evidence for a Divinely Created Universe*. Colorado Springs: David C Cook, 2015.

Ward, Peter, and Donald Brownlee. *Rare Earth: Why Complex Life Is Uncommon in the Universe*. New York: Copernicus, 2000.

Guide for Group Discussion
and Personal Reflection

Introduction

1. What prompted you to pick up this book? Did some experience or question encourage you to select a book on miracles? Describe what generates your interest in this topic.

2. On a scale of one to ten, with one being "totally skeptical" and ten being "completely convinced," how would you rate your current stance concerning the miraculous? Why did you choose that number? What would it take for you to move higher on the scale?

3. The book begins with several short stories about some very unusual events. Do any of them seem like actual miracles to you? Which ones and why?

4. Do you believe the miracles of Jesus occurred as described in the New Testament gospels (Matthew, Mark, Luke, and John)? Are any of Jesus' supernatural acts more difficult to believe than others? Please elaborate.

5. Have you ever had an experience you can only explain as a divine intervention in your life? Please describe it. What makes it seem supernatural to you? How did this miracle make you feel? Did it change your view of God? If so, how?

6. How would you distinguish between an unusual coincidence and a real miracle?

Chapter 1: The Making of a Skeptic

1. Describe your spiritual journey. What factors influenced your faith as a child? How have your beliefs changed over the years? What is your current spiritual viewpoint?

2. Skeptic Michael Shermer tells the heartbreaking story of how his girlfriend was paralyzed in an accident. He said his prayers for her healing went unanswered. How do you think you would have responded in a similar situation?

3. American patriot Thomas Paine wrote, "Is it more probable that nature should go out of her course, or that a man should tell a lie? We have never seen, in our time, nature go out of her course; but we have good reason to believe that millions of lies have been told in the same time; it is therefore, at least millions to one, that the reporter of a miracle tells a lie."[1] Do you agree? Why or why not?

4. What kind of evidence would be necessary to convince you that a miracle has actually taken place?

5. Shermer describes some questions that troubled his faith. Are there any issues that cause you to hesitate in fully embracing Christianity? What are they? Where might you find good answers to your concerns?

Chapter 2: The Knockdown Argument

1. How would you define *faith*? There's an old joke about a Sunday school student who said, "Faith is believing something even though you know in your heart it can't be true." Some

skeptics say faith involves believing something despite a lack of evidence for it—or even evidence to the contrary. Most Christians define faith as taking a step in the same direction the evidence is pointing. Which of these definitions resonates with you? How would *you* define faith?

2. Skeptic Michael Shermer believes that Scottish philosopher David Hume's arguments against miracles are decisive. Based on what you've read, how strong do you believe Hume's position is?

3. Atheist Jerry Coyne said, "To have real confidence in a miracle, one needs evidence—massive, well-documented, and either replicated or independently corroborated evidence from multiple and reliable sources." His conclusion: "No religious miracle even comes close to meeting those standards." Do you agree or disagree? Why?

4. Shermer said it would take an amputee growing back a limb to convince him that God had healed the person. Is that a reasonable threshold for belief? Why or why not?

5. How might psychological or emotional factors play into a person believing that God has healed them of a disease? What kind of miracle would defy an explanation based on these factors?

Chapter 3: Myths and Miracles

1. Skeptic Michael Shermer believes the four gospels—Matthew, Mark, Luke, and John—were written to make moral points rather than to record what actually occurred. Do you agree or disagree? Why?

2. Shermer raises the question of why Jews don't accept the resurrection story, even though they share much of the same Holy Book as Christians. Why do you think this is the case?

3. If God brought the universe into existence from nothing, this would be the most spectacular miracle of all. Are you convinced that the universe was created by God? Why or why not?

4. Shermer believes that heaven, as described by Christians, would be "boring." Do you agree or disagree? Why?

5. If it turned out God *does* exist, Shermer said he would tell him that he followed the Golden Rule as best he could. How do you believe God would respond? Can you think of any biblical passages that address this issue?

6. Shermer tells an intriguing story about the transistor radio that started playing after his wedding. What do you make of that incident? Was it simply an extraordinary coincidence, or something more?

Chapter 4: From Skepticism to Belief

1. What do you think C. S. Lewis meant when he wrote, "Miracles are in fact a retelling in small letters of the very same story which is written across the whole world in letters too large for some of us to see"?

2. Christian scholar Craig Keener came to faith in an emotional experience as a teenager and then subsequently studied the evidence that supports Christianity. Can you relate to that? Why or why not? How has evidence influenced your own faith journey—or has it?

3. Would you consider Keener's conversion experience to be "miraculous"? In what way might all spiritual rebirths be viewed as miracles?

4. The young people who shared Jesus with Keener weren't exactly adept at "friendship evangelism." However, God still used their imperfect interactions with him to bring him to

faith. Describe a time when you shared your spiritual beliefs with someone else. Did you feel awkward? What was the result? What would make it easier for you to talk about your faith with others?

5. Keener describes a professor who said he wouldn't believe in God even if someone were raised from the dead right in front of him. What could cause someone to be so closed-minded? What is needed besides evidence to bring such people to faith?

Chapter 5: From Hume to Jesus

1. New Testament professor Craig Keener defends Matthew, Mark, Luke, and John as being in the genre of "ancient biographies" rather than mythology or legend. Does this change the way you view these gospels? What does Keener's observation mean in terms of the historical accuracy of these writings?

2. The miracles of Jesus are present in the very earliest records of his life and ministry. Does this bolster their credibility to you? Why or why not?

3. Keener refutes skeptic David Hume, who was cited by Michael Shermer as making a "knockdown argument" against miracles. How does Hume fall into the trap of circular reasoning? Philosopher John Earman, who is not a Christian, titled his book *Hume's Abject Failure*. Does that seem like an accurate title? Why?

4. Some skeptics demand "extraordinary evidence" for miracles, but Keener said "sufficient and credible evidence" is all that should be needed. Is this a reasonable standard in your opinion? Why or why not?

5. If someone reports that a miracle took place, what evidence would you need to see to back up their claim? What kind of eyewitnesses would you find convincing? If you had the chance, what questions might you ask an eyewitness to try to determine if they were being truthful? What kind of documentation of the supposed miracle would you consider helpful?

6. Do you think Christians are too quick to describe unusual events as miracles? Are they too credulous? Should they be more skeptical? Why or why not? What's the difference between healthy skepticism and a closed mind?

Chapter 6: A Tide of Miracles

1. Craig Keener tells the story of his wife's older sister, Thérèse, who was bitten by a snake and stopped breathing for more than three hours. What is your reaction to the story? Was this a miracle, or merely a remarkable resuscitation? Why didn't she suffer the kind of brain damage that normally happens after six minutes without oxygen?

2. Keener's story about Barbara, a multiple sclerosis patient on the edge of death, seems particularly compelling. What is your reaction to it? Did any aspect of her story especially amaze you? Can you think of any naturalistic explanation that would account for everything that happened?

3. Keener recounts several stories from the research for his book, including the healing of a broken ankle, deafness, and a heart condition. What's your response to these reports? Do you find them believable? Why or why not?

4. Why do you think there are no reports of limbs being restored to amputees? Are there other credible healings that are clearly visible, as the healing of an amputee would be? Which ones?

5. Miraculous healings are fueling the growth of Christian churches in countries around the world, including China, the Philippines, Brazil, and Ethiopia. What are some possible reasons that God is manifesting his power in such a dramatic way in these places?

6. Keener says, "Anti-supernaturalism has reigned as an inflexible Western academic premise for far too long." Do you agree? What attitude should scholars take toward claims of the miraculous? Why?

Chapter 7: The Science of Miracles

1. Harvard scientist Stephen Jay Gould said science and faith occupy "nonoverlapping magisteria"—in other words, science deals with the empirical universe, facts, and theories, while faith focuses on questions of moral meaning and values. Why doesn't this distinction work in the case of Christianity?

2. The textbook *Psychology of Religion* reads, "The evidence of the effectiveness of prayers . . . remains outside the domain of science." Do you agree or disagree? Should scholars try to study apparent miracles? What tools might scientists use in determining whether a miracle claim is credible?

3. Skeptic Michael Shermer relied heavily on the 2006 STEP research that showed no effect of prayer—or perhaps even a small negative impact—on the healing of heart patients. However, Indiana University professor Candy Gunther Brown revealed that the people praying in that study were part of a non-Christian sect that doesn't even believe God performs miracles. Her conclusion is that this study tells us nothing about the impact of authentic Christian prayer on healing. Do you agree with her? Why or why not?

4. What is your reaction to the prayer studies Brown conducted in Mozambique and Brazil, where people with vision and

hearing impairments were examined, prayed for, and then examined again—with sudden improvements frequently reported? What about the other studies she cited that showed prayer to have a positive impact? Do they seem credible to you?

5. If you could design a new study to try to determine whether miraculous healings have taken place, what might it look like?

6. Brown distinguishes between *distant* intercessory prayer and *proximal* intercessory prayer. Why is this important?

Chapter 8: Dreams and Visions

1. Do you believe that God sometimes guides people through dreams? Have you ever had a dream that you believe came from beyond yourself? Was there any outside corroboration of that belief? Describe your experience.

2. What are some dangers of Christians focusing too much on dreams? How can they safeguard against being misled?

3. Tom Doyle, a missionary to the Middle East, describes several examples of extraordinary dreams and visions among Muslims. Did one of his stories especially resonate with you? Why?

4. In the Middle East, a person who is coming to faith in Christ is often asked, first, if they are willing to suffer for Jesus and, second, if they are willing to die for him. Honestly, how would you answer those questions?

5. Lee Strobel talks about the only dream he remembers from his childhood—the appearance of an angel who told him that someday he would understand the message of grace. How do you view this experience? Miraculous? Coincidental? Why?

6. Why do you suppose God doesn't use dreams and visions to reach millions more people with the gospel?

Chapter 9: The Astonishing Miracle of Creation

1. Do your interests gravitate more toward science, history, the humanities, or something else? What aspect of science most intrigues you? Why? In addition to using the scientific method, what are some other ways we can determine whether something is true or not?

2. Romans 1:20 reads, "For since the creation of the world God's invisible qualities—his eternal power and divine nature—have been clearly seen, being understood from what has been made, so that people are without excuse." Based on this verse, physicist Michael Strauss points out that miracles aren't necessary for us to know there's a God; rather, we see evidence for him more commonly through the world he has made. In your opinion, what aspects of nature point most strongly toward God's existence? Why?

3. Strauss says that because of the overwhelming amount of scientific data, failing to believe in the big bang would be like believing the earth is flat. How confident are you that the world began with the big bang? Do you think this event contradicts or supports the Bible's assertion that God created everything?

4. The *kalam* cosmological argument says that whatever begins to exist has a cause; the universe began to exist; and therefore the universe has a cause. How strong does this argument seem to you? Can you think of any examples of something that has a beginning but lacks a cause?

5. Philosopher William Lane Craig says if God created the universe, then miracles like the virgin birth are mere child's play. Do you agree? Why or why not?

6. Strauss said, "We don't live our lives based on obscure possibilities; we live our lives based on probabilities. Is it

possible my wife poisoned my cereal this morning? Anything is possible, but not everything is probable." How is this statement relevant to the investigation of miracle claims?

Chapter 10: Our Miraculous Universe and Planet

1. Atheist Christopher Hitchens conceded that the fine-tuning of the universe is the most intriguing argument Christians make for the existence of God. How strong does this evidence seem to you?

2. Which example of fine-tuning made the biggest impact on you and why?

3. Oxford's Richard Swinburne said that when it comes to explaining the fine-tuning of the universe, it's "the height of irrationality" to postulate a proliferation of other universes— for which there is no physical evidence—rather than to believe in the existence of one God. Do you agree? Why or why not?

4. Astrophysicist Hugh Ross said, "It is worth noting that Scripture speaks about the transcendent beginning of physical reality, including time itself (Genesis 1:1; John 1:3; Colossians 1:15–17; Hebrews 11:3); about continual cosmic expansion, or "stretching out" (Job 9:8; Psalm 104:2; Isaiah 40:22; 45:12; Jeremiah 10:12); about unchanging physical laws (Jeremiah 33:25), one of which is the pervasive law of decay (Ecclesiastes 1:3–11; Romans 8:20–22)." Take some time to look up the biblical references that intrigue you the most. How does science confirm what the Scriptures tell us about creation?

5. Science philosopher Tim Maudlin says there are just two plausible explanations for the universe's fine-tuning: a multiverse

or a designer. In your view, which explanation fits the overall evidence the best? What facts support your conclusion?

6. A common objection by skeptics is, "If God created the universe, then who created God?" How convincing are the answers offered by Michael Strauss and William Lane Craig? Why?

Chapter 11: The Miracle of the Resurrection

1. Have you ever watched TV programs on how investigators cracked old murder cases that others hadn't been able to figure out? What are some of the essential skills a detective would need to successfully solve these "cold" cases? How might this expertise be relevant to determining whether Jesus really rose from the dead?

2. Detective J. Warner Wallace used the example of a stabbing victim to illustrate how presuppositions can deter detectives from pursuing the truth. How can preformed opinions influence whether a person is open to the possibility of miracles? Have you ever had a closed mind toward the miraculous? What happened?

3. When he was an atheist, Wallace's evaluation of the four gospels convinced him that the writers intended to record what took place. Skeptic Michael Shermer believes the gospels are fanciful stories that were told to make a moral point. Now that you have read both their explanations, which viewpoint do you believe is best supported by the evidence and why?

4. Wallace said that when witnesses experience something that's unique, unrepeated, and personally important or powerful, they are much more likely to remember it. Can you think of an example of this from your own life? How does this observation apply to the reliability of the gospels?

5. Investigating the historicity of the resurrection can be reduced to two issues: Was Jesus dead after his crucifixion, and was he reliably encountered alive again afterward? Do you believe Wallace sufficiently established both points? What facts did you find the most persuasive?

6. Wallace considered several popular challenges to the resurrection: that Jesus' tomb was empty because his body was discarded and never buried; that the disciples conspired to lie about having seen Jesus alive after his crucifixion; that the disciples were having visions or hallucinations when they saw him; and that Jesus (according to the Qur'an) was never executed in the first place. Which of these challenges was strongest to you and why? How did Wallace answer the objection? How satisfied are you with his explanation?

7. Wallace said that after becoming convinced of Jesus' identity, "the more I understood the true nature of Jesus, the more my true nature was exposed—and I didn't like what I saw." Can you relate to that uncomfortable experience? How?

Chapter 12: Embarrassed by the Supernatural

1. Have you ever had a seemingly supernatural experience you were reluctant to share because you didn't want others to think you were a religious fanatic? Please tell the story. Even if you've never had that happen personally, can you understand why people might feel that way? What would be some possible reasons for their reluctance?

2. More than thirty years ago, two respected Christian thinkers wrote an article called "Embarrassed by God's Presence," in which they accused some churches of operating as if God

didn't really matter. "The central problem for our church, its theology, and its ethics is that it is simply atheistic," they wrote. Do you think that assessment, though harsh, still holds today? How so? Have you seen examples of churches or individual Christians who affirm the doctrines of faith but who live as if God is irrelevant to them?

3. Do you agree with Roger Olson that some churches and Christians are not fully convinced that God is still supernaturally active? How might this be reflected in their lives and attitudes?

4. Said Olson, "The richer we get, the more education we attain, the less comfortable we are with the miraculous." Do you agree or disagree? Olson said the quest for respectability prompts some Christians to feel embarrassed by the supernatural. "We are desperate to fit in," he said. What do you think of this observation?

5. Pastor Bill Hybels talks about "the whispers of God"—gentle nudgings of the Holy Spirit through which God leads us. Hybels said these divine leadings are an integral part of his life. Can you describe an experience where you believe God was leading you?

6. Olson said that balance is important—not to be too credulous about the miraculous, while still being open to God's supernatural activity. How might that balance play out in your own life? How can Christians safeguard against tipping too far toward skepticism or gullibility?

7. Olson describes an intriguing experience he had concerning a hymn. In the end, he concludes this may have been a coincidence, or it may have been God subtly sending him a message. Which do you think it was and why?

Chapter 13: When Miracles *Don't* Happen

1. Have you ever prayed fervently for God to perform a miracle in your life, but the miracle you requested never came? Describe the circumstances. How did you react? What emotions did you feel? How did this experience affect your view of God?

2. In struggling with his wife's dementia, Douglas Groothuis has never questioned whether God exists, but at times he has questioned God's goodness. Can you relate to that? If so, how did you grapple with your feelings? Groothuis added that pondering Jesus hanging on the cross for him "brings me back to spiritual sanity." Why do you think that is?

3. Groothuis said, "We may not know what God is achieving in the short run, but given the credibility of Christianity and my forty years as a Christian, I am justified in believing there can be significance and purpose in suffering." What kind of "significance and purpose" do you believe can be found in our suffering? What good might God draw from such experiences?

4. Groothuis said he is learning how to "suffer well." What might that look like? How can a person lament without sinning? On the cross, Jesus cried out, "My God, my God, why have you forsaken me?" His lament was answered by his resurrection. Why is the resurrection of Jesus the ultimate answer for us as well?

5. Groothuis draws a distinction between *meaningless* suffering and *inscrutable* suffering. How would you describe the difference between them? Was this delineation helpful for you? In what way?

6. What did you think of the "prayer of relinquishment" that Groothuis prayed? When is it appropriate to offer such a prayer? When I asked Groothuis how this prayer changed his

attitude toward healing, he said, "Rather than feeling like I'm always beating God with my fists, now I feel more like I'm resting in his arms." Which of these feelings best describes you when the answer you've sought hasn't come?

Conclusion: Reaching Your Verdict

1. Have you ever prayed aloud in the presence of someone who was sick? What thoughts ran through your mind as you did so? How boldly and confidently did you specifically ask God to heal him or her? Did you feel more comfortable praying for God to guide their doctor or work through their medication? Why?

2. Adrian Holloway pointed out that even Jesus didn't heal people automatically; the disciples failed to cure an epileptic boy even after they had been given the authority to heal; and Paul was never relieved of his thorn in the flesh. Said Holloway, "So there are biblical reasons that we shouldn't be surprised when everyone isn't healed in each and every instance." Does this help you with the question of why many people remain sick despite prayers for their healing? Why or why not?

3. Tricia Lott Williford, who was widowed with two young children, said, "Faith is not measured by our ability to manipulate God to get what *we want*. It is measured by our willingness to submit to what *he wants*." What's your take on her observation? How might this impact your own attitude when requested miracles don't come?

4. For skeptic Harriet Hall, it would take a chicken who spoke English, learned to read, and beat a grandmaster in chess for her to "provisionally conclude" that something occurred that was "impossible to explain without appealing to supernatural forces." Is that a reasonable place to set the bar of belief?

What might motivate someone to demand that level of proof for the miraculous?

5. Lee Strobel's conclusion is that "the case *against* miracles falls short." Do you share his opinion? Describe why or why not. How about the case *for* miracles? After reading this book, are you convinced that God continues to supernaturally intervene in people's lives? What was the most persuasive element for you in the case for miracles and why?

6. Michael Shermer believes that God—if he exists—won't judge him harshly due to his efforts to lead a good life. But Romans 3:23 warns that "all have sinned and fall short of the glory of God." The Bible makes it clear that salvation cannot be earned by our good deeds, but must be received as a gift of grace through faith. Romans 6:23 explains, "For the wages of sin is death, but the gift of God is eternal life in Christ Jesus our Lord." Why is it difficult for people to receive this gift of forgiveness and eternal life? Have you taken that step? If not, why not do so now?

Notes

Quotes (pages 11–12)

1. "Thomas A. Edison on Immortality: The Great Inventor Declares Immortality of the Soul Improbable," interview with Edward Marshall, *Columbian Magazine* 3.4 (January 1911).

2. Richard Dawkins, *The Blind Watchmaker: Why the Evidence of Evolution Reveals a Universe without Design* (New York: Norton, 1996), 139.

3. Stephen Hawking and Leonard Mlodinow, *The Grand Design* (New York: Bantam, 2010), 30.

4. C. S. Lewis, *God in the Dock: Essays on Theology and Ethics* (Grand Rapids: Eerdmans, 2014), 13.

5. Fyodor Dostoyevsky, *The Brothers Karamazov* (New York: New American Library, 1957), 34.

6. John C. Lennox, *Miracles: Is Belief in the Supernatural Irrational?* (Cambridge, MA: Veritas Forum, 2013), 25. This booklet contains the text of Lennox's talk under the same title at a Veritas Forum at Harvard University in 2012.

7. Eric Metaxas, *Miracles: What They Are, Why They Happen, and How They Can Change Your Life* (New York: Dutton, 2014), 16.

8. G. K. Chesterton, *The Innocence of Father Brown* (London: Cassell, 1911), 2.

Introduction: Investigating the Miraculous

1. See Anugrah Kumar, "Ben Carson Says God Helped Him Ace College Chemistry Exam by Giving Answers in a Dream," *Christian Post*, May 9, 2015, www.christianpost.com/news/ben

-carson-says-God-helped-him-ace-college-chemistry-exam-by
-giving-answers-in-dream-138913.

2. Helen Roseveare, *Living Faith* (Minneapolis: Bethany House, 1980),
44–45.

3. Miller tells his story in *Speechless* (Houston: Worldwide, 2017) and
Out of the Silence (Nashville: Thomas Nelson, 1996).

4. Visit NuVoice Ministries at www.nuvoice.org.

5. See Joel Landau, "'Mysterious Voice' Led Utah Cops to Discover
Child Who Survived for 14 Hours in Submerged Car after
Mom Drowned," *New York Daily News*, March 9, 2015, www.
nydailynews.com/news/national/mysterious-voice-leads-police-
baby-car-crash-article-1.2142732; Leonard Greene, "Baby Survives
Being Trapped 14 Hours in Submerged Car," *New York Post*,
March 9, 2015, http://nypost.com/2015/03/09/baby-survives-14
-hours-trapped-in-car-submerged-in-icy-river; Billy Hollowell,
"Police Can't Explain the Mysterious Voice That They Claim Led
Them to the Baby Girl Trapped for 14 Hours in Frigid Waters,"
The Blaze, March 10, 2015, www.theblaze.com/news/2015/03/10/
police-cant-explain-the-mysterious-voice-that-they-claim-led-them
-to-the-baby-girl-trapped-for-14-hours-in-frigid-waters.

6. Justin Brierley, "Derren Brown: The Miracle Maker Reveals His
Christian Past," *Premier Christianity*, September 2016, www
.premierchristianity.com/Past-Issues/2016/September-2016/Derren
-Brown-The-miracle-maker-reveals-his-Christian-past.

7. Nicholas Kristof, "Am I a Christian, Pastor Timothy Keller?" *New
York Times*, December 23, 2016, www.nytimes.com/2016/12/23/
opinion/sunday/pastor-am-i-a-christian.html.

8. For a good analysis of this issue, see John Piper, "Are Signs and
Wonders for Today?" *Desiring God*, February 25, 1990, www
.desiringgod.org/messages/are-signs-and-wonders-for-today.

9. Miller, *Speechless*, 122.

10. Miller, *Speechless*, 141.

11. For these and many other definitions and their citations, see
Michael R. Licona, *The Resurrection of Jesus: A New Historiographical
Approach* (Downers Grove, IL: InterVarsity, 2010), 134–36.

12. Richard L. Purtill, "Defining Miracles," in *In Defense of Miracles: A Comprehensive Case for God's Action in History*, ed. R. Douglas Geivett and Gary R. Habermas (Downers Grove, IL: InterVarsity, 1997), 72.

13. Purtill, "Defining Miracles," 61–62.

14. Noah Berlatsky, "Is It Immoral to Believe in Miracles?" *Religion Dispatches*, December 22, 2016. www.religiondispatches.org/miracle-myth-review.

15. Timothy McGrew, "Do Miracles Really Violate the Laws of Science?" *Slate*, undated, www.slate.com/bigideas/are-miracles-possible/essays-and-opinions/timothy-mcgrew-opinion.

16. A random representative sample of 1,000 US adults completed this questionnaire. The sample error is +/-3.1 percentage points at the 95 percent confidence level. The response rate was 55 percent. The survey was conducted as the research for this book began in 2015.

17. Based on 2016 US government estimate of population over the age of eighteen at 249,454,440. See www.census.gov/quickfacts/fact/table/US/.

18. Harriet Hall, "On Miracles," *Skeptic* 19.3 (2014): 18.

19. This survey was conducted by HCD Research and the Louis Finkelstein Institute for Religious and Social Studies of the Jewish Theological Seminary; see "Science or Miracle? Holiday Season Survey Reveals Physicians' Views of Faith, Prayer and Miracles," BusinessWire, December 20, 2004, www.businesswire.com/news/home/20041220005244/en/Science-Miracle-Holiday-Season-Survey-Reveals-Physicians.

20. See "Science or Miracle?"

Chapter 1: The Making of a Skeptic

1. Cathy Lynn Grossman, "Richard Dawkins to Atheist Rally: 'Show Contempt' for Faith," *USA Today*, March 24, 2012, http://content.usatoday.com/communities/Religion/post/2012/03/-atheists-richard-dawkins-reason-rally/1.

2. Another rendering: "I have labored carefully not to mock, lament, or denounce human actions, but to understand them" (Baruch Spinoza, *Tractatus Politicus*, trans. A. H. Gossett [1667; repr.,

London: Bell, 1883]), quoted in Michael Shermer, *The Mind of the Market: How Biology and Psychology Shape Our Economic Lives* (New York: Holt, 2008), xxiv.

3. Letter from Alfred Russel Wallace to brother-in-law Thomas Sims in 1861, quoted in James Marchant, ed., *Alfred Russel Wallace: Letters and Reminiscence* (1916; repr., New York: Qontro, 2010), 1:94.

4. All interviews are edited for conciseness, clarity, and content.

5. See Michael Shermer, *How We Believe: Science, Skepticism, and the Search for God*, 2nd ed. (New York: Holt, 2003), 4–5.

6. "God whispers to us in our pleasures, speaks in our conscience, but shouts in our pain: it is His megaphone to rouse a deaf world" (C. S. Lewis, *The Problem of Pain* [1940; repr., New York: HarperCollins, 1996], 91).

7. Richard Dawkins, *River Out of Eden: A Darwinian View of Life* (New York: Basic Books, 1995), 133.

8. Today, Maureen, still a paraplegic, is married with two children.

Chapter 2: The Knockdown Argument

1. Huxley said, "They [believers] were quite sure they had attained a certain 'gnosis'—had, more or less successfully, solved the problem of existence; while I was quite sure I had not, and had a pretty strong conviction that the problem was insoluble" (*Collected Essays* [New York: Appleton, 1894], 237–38).

2. See Michael Shermer, *The Believing Brain* (New York: Holt, 2011), 2.

3. Jerry A. Coyne, *Faith vs. Fact: Why Science and Religion Are Incompatible* (New York: Viking, 2015), 124.

4. Richard L. Purtill, "Defining Miracles," in *In Defense of Miracles: A Comprehensive Case for God's Action in History*, ed. R. Douglas Geivett and Gary R. Habermas (Downers Grove, IL: InterVarsity, 1997), 72.

5. I'm not related to forward Eric Strobel from Rochester, Minnesota, who played on that historic team.

6. Herbert Benson et al., "Study of the Therapeutic Effects of Intercessory Prayer (STEP) in Cardiac Bypass Patients: A Multicenter Randomized Trial of Uncertainty and Certainty of Receiving Intercessory Prayer," *American Heart Journal* 151.4 (April 2006): 934–42.

7. Quoted in Ernest C. Mossner, *The Life of David Hume* (Oxford: Clarendon, 1980), 117.

8. William Edward Morris and Charlotte R. Brown, "David Hume," *Stanford Encyclopedia of Philosophy*, https://plato.stanford.edu/entries/hume.

9. Michael Shermer, *Why People Believe Weird Things: Pseudoscience, Superstition, and Other Confusions of Our Time*, rev. ed. (New York: Holt, 2002), 45.

10. See David Hume, *Enquiries Concerning the Human Understanding and Concerning the Principles of Morals*, 2nd ed., ed. L. A. Selby-Bigge (Oxford: Clarendon, 1902), 116–17, http://oll.libertyfund .org/titles/hume-enquiries-concerning-the-human-understanding -and-concerning-the-principles-of-morals.

11. Graham H. Twelftree, *Jesus the Miracle Worker: A Historical and Theological Study* (Downers Grove, IL: InterVarsity, 1999), 40.

Chapter 3: Myths and Miracles

1. John 21:25 reads, "Jesus did many other things as well. If every one of them were written down, I suppose that even the whole world would not have room for the books that would be written."

2. Graham H. Twelftree, *Jesus the Miracle Worker* (Downers Grove, IL: InterVarsity, 1999), 19.

3. Marcus J. Borg, *Jesus: A New Vision* (San Francisco: HarperSan Francisco, 1987), 61.

4. The Gospel of Thomas, consisting of 114 sayings supposedly attributed to Jesus, has no actual link to the disciple by that name. It was written between AD 175 and 200—long after the canonical gospels of Matthew, Mark, Luke, and John. See Lee Strobel, *In Defense of Jesus* (Grand Rapids: Zondervan, 2007), 23–67.

5. See Strobel, *In Defense of Jesus*, 165–98.

6. Tim Callahan, "Did Jesus Exist? What the Evidence Reveals," *Skeptic* 19.1 (January 2014).

7. First Corinthians 15:17 reads, "And if Christ has not been raised, your faith is futile; you are still in your sins."

8. Michael Shermer, Twitter post, August 31, 2016, 9:01 a.m., http://twitter.com/michaelshermer.

9. Michael Shermer, "Anomalous Events That Can Shake One's Skepticism to the Core," *Scientific American*, October 1, 2014, www.scientificamerican.com/article/anomalous-events-that-can-shake-one-s-skepticism-to-the-core.

Chapter 5: From Hume to Jesus

1. See Matthew 11:21; Luke 10:13.

2. See Matthew 11:4–6; Luke 7:22.

3. See 1 Corinthians 15.

4. For example, see Gary R. Habermas, "The Case for Christ's Resurrection," in *To Everyone an Answer*, ed. Francis J. Beckwith, William Lane Craig, and J. P. Moreland (Downers Grove, IL: InterVarsity, 2004), 180–98. According to Ulrich Wilckens, the creed "indubitably goes back to the oldest phase of all in the history of primitive Christianity" (*Resurrection: Biblical Testimony to the Resurrection* [Edinburgh: St. Andrews Press, 1977], 2).

5. See Geza Vermes, "The Jesus Notice of Josephus Re-examined," *Journal of Jewish Studies* 38.1 (Spring 1987): 1–10; see also Geza Vermes, *Jesus the Jew: A Historian's Reading of the Gospels* (Minneapolis: Fortress, 1981), 79.

6. Raymond Brown, *The Death of the Messiah* (New York: Doubleday, 1994), 2:144.

7. Luke 11:20.

8. Gerd Theissen and Annette Merz, *The Historical Jesus: A Comprehensive Guide* (Minneapolis: Fortress, 1998), 281.

9. Larry Shapiro, *The Miracle Myth: Why Belief in the Resurrection and the Supernatural Is Unjustified* (New York: Columbia University Press, 2016), 148, xiv–xv.

10. For example, see David Johnson, *Hume, Holism, and Miracles* (Ithaca, NY: Cornell University Press, 1999), 76–78.

11. See Mark J. Larson, "Three Centuries of Objections to Biblical Miracles," *Bibliotheca Sacra* 160.637 (January 2003): 87.

12. John Earman, *Hume's Abject Failure: The Argument against Miracles* (Oxford: Oxford University Press, 2000), 3.

13. Earman, *Hume's Abject Failure*, 5.

14. Writes Earman, "In criticizing Hume's argument against miracles, I have occasionally been subjected to a kind of reverse inquisition: since I attack Hume, must I not have some hidden agenda of Christian apologetics? I find such inquisitions profoundly distasteful since they deflect attention from the real issues. I am not averse, however, to laying my cards on the table. I find much that is valuable in the Judeo-Christian heritage, but I find nothing attractive, either intellectually or emotionally, in the theological doctrines of Christianity" (*Hume's Abject Failure*, viii).

15. Jeffrey Koperski, "Review of John Earman, *Hume's Abject Failure: The Argument against Miracles*," *Philosophia Christi* 4.2 (2002): 558.

16. Johnson, *Hume, Holism, and Miracles*, front flap.

17. Johnson, *Hume, Holism, and Miracles*, 4.

18. Keith Ward, "Believing in Miracles," *Zygon* 37.3 (September 2002): 742.

19. Jerry A. Coyne, *Faith vs. Fact* (New York: Viking, 2015), 124.

20. For physicist Michael G. Strauss's response to this contention, "Extraordinary Claims and Extraordinary Evidence," Dr. Michael G. Strauss blog, May 21, 2017, www.michaelgstrauss.com/2017/05/extraordinary-claims-and-extraordinary.html.

Chapter 6: A Tide of Miracles

1. See Philip Yancey, "Jesus and Miracles," Philip Yancey blog, August 20, 2015, www.philipyancey.com/Jesus-and-miracles, emphasis added.

2. Gardner was a Fellow of the Royal College of Obstetricians and Gynecologists and of the Association of Surgeons in East Africa. He served as an examiner to the University of Newcastle-upon-Tyne. He was ordained in the United Free Church of Scotland. See Rex Gardner, *Healing Miracles: A Doctor Investigates* (London: Darton, Longman & Todd, 1986), back cover.

3. Gardner, *Healing Miracles*, 202–5.

4. Gardner, *Healing Miracles*, 206.

5. Gardner, *Healing Miracles*, 165.

6. See Harold P. Adolph, *Today's Decisions, Tomorrow's Destiny* (Spooner, WI: White Birch, 2006), 48–49; Scott J. Kolbaba, MD, *Physicians' Untold Stories* (North Charleston, SC: CreateSpace, 2016), 115–22.
7. "I can do all this through him who gives me strength."
8. Interestingly, the visiting minister, Wesley Steelberg Jr., had himself been healed of a heart condition when he had been given just hours to live; see Craig S. Keener, *Miracles: The Credibility of the New Testament Accounts* (Grand Rapids: Baker Academic, 2011), 1:431–32.
9. See Chauncey W. Crandall IV, MD, *Raising the Dead: A Doctor Encounters the Miraculous* (New York: FaithWords, 2010), 1–5.
10. Crandall, *Raising the Dead*, 171–73.
11. Robert A. Larmer, *Dialogues on Miracle* (Eugene, OR: Wipf & Stock, 2015), 117–19.
12. See Matthew 12:9–14.
13. J. P. Moreland, *Kingdom Triangle: Recover the Christian Mind, Renovate the Soul, Restore the Spirit's Power* (Grand Rapids: Zondervan, 2007), 168.
14. Allan Anderson and Edmond Tang, eds., *Asian and Pentecostal: The Charismatic Face of Christianity in Asia*, rev. ed. (Eugene, OR: Wipf & Stock, 2011), 391.
15. Jim Rutz, *Megashift* (Colorado Springs: Empowerment, 2005), 4.
16. "I would like to use my rudimentary French by talking with her." The French version looks better in print than when I stumbled through it aloud.

Chapter 7: The Science of Miracles

1. Paul Copan et al., eds., *Dictionary of Christianity and Science* (Grand Rapids: Zondervan, 2017), 621.
2. Stephen Jay Gould, "Nonoverlapping Magisteria," *Natural History* 106 (March 1997): 19.
3. Gould, "Nonoverlapping Magisteria," 22; see also Stephen Jay Gould, *Rocks of Ages: Science and Religion in the Fullness of Life* (New York: Ballantine, 1999).
4. Matthew 11:4–5.

5. Mark 1:44.

6. Candy Gunther Brown, *Testing Prayer: Science and Healing* (Cambridge, MA: Harvard University Press, 2012), 7.

7. Mary Jo Meadow and Richard D. Kahoe, *Psychology of Religion: Religion in Individual Lives* (New York: Harper & Row, 1984), 120.

8. Jesus answered him: "It is also written: 'Do not put the Lord your God to the test'" (Matthew 4:7).

9. Not to be confused with the Unification Church or Unitarian Universalism. For more on the Unity School of Christianity, visit www.unity.org.

10. Ron Rhodes, *The Challenge of the Cults and New Religions* (Grand Rapids: Zondervan, 2001), 118.

11. Ruth A. Tucker, *Another Gospel: Cults, Alternative Religions, and the New Age Movement* (Grand Rapids: Zondervan, 1989), 189, emphasis added.

12. See Ron Rhodes, ed., *Christian Research Newsletter* 5.2 (1994), www.iclnet.org/pub/resources/text/cri/cri-nwsl/web/crn0052a.html, emphasis added.

13. See "Unity School of Christianity," Probe, May 27, 1995, www .probe.org/unity-school-of-christianity. Used in this theological sense, the term *cult* is not meant to be derogatory or pejorative, and it does not necessarily suggest an authoritarian, mind-controlling, abusive, or secretive sect. An expert on alternative religions, the late Walter Martin, defined a theological cult this way: "By 'cult,' we mean a group, religious in nature, which surrounds a leader or a group of teachings which either denies or misrepresents essential biblical doctrine" (*The New Cults* [Ventura, CA: Regal, 1980], 16). Another expert, Alan Gomes, defined cults as "a group of people who claim to be Christian, yet embrace a particular doctrinal system taught by an individual leader, group of leaders, or organization, which (system) denies (either explicitly or implicitly) one or more of the central doctrines of the Christian faith as taught in the sixty-six books of the Bible" (*Unmasking the Cults* [Grand Rapids: Zondervan, 1995], 7). For a discussion on how cults should be defined, see Rhodes, *Challenge of the Cults*, 19–35.

14. Quoting May Rowland, Silent Unity's director from 1916 to 1971; see Neal Vahle, *The Unity Movement: Its Evolution and Spiritual Teachings* (Philadelphia: Templeton Foundation Press, 2002), 246–47.

15. Charles Fillmore, *Christian Healing* (Lee's Summit, MO: Unity School of Christianity, 1954), 162, quoted in Tucker, *Another Gospel*, 184–85.

16. Myrtle Fillmore, *Myrtle Fillmore's Healing Letters* (Unity Village, MO: Unity Books, 1988), 106.

17. "What Is Affirmative Prayer?" www.unity.org/prayer/what-affirmative-prayer, emphasis added.

18. See James 5:14.

19. "Religions," World Factbook, www.cia.gov/library/publications/the-world-factbook/fields/2122.html.

20. Tim Stafford, *Miracles: A Journalist Looks at Modern-Day Experiences of God's Power* (Bloomington, MN: Bethany House, 2012), 150–51.

21. "Comparitive [sic] Examples of Noise Levels," www.industrialnoisecontrol.com/comparative-noise-examples.htm.

22. "Understanding the Eye Chart," www.pearsoneyecare.com/2013/06/30/understanding-the-eye-chart.

23. Brown, *Testing Prayer*, 217.

24. See Brown, *Testing Prayer*, 214.

Chapter 8: Dreams and Visions

1. Luke 13:22–29.

2. See Nabeel Qureshi, *Seeking Allah, Finding Jesus: A Devout Muslim Encounters Jesus*, 2nd ed. (Grand Rapids: Zondervan, 2016). My friend Nabeel died of stomach cancer in 2017 at age thirty-four after writing bestselling books about Jesus and traveling the world to talk about his Christian faith.

3. See Tom Doyle, *Dreams and Visions: Is Jesus Awakening the Muslim World?* (Nashville: Nelson, 2012), 127.

4. Lee Strobel, *The Case for Faith* (Grand Rapids: Zondervan, 2000), 162.

5. Doyle, *Dreams and Visions*, v.

6. Tom Doyle, *Killing Christians: Living the Faith Where It's Not Safe to Believe* (Nashville: W Publishing, 2015), back cover.

7. Doyle changes the names of the people he talks about in the Middle East to protect their identity and keep them from potential danger. The name Rachel at the end of this chapter is also fictitious to avoid conflict with her Muslim relatives.

8. John 14:27.

9. Doyle tells a more complete story about Noor in his *Dreams and Visions*, 3–12.

10. Genesis 18:25.

11. John 1:1.

12. John 14:6.

Chapter 9: The Astonishing Miracle of Creation

1. Geraint F. Lewis and Luke A. Barnes, *A Fortunate Universe: Life in a Finely Tuned Cosmos* (Cambridge, UK: Cambridge University Press, 2016), 291.

2. Genesis 1:1.

3. In referring to creation as a "miracle," I'm using the term in the broad sense of being an amazing event instigated by God. As Oxford professor John C. Lennox observes, "Strictly speaking, miracles concern events that are exceptions to recognized laws. As such they clearly *presuppose* the existence of the normal course of things. It follows, then, that it does not really make sense to think of the creation of the normal course of things as a miracle" (*Gunning for God* [Oxford: Lion, 2011], 167).

4. Quoted in Lee Strobel, *The Case for Faith* (Grand Rapids: Zondervan, 2000), 60–61.

5. Robert Evans, "Key Scientist Sure 'God Particle' Will Be Found Soon," Reuters Science News, April 7, 2008, www.reuters.com/article/us-science-particle-idUSL0765287220080407; see also Leon Lederman and Dick Teresi, *God Particle: If the Universe Is the Answer, What Is the Question?* (New York: Dell, 1993). The precise origin of the nickname is, a little like the boson itself, difficult to pin down. But experimental physicist Lederman wrote, "This boson is so central to the state of physics today, so crucial to our final understanding of the structure of matter, yet

so elusive, that I have given it a nickname: the God Particle. Why God Particle? Two reasons. One, the publisher wouldn't let us call it the [expletive deleted] Particle, though that might be a more appropriate title, given its villainous nature and the expense it is causing. And two, there is a connection, of sorts, to another book, a *much* older one . . ." (p. 22).

6. See Ken Boa and Larry Moody, *I'm Glad You Asked: In-Depth Answers to Difficult Questions about Christianity* (Colorado Springs: David C Cook, 1995).

7. "For since the creation of the world God's invisible qualities—his eternal power and divine nature—have been clearly seen, being understood from what has been made, so that people are without excuse."

8. Cited in George Gamow, *My World Line: An Informal Autobiography* (New York: Viking, 1970), 44.

9. Stephen Hawking, *A Brief History of Time*, rev. ed. (New York: Bantam, 1998), 146.

10. See William Lane Craig and Kevin Harris, "The First Split Second of the Universe," Reasonable Faith, March 15, 2016, www .reasonablefaith.org/the-first-split-second-of-the-universe.

11. Arvind Borde, Alan Guth, and Alexander Vilenkin.

12. Michael Martin, ed., *The Cambridge Companion to Atheism* (Cambridge, UK: Cambridge University Press, 2007), 183.

13. William Lane Craig, *On Guard: Defending Your Faith with Reason and Precision* (Colorado Springs: David C Cook, 2010), 70–71.

14. Craig, *On Guard*, 74.

15. Strauss elaborated: "Some scientists say quantum fluctuations are 'uncaused' events. First, there are some interpretations of quantum mechanics that may be correct that still require all events to be caused, such as Bohm's interpretation. Second, these 'uncaused' events obey the laws of physics, even if only probabilistically. Is an event that obeys precise laws 'uncaused'? Third, these events still occur within our space-time fabric, so again, there is a required foundation for them to occur. Fourth, we really don't know how to interpret the quantum mechanical wave function since

all we can do is make measurements, and those measurements precisely follow known laws. It is the process of the wave function to the measurement, which we don't know how it really works, that is used to claim uncaused events. These arguments are not irrefutable, but I think it is a real stretch to claim that an event that is bound by our space-time laws of physics and explained by mathematics we don't unambiguously know how to interpret, is truly 'uncaused.'"

16. Craig, *On Guard*, 91–92.
17. Alexander Vilenkin, *Many Worlds in One: The Search for Other Universes* (New York: Hill and Wang, 2006), 176.

Chapter 10: Our Miraculous Universe and Planet

1. "Christopher Hitchens Makes a Shocking Confession," www.you tube.com/watch?v=E9TMwfkDwIY.
2. Cambridge astrophysicist Geraint F. Lewis and Luke A. Barnes, a Cambridge-educated postdoctoral researcher at the Sydney Institute for Astronomy, responded to the claim that "fine-tuning has been debunked" by replying, "No, it hasn't." Barnes reviewed the scientific literature on the topic, summarizing the conclusions of more than two hundred published papers in the field. "On balance, the fine-tuning of the Universe for life has stood up well under the scrutiny of physicists," they wrote. They added that it is "not the case" that "fine-tuning is the invention of a bunch of religious believers who hijacked physics to their own ends." Rather, they said, "physics has tended to consolidate our understanding of fine-tuning" (*A Fortunate Universe: Life in a Finely Tuned Cosmos* [Cambridge, UK: Cambridge University Press, 2016], 241–42).
3. Credit to Daniel Bakken, a Christian apologist who has a degree in physics.
4. Paul Davies, *The Edge of Infinity* (New York: Simon & Schuster, 1982), 90.
5. See Hugh Ross, *The Creator and the Cosmos: How the Greatest Scientific Discoveries of the Century Reveal God* (Colorado Springs: NavPress, 1995), 117.

6. Roger Penrose, *The Emperor's New Mind* (Oxford: Oxford University Press, 1989), 344.

7. Paul Davies, *The Cosmic Blueprint* (New York: Simon & Schuster, 1988), 203.

8. Edward Harrison, *Masks of the Universe: Changing Ideas on the Nature of the Universe* (New York: Macmillan, 1985), 252.

9. Peter D. Ward and Donald Brownlee, *Rare Earth: Why Complex Life Is Uncommon in the Universe* (New York: Copernicus, 2000), 220. For an excellent discussion of the importance of plate tectonics, see pages 191–220.

10. Hugh Ross, "Probability for Life on Earth," Reasons to Believe, April 1, 2004, www.reasons.org/articles/probability-for-life-on -earth; see also Hugh Ross, *Improbable Planet: How Earth Became Humanity's Home* (Grand Rapids: Baker, 2016).

11. See John D. Barrow and Frank J. Tipler, *The Anthropic Cosmological Principle* (Oxford: Oxford University Press, 1996).

12. Quoted in Lewis and Barnes, *A Fortunate Universe*, 355.

13. Quoted in Lee Strobel, *The Case for Faith* (Grand Rapids: Zondervan, 2000), 78.

14. Quoted in Lee Strobel, *The Case for a Creator* (Grand Rapids: Zondervan, 2004), 136.

15. Quoted in Lewis and Barnes, *A Fortunate Universe*, preface material.

16. John Horgan, "Cosmic Clowning: Stephen Hawking's 'New' Theory of Everything Is the Same Old Crap," *Scientific American* blog post, September 13, 2010, https://blogs.scientificamerican. com/cross-check/cosmic-clowning-stephen-hawkings-new-theory -of-everything-is-the-same-old-crap.

17. "Besides," Strauss added, "even if it turns out the multiverse idea is true, it would actually support the case for a creator." Why? He explained: "Not only would the Borde-Guth-Vilenkin theorem point toward a beginning that would need a creator, but the extra dimensions of string theory would require that any creator exist in multiple dimensions. That would mean he could easily perform miraculous acts in our four dimensions. In fact, a discovery of

other universes or extra dimensions would, in some sense, increase the necessary magnitude of any creator. One could legitimately ask the question, 'How many universes would an infinite God create?'"

18. John Polkinghorne, *Science and Theology* (Minneapolis: Fortress, 1998), 38.

19. Richard Swinburne, *Is There a God?* (Oxford: Oxford University Press, 1995), 68.

20. John Leslie, *Universes* (New York: Routledge, 1989), 198.

21. Quoted in Strobel, *Case for a Creator*, 109.

22. Quoted in Strobel, *Case for Faith*, 77.

23. Quoted in Paul Copan et al., eds., *Dictionary of Christianity and Science* (Grand Rapids: Zondervan, 2017), 66.

24. Isaiah 55:8–9 reads, "'For my thoughts are not your thoughts, neither are your ways my ways,' declares the Lord. 'As the heavens are higher than the earth, so are my ways higher than your ways and my thoughts than your thoughts.'"

Chapter 11: The Miracle of the Resurrection

1. See Richard Whitehead, "Forensic Statement Analysis: Deception Detection," Law Enforcement Learning, undated, www.law enforcementlearning.com/course/forensic-statement-analysis.

2. This is a paraphrase of the C. S. Lewis quote, "One must keep pointing out that Christianity is a statement which, if false, is of *no* importance, and, if true, of infinite importance" (1970; repr., *God in the Dock: Essays on Theology and Ethics* [Grand Rapids: Eerdmans, 2014], 102).

3. See Luke 1:1–3.

4. See 1 Peter 5:1; 2 Peter 1:16–17.

5. 1 John 1:1.

6. Acts 4:20.

7. Acts 10:39.

8. See 1 Corinthians 15.

9. Simon Greenleaf, *The Testimony of the Evangelists: The Gospels Examined by the Rules of Evidence* (Grand Rapids: Baker, 1984), 34.

10. See Michael R. Licona, *Why Are There Differences in the Gospels?*

What We Can Learn from Ancient Biography (Oxford: Oxford University Press, 2017).

11. John 20:2. "Beloved disciple" ("the one Jesus loved") is the way the apostle John refers to himself.

12. Luke 24:24 reads, "Then some of our companions went to the tomb and found it just as the women had said, but they did not see Jesus."

13. Licona quotes are from "Why Are There Differences in the Gospels? An Interview with Michael R. Licona," Bible Gateway, June 27, 2017, www.biblegateway.com/blog/2017/06/why-are-there -differences-in-the-gospels-an-interview-with-michael-r-licona, emphasis added.

14. See J. J. Blunt, *Undesigned Coincidences in the Writings of Both the Old and New Testament: An Argument of Their Veracity* (1847; repr., London: Forgotten Books, 2017); Lydia McGrew, *Hidden in Plain View: Undesigned Coincidences in the Gospels and Acts* (Chillicothe, OH: DeWard, 2017).

15. See Matthew 4:18–22.

16. See Luke 5:1–11.

17. Matthew 26:67–68.

18. See 1 Corinthians 15:17.

19. Surah 4:157–158 in the Qur'an: "That they said (in boast) 'We killed Christ Jesus, the son of Mary, the Messenger of Allah'—but they killed him not, nor crucified him, but so it was made to appear to them, and those who differ therein are full of doubts, with no (certain) knowledge, but only conjecture to follow, for of a surety they killed him not—Nay, Allah raised him up unto Himself; and Allah is exalted in Power, Wise . . ."

20. Josephus, Tacitus, Mara bar Serapion, Lucian, and the Talmud.

21. See Gary R. Habermas and Michael R. Licona, *The Case for the Resurrection of Jesus* (Grand Rapids: Kregel, 2004).

22. Bart Ehrman, *How Jesus Became God: The Exaltation of a Jewish Preacher from Galilee* (New York: HarperOne, 2014), 7, 157, italics in original.

23. Craig A. Evans, "Getting the Burial Traditions and Evidences

Right," in *How God Became Jesus: The Real Origins of Belief in Jesus' Divine Nature*, ed. Michael F. Bird et al. (Grand Rapids: Zondervan, 2014), 73.

24. Evans, "Getting the Burial Traditions and Evidences Right," 76.

25. Evans, "Getting the Burial Traditions and Evidences Right," 89.

26. Evans, "Getting the Burial Traditions and Evidences Right," 93.

27. See 1 Corinthians 15:4. Wallace also noted that a 2007 documentary, *The Lost Tomb of Jesus*, claimed to have found the family tomb of Jesus, including an ossuary labeled in Aramaic "Jesus, Son of Joseph." Subsequently, scholars have undermined the film's credibility. However, said Wallace, embrace of the movie by skeptics at the time shows their inconsistency. "Often skeptics deny the fact Jesus would be buried in a grave—until, of course, it serves their purpose to claim there is a grave of Jesus. You can't have it both ways."

28. Jodi Magness, "Jesus' Tomb: What Did It Look Like?" in *Where Christianity Was Born*, ed. Hershel Shanks (Washington, DC: Biblical Archaeology Society, 2006), 224.

29. Acts, Clement of Rome, Polycarp, Ignatius, Dionysius of Corinth (quoted by Eusebius), Tertullian, and Origen.

30. See Sean McDowell, *The Fate of the Apostles: Examining the Martyrdom Accounts of the Closest Followers of Jesus* (New York: Routledge, 2016).

31. 2 Corinthians 5:17.

32. See Lee Strobel, *The Case for Christ* (Grand Rapids: Zondervan, 1998), 187–201.

33. See Stan Telchin, *Betrayed!* (Grand Rapids: Chosen, 1982).

Chapter 12: Embarrassed by the Supernatural

1. Asked in my interview how he defines an Arminian, Olson replied, "An Arminian is a Protestant Christian who believes that God grants us free will to accept or reject his offer of salvation. He does not make that decision for us, but he does give us the ability to decide, which we don't have on our own." He added, "I consider anyone an Arminian who fits that profile, even if they don't call themselves an Arminian."

2. Stanley Hauerwas and William H. Willimon, "Embarrassed by God's Presence," *Christian Century* 102 (January 30, 1985): 98–100.

3. Hauerwas and Willimon, "Embarrassed by God's Presence,"100.

4. Hauerwas and Willimon, "Embarrassed by God's Presence," 100, emphasis added.

5. Hauerwas and Willimon, "Embarrassed by God's Presence," 100.

6. For more detail about this health episode and the spiritual lessons I learned from it, see Lee Strobel, *The Case for Grace* (Grand Rapids: Zondervan, 2016), 163–70.

7. Bill Hybels, *The Power of a Whisper: Hearing God, Having the Guts to Respond* (Grand Rapids: Zondervan, 2010), 16.

8. Hybels, *Power of a Whisper*, 16.

9. Hybels, *Power of a Whisper*, 17.

Chapter 13: When Miracles Don't Happen

1. Douglas Groothuis, *Walking through Twilight: A Wife's Illness—A Philosopher's Lament* (Downers Grove, IL: InterVarsity, 2017).

2. James F. Sennett and Douglas Groothuis, *In Defense of Natural Theology: A Post-Humean Assessment* (Downers Grove, IL: IVP Academic, 2005). The book's thesis: "Natural theology is alive and well in contemporary philosophy; the supposed Humean refutation of the enterprise is a myth whose exposure is long overdue" (p. 15).

3. See my interview with philosopher Peter Kreeft of Boston College in *The Case for Faith* (Grand Rapids: Zondervan, 2000), 30–54.

4. Matthew 27:46; see Psalm 22:1.

5. Bernard Schweizer, *Hating God: The Untold Story of Misotheism* (Oxford: Oxford University Press, 2010).

6. See John 11:1–44.

7. Ecclesiastes 3:1, 6 reads, "There is a time for everything, and a season for every activity under the heavens . . . a time to search and a time to give up . . ."

8. See Paul Tournier, *To Resist or to Surrender* (Eugene, OR: Wipf & Stock, 1964).

9. See John 6:67–68.

10. Catherine Marshall, *Adventures in Prayer* (New York: Ballantine, 1975), 62–63, italics in original.

11. Marshall, *Adventures in Prayer*, 70–71.

12. See Romans 5:3–5.

13. Matthew 5:4 reads, "Blessed are those who mourn, for they will be comforted."

14. Mark 12:30 reads, "Love the Lord your God with all your heart and with all your soul and with all your mind and with all your strength."

Conclusion: Reaching Your Verdict

1. Matthew 13:58; see Mark 6:1–6.

2. See Matthew 17:14–16.

3. See 2 Timothy 4:20.

4. 2 Corinthians 12:7.

5. Tricia Lott Williford, "When Everyone Else Is Getting Their Miracle: How to Deal with Feeling Overlooked," Ann Voskamp blog, July 10, 2017, www.annvoskamp.com/2017/07/when-everyone -else-is-getting-their-miracle-how-to-deal-with-feeling-overlooked.

6. Nancy Guthrie, *Hearing Jesus Speak into Your Sorrow* (Carol Stream, IL: Tyndale, 2009), 19, emphasis in original.

7. Harriet Hall, "On Miracles," *Skeptic* 19.3 (2014): 17–23. All quotes from Hall in this chapter are from this article.

8. See John Earman, *Hume's Abject Failure: The Argument against Miracles* (Oxford: Oxford University Press, 2000).

9. See 1 Corinthians 15:12–19.

10. Ephesians 2:8–9 reads, "For it is by grace you have been saved, through faith—and this is not from yourselves, it is the gift of God—not by works, so that no one can boast."

11. Romans 3:23: "For all have sinned and fall short of the glory of God." Romans 5:8: "But God demonstrates his own love for us in this: While we were still sinners, Christ died for us." Romans 6:23: "For the wages of sin is death, but the gift of God is eternal life in Christ Jesus our Lord." Romans 10:9–10: "If you declare with your mouth, 'Jesus is Lord,' and believe in your heart that God raised

him from the dead, you will be saved. For it is with your heart that you believe and are justified, and it is with your mouth that you profess your faith and are saved." Romans 10:13: "Everyone who calls on the name of the Lord will be saved."

12. Proverbs 2:3–5, paraphrase.

Guide for Group Discussion and Personal Reflection

1. Thomas Paine, *The Age of Reason: The Definitive Edition* (Grand Rapids: Michigan Legal Publishing, 2014), 54.

Index

The Case for Miracles for Kids

New York Times *bestselling author Lee Strobel with Jesse Florea*

From bestselling author Lee Strobel's well-renowned, bestselling series exploring the life of Jesus and what it means to be a Christian, *The Case for Miracles for Kids* tackles the tough questions kids ask about God, Jesus, and miracles, as well as providing information for kids who want to learn more so they can share their faith and knowledge with others. Mixing lighthearted prose and a conversational style with historical facts, research, and true stories, this book brings the miracles and ministry of Jesus to life and shows why they still matter today.

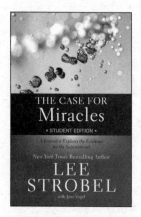

The Case for Miracles Student Edition

A Journalist Explores the Evidence for the Supernatural

New York Times *bestselling author Lee Strobel with Jane Vogel*

From the well-renowned, bestselling series exploring the life of Jesus and what it means to be a Christian, *The Case for Miracles Student Edition* tackles tough questions about God, Jesus, and miracles, offering historical evidence that miracles are possible. With content tied to Lee Strobel's adult title, *The Case for Miracles*, this book is ideal for students who want to learn how to share their faith and knowledge about God with others. Mixing lighthearted prose and a conversational style with facts, research, and true stories, *The Case for Miracles Student Edition* brings the miracles and ministry of Jesus to life.

Available in stores and online!